SARAH BERNHARDT

TRAGIQUE HISTOIRE D'HAMLET
PRINCE DE DANEMARK
SARAH BERNHARDT

THÉÂTRE SARAH BERNHARDT

SARAH BERNHARDT

The Art of High Drama

Carol Ockman and Kenneth E. Silver

With contributions by
Janis Bergman-Carton
Karen Levitov
Suzanne Schwarz Zuber

The Jewish Museum, New York
Under the auspices of the Jewish Theological Seminary of America

Yale University Press
New Haven and London

This book has been published in conjunction with the exhibition *Sarah Bernhardt: The Art of High Drama*, organized by The Jewish Museum and presented from December 2, 2005, to April 2, 2006.

This exhibition was realized with the generous participation of the Bibliothèque Nationale de France.

{BnF

Exhibition Curators: Carol Ockman and Kenneth E. Silver
Manager of Curatorial Publications: Michael Sittenfeld
Associate Curator: Karen Levitov
Curatorial Assistant: Suzanne Schwarz Zuber
Manuscript Editor: Anna Jardine
Publications Assistant: Beth Turk
Exhibition Design: Abbott Miller and Michelle Reeb, Pentagram Design, with the assistance of Barbara Suhr

Publisher, Art & Architecture, Yale: Patricia Fidler
Associate Editor, Art & Architecture, Yale: Michelle Komie
Manuscript Editor, Yale: Laura Jones Dooley
Production Manager, Yale: Mary Mayer
Photo Editor, Yale: John Long
Designed by Abbott Miller with Jeremy Hoffman, Pentagram Design
Set in the font Seria and Seria Sans designed by Martin Majoor
Printed in Italy by Conti Tipocolor

Cover illustrations: front, Félix Nadar, *Sarah Bernhardt*, c. 1860. Bibliothèque Nationale de France, Département des Estampes, Paris; back, Paul François Berthoud, *Jardinière of Sarah Bernhardt*, 1905. Collection of Raphael Benjamin Sinai, London
Frontispiece: Alphonse Mucha, *Tragique histoire d'Hamlet*, 1899. Collection of Mr. and Mrs. Ivan Lendl, New York

The Jewish Museum
1109 Fifth Avenue
New York, New York 10128
www.thejewishmuseum.org

Yale University Press
PO Box 209040
New Haven, Connecticut 06520–9040
www.yalebooks.com

Library of Congress Cataloging-in-Publication Data
Ockman, Carol.
Sarah Bernhardt : the art of high drama / Carol Ockman and Kenneth E. Silver ; with contributions by Janis Bergman-Carton, Karen Levitov, Suzanne Schwarz Zuber.
    p.   cm.
  Published in connection with an exhibition held at the Jewish Museum, New York, Dec. 2, 2005–Apr. 2, 2006.
  Includes bibliographical references and index.
  ISBN-13: 978-0-300-10919-1 (clothbound : alk. paper)
  ISBN-10: 0-300-10919-9 (clothbound : alk. paper)
  ISBN-13: 978-0-300-11343-3 (paperbound : alk. paper)
  ISBN-10: 0-300-11343-9 (paperbound : alk. paper)
  1. Bernhardt, Sarah, 1844–1923—Exhibitions. 2. Actors—France—Exhibitions. I. Silver, Kenneth E. II. Bergman-Carton, Janis. III. Levitov, Karen. IV. Zuber, Suzanne Schwarz, 1976– V. Bernhardt, Sarah, 1844–1923. VI. Jewish Museum (New York, N.Y.) VII. Title.
  PN2638.B5O35 2005
  792.02'8'092—dc22   2005011076

A catalogue record for this book is available from the British Library.

The paper in this book meets the guidelines for permanence and durability of the Committee on Production Guidelines for Book Longevity of the Council on Library Resources.

10 9 8 7 6 5 4 3 2 1

Contents

Donors to the Exhibition

Sarah Bernhardt: The Art of High Drama is made possible through a leadership grant from the Jerome L. Greene Foundation. Major support was provided by Mildred and George Weissman.

Generous funding was also provided by the Blanche and Irving Laurie Foundation, the estate of Jordan Mayro, The Grand Marnier Foundation, the Georges Lurcy Charitable and Educational Trust, Barbara G. Fleischman, The Mailman Foundation, Inc., Rita and Burton Goldberg, Fanya Gottesfeld Heller, the Maurice I. Parisier Foundation, Inc., the New York Council of the Humanities, a state program of the National Endowment for the Humanities, and other donors.

The catalogue was made possible through the Dorot Foundation publications endowment.

Lenders to the Exhibition

Ariodante, Paris
Armand Hammer Museum of Art and
    Cultural Center, at UCLA
Bibliothèque Forney, Paris
Bibliothèque Nationale de France, Paris
Bibliothèque-Musée de la Comédie
    Française, Paris
Bibliothèque-Musée de l'Opéra, Paris
Billy Rose Theatre Collection, The New York
    Public Library for the Performing Arts
British Library, London
Cinémathèque Française, Paris
Dahesh Museum of Art, New York
Garrick Club, London
Gaumont-Pathé Archives, Paris
The Hampden-Booth Theatre Library,
    New York
Harry Ransom Humanities Research
    Center, The University of Texas at Austin
Harvard Theatre Collection, Cambridge,
    Massachusetts
Jane Voorhees Zimmerli Art Museum,
    Rutgers, The State University of New
    Jersey, New Brunswick
The Jewish Museum, New York
Library of Congress, Washington, D.C.
The Metropolitan Museum of Art,
    New York
Mucha Trust, London
Musée Carnavalet—Histoire de Paris
Musée Galliera, Musée de la Mode de la
    Ville de Paris
Musée de la Publicité, Paris
Musée des Arts Décoratifs, Paris
Musée des Beaux-Arts de Tourcoing
Musée d'Orsay, Paris
Petit Palais, Musée des Beaux-Arts de la
    Ville de Paris
Museum of Fine Arts, Boston
Museum of the City of New York
Mutuelle Nationale des Artistes,
    Couilly-Pont-aux-Dames, France
The New York Public Library
Posters Please, Inc., New York
The Shubert Archive, New York

Sterling and Francine Clark Art
    Institute, Williamstown, Massachusetts
Twentieth Century Fox
Victoria and Albert Museum, London

Private Collections
Anonymous lenders
Victor Arwas, London
Amy Bedik, New York
Lorraine and Martin Beitler, Edgewater,
    New Jersey
Alain Campignon, Paris
Ralph Esmerian
Laura Gold, Park South Gallery at
    Carnegie Hall, New York
Olivier Hurstel, Paris
Cherry Jones, New York
Philippe Lechat, Paris
Mr. and Mrs. Ivan Lendl, New York
Mr. Albert Malumed and Ms. Jacqueline
    Morris, New York
Beatrix Ost and Ludwig Kuttner, New York
Mr. and Mrs. Jack Rennert, New York
Norma Canelas and William D. Roth,
    Winter Haven, Florida, and New York
Mr. and Mrs. Joel Schur, Greenwich,
    Connecticut
Laurence Senelick Collection of
    Theatrical Imagery, West Medford,
    Massachusetts
Raphael Benjamin Sinai, London
Robert A. Zehil, Monte Carlo

Foreword

The Divine Sarah and The Jewish Museum? What is the connection between the two? *Sarah Bernhardt: The Art of High Drama* explores the intersections of art and Jewish culture as reflected in the life and artistry of Sarah Bernhardt in turn-of-the-century France—a time and place that has been fertile ground for developing exhibitions at The Jewish Museum. From the museum's *The Dreyfus Affair: Art, Truth, and Justice* in 1987 to its exhibition *The Power of Conversation: Jewish Women and Their Salons* in 2005, we have presented art against the backdrop of contradictory tensions and opportunities that emerged for Jews in this post-Emancipation period. Art and social history merge in both the recent *Salons* exhibition and *Sarah Bernhardt* as they explore the confluence of a newly assimilated urban Jewish population with novel forms of art and a new feminism. *Sarah Bernhardt* brings us into the world of a woman who was an idolized beauty and famous actress as well as a woman whose opinions affected politics, whose acting roles challenged representations of gender, and whose career had an international reach in the worlds of art and commerce.

This exhibition showcases an enormous range of media, including early film, photography, and decorative and fine arts. Also included are the artifacts of popular culture, for this was an era of photomechanical reproduction that generated innovative means of mass communication and new forms of manipulating and creating public opinion. Sarah Bernhardt used the nascent modern press to reach a vast audience. She promoted herself as a classical actress with an audacious personality and benefited from the blurring of boundaries between her life and her art.

The Industrial Revolution and the democratization of cities created a new mobility for Jews. The proliferation of public theaters, cafés, and art galleries encouraged their denizens to cross class, gender, and religious boundaries. Yet within this secular society, religious anti-Semitism was replaced with a new and equally virulent political anti-Semitism. In this world of conflicting views, Sarah Bernhardt's popularity and power is extraordinary. She was able to enthrall France even as she challenged its assumptions, emerging as the most popular figure of her time.

The Jewish Museum is pleased to be able to bring to light a new investigation of this extraordinary woman in the form of an exhibition and catalogue. We are delighted to benefit from the knowledge and creative imaginations of two guest curators, Carol Ockman and Kenneth E. Silver. I extend tremendous thanks to them for their diligence, thoughtfulness, and imagination in working on this project. I also thank Jewish Museum Associate Curator Karen Levitov for her patient and thorough work on all aspects of the project. Together this curatorial team has created the first major museum exhibition of its kind devoted to Sarah Bernhardt.

Projects that involve ambitious catalogues and extensive international loans are costly endeavors requiring the endorsement of potential supporters and participants. We are exceedingly grateful to the Jerome L. Greene Foundation, whose President and CEO, Dawn Greene, is also a member of the Jewish Museum Council, for leadership support of Sarah Bernhardt. And we greatly appreciate the generous contributions of all of the donors listed on page vi.

The Board of Trustees of The Jewish Museum has enthusiastically supported an exhibition program that explores the nexus of art and Jewish culture. The trustees' leadership and support allows the museum to seek continuously to break new ground with such exhibitions as Sarah Bernhardt: The Art of High Drama. With their cooperation and that of the guest curators, museum staff, donors, and lenders, this has been a particularly gratifying project. Learning about Bernhardt inspires courage and creativity in all our lives. We feel grateful to this extraordinary figure of modernity for the inspiration she gives us today, and we thank the curators for revealing her artistry and personality in this pleasurable and stimulating presentation.

JOAN ROSENBAUM
Helen Goldsmith Menschel Director
The Jewish Museum

Acknowledgments

The preparation of a major international loan exhibition and its catalogue depends on the generosity of many people. The Jewish Museum makes possible unique exhibitions that present great works of art in innovative contexts. As always, the vision of its Helen Goldsmith Menschel Director, Joan Rosenbaum, is the starting point for exciting curatorial projects like *Sarah Bernhardt: The Art of High Drama*. We are deeply indebted to her commitment to this exhibition from its inception. Norman L. Kleeblatt, Susan and Elihu Rose Chief Curator, first proposed the idea of an exhibition about Sarah Bernhardt to us; we thank him for this remarkable opportunity. Ruth Beesch, Deputy Director for Program, has been both a constant advocate for this project and a creative problem-solver. Her guidance and friendship have been invaluable. Associate Curator Karen Levitov has been our direct link to the museum; guest curators could not ask for a more subtle and intelligent facilitator in the endless variety of challenges that face anyone organizing an exhibition of this complexity. Our shared three-year journey has been a great pleasure. We are deeply grateful to Suzanne Schwarz Zuber, Curatorial Assistant, who stepped in at a critical juncture in the show's preparation; her diligence has been exceptional.

At The Jewish Museum many other individuals have been crucial to this exhibition. We would like to thank Jane Rubin, Head Registrar, and her staff, especially Julie Maguire, Associate Registrar; Aviva Weintraub, Director of Media and Public Programs; Andrew Ingall, Assistant Curator, Broadcast Archive and Media; Nelly Silagy Benedek, Director of Education; Lynn Thommen, Deputy Director for External Affairs; Sarah Himmelfarb, Associate Director of Development, Institutional Giving; Susan Wyatt, Senior Grants Writer; and interns Amy Sande-Friedman, Sandy Pearl, Sandra Roemermann, and Shira Farber.

The professionalism and dedication of Michael Sittenfeld, Manager of Curatorial Publications, have been exemplary. We thank him for his central role in the realization of this catalogue, along with Project Assistant Beth Turk. A writer's best friend is a great editor: we were fortunate to work with Anna Jardine, whose incisive queries were both stimulating and efficacious. We are grateful to Janis Bergman-Carton, Professor at Southern Methodist University, Karen Levitov, and Suzanne Schwarz Zuber for their contributions to the catalogue. The superb design of the catalogue is the result of Abbott Miller's sophisticated graphic sensibility. Miller and his colleagues at Pentagram also created the remarkable installation of the exhibition, a multimedia tour de force, for which Barbara Suhr provided crucial expertise. We are indebted to Robin White Owen of MediaCombo for her assistance with film and video and to Sarah Schraeger for her lighting design. The Jewish Museum's Director of Operations, Al Lazarte, and his staff, have anticipated the myriad problems attending an exhibition of this scope.

This show would not have happened without the support of numerous individuals at museums, public and private collections, and galleries. In France our greatest debt is to the Bibliothèque Nationale and especially to Noëlle Guibert, Directeur du Département des Arts du Spectacle, who opened the doors of her incomparable theater collection to us and made available the assistance of her dedicated staff, including Noëlle Giret, Danielle Chamaillard, Tifenn Martinot-Lagarde, and Cécile Coutin. At the Bibliothèque Nationale we would also like to thank Sylvie Aubénas, Anne-Marie Sauvage, Valérie Sueur, Jacqueline Martinet, and Jocelyn Bouquillard at the Département des Estampes, who have facilitated the loan of some of the world's rarest works on paper; Monique Cohen and Mauricette Berne of the Département des Manuscrits; Bruno Sebald of the Département de l'Audiovisuel; and Dominique Saligny, of the Département des Travaux d'Art. We owe particular thanks to Claudette Joannis, Conservateur en Chef du Patrimoine, Château de Malmaison, who oversees the collection of the Mutuelle Nationale des Artistes. Her time and generosity of spirit have been indispensable. At the Bibliothèque-Musée de la Comédie Française, Joël Huthwohl, Conservateur-Archiviste, has been extremely gracious, as has Brigitte Levoyet. At the Musée Carnavalet we are indebted to the efforts of Roselyne Hurel, Conservateur en Chef; we also thank Director Jean-Marc Léri and Curators of Photography Catherine Tambrun and Françoise Reynaud. At the Musée d'Orsay we are grateful to Curators Anne Distel, Emmaneulle Héran, Caroline Mathieu, Marie-Pierre Salé, and Laure de la Majorie. Quentin Bajac, now Curator at the Musée Nationale d'Art Moderne, Centre Georges Pompidou, offered welcome assistance. Curators Isabelle Collet, Dominique Morel, and Amélie Simier at the Musée du Petit Palais and Director Gilles Chazal have been most generous, as has Catherine Join-Dieterle, Curator at the Musée de la Mode de la Ville de Paris. At the Musée des Arts Décoratifs we gratefully acknowledge the help of Béatrice Salmon, Odile Nouvel, and Evelyne Possémé, as well as Réjane Bargiel at the Musée de la Publicité. We thank Bernard Benoliel, Laure Bouissou, and Gaëlle Vidalie at the Cinémathèque Française, as well as Patrice Flamme for technical assistance; Pierre Vidal at the Musée et Bibliothèque de l'Opéra; Anne-Claude Lelieur and Thierry Devynck at the Bibliothèque Forney; Catherine Vincent-Delors at the Musée Lalique; and Monsieur Serban at the Théâtre de la Ville. We have been extremely fortunate to receive loans from important private collectors and dealers, including Alain Campignon, great-grandson of Sarah Bernhardt; François-Joseph Graf and his assistant Marie-Laurence Gemino; Jane Roberts; and Robert Zehil of Monte Carlo. For their efforts on our behalf in Paris, we thank Roberto Pollo, Lucile Audouy of the Galerie Elstir, Michel Périnet, and our friends the late Liliane de Rothschild, Madeleine Walter, Catherine Cozzano, Françoise and Francis Neher, and Ellen McBreen and Josh Clark. We are indebted to Fritz Falk, Kazumi Arikawa, and Haruko Itotagawa and to Guy Cocheval, Director, Musée des Beaux-Arts, Montreal.

In Britain, many people at the Victoria and Albert Museum have provided indispensable assistance: Director Geoff Marsh, Deputy Head Jim Fowler, Catherine Haill, and Guy Baxter of the Theatre Museum; Linda Parry, Marjorie Trusted, Martin Barnes, Margaret Timmers, Rachel Nesbit, and Mark Haworth-Booth; and John Baskett and Betty Beazley at The Garrick Club. We owe special debts to John and Sara Mucha at the Mucha Foundation and to Victor Arwas and Jane Abdy. We also thank Miranda Mason, who has more than once provided useful information about objects and resources.

In the United States, our gratitude extends first and foremost to the Harvard Theatre Collection and to its Curator, Frederic Woodbridge Wilson, who made available his incomparable holdings. We also thank Annette Fern and Luke Dennis, who guided us through Harvard's wealth of material. At the Museum of Fine Arts, Boston, we thank Malcolm Rogers, Ann and Graham Gund Director; Tracy Albainy, Chief Curator of Decorative Arts and Sculpture of Europe; Marietta Cambareri, Assistant Curator of Decorative Arts and Sculpture, Arts of Europe; and Bet McLeod, Meghan Melvin, Christopher Newth, and Sue Walsh, Curator of Prints and Drawings. Kurt Heinzelman, Executive Curator for Academic Programs at the Harry Ransom Humanities Research Center, The University of Texas, Austin, was generous with his time and facilities, as was Helen Adair, Performing Arts Librarian. We thank Michael Conforti, Director, Richard Rand, Curator, and Sarah Lees, Assistant Curator of Paintings, at the Clark Art Institute; Karen Bucky and Bonghee Lis at the Clark Art Institute Library; Phillip Dennis Cate, the Zimmerli Art Museum, Rutgers University; Elena Millie, Carol Johnson, and Rachel Waldron of the Library of Congress; and Nancy M. Shawcross of the Philip H. Ward Collection of Theatrical Images, Rare Book and Manuscript Library, University of Pennsylvania. We owe a special debt to Laurence Senelick, Fletcher Professor of Drama and Oratory, Tufts University: he has generously loaned us works from his collection and shared with us his great knowledge of theater history. For most generous assistance pertaining to Sarah Bernhardt's handkerchief, we gratefully applaud Julie Harris and Cherry Jones, and John Erman.

In New York, we thank Marty Jacobs, Curator of the Theater Collections, and Assistant Registrar Kerry L. McGinnity at the Museum of the City of New York, as well as its Director, Susan Henshaw-Jones. Colta Ives, Curator of Drawings and Prints at The Metropolitan Museum of Art, was particularly generous, and we also thank Mia Fineman of the Department of Photographs and Robert Kaufmann, Librarian of the Department of European Decorative Arts. At The New York Public Library we greatly appreciate the assistance of Bob Taylor, Lewis and Dorothy Cullman Curator, Billy Rose Theater Collection; Barbara Cohen-Stratyner, Judy R. and Alfred A. Rosenberg Curator of Exhibitions; and Clayton Kirking, Chief, Art Information Services. At the Dashesh Museum of Art, Stepen Ediden, Chief Curator, and Roger Diederen, Curator, have been most accommodating, and we are grateful to the museum's Director, Peter Trippi. We are equally indebted to Sonya Bekkerman and Holly Congdon at Sotheby's; Maryann Chach and Vicki Reiss at the Shubert Archive; Raymond Wemmlinger at the Players' Club; and Charles Silver of the Department of Film and Video at The Museum of Modern Art. Jack Rennert of Posters Please Gallery has been generous, thoughtful, and informative, and we also thank his assistant, Terry Shargel.

Many others in the United States have helped us track down leads and provided invaluable assistance. We are indebted to Joseph Baillio and Philip Dempsey, Wildenstein & Co.; to Robert Cashey, Shepherd Gallery; to Elizabeth Hayes and Blanche Tannery of the Cultural Service, Embassy of France; and to Edgar LaMance, Julie Wilder, Joan Talkowsy, Lisa Lindstrom, Robert Rosenblum, Michael Friend, Mary McLeod, Christiane Andersson, Elizabeth Kley, Joan Stern, Susan Dalsimer, Sarah Bradford Landau, Chiori Miyagawa, Richard Schechner, Ethelyne Staley, Annemarie Bean, Elizabeth Kihara, Leonard Finger, Elizabeth Ely, Ann McCauley, Aimée Brown Price, Raymond Wapner, George Mangini, Francine Goldenhaar, Christopher Lyon, Jan McCullagh, Patricia Grossman, Ann Pellegrini, David Menefee, Beth Gersh-Nesic, Jeremy Benjamin, Rizvana Braxton, Chester Collins, Deborah Berke, Christine Kondoleon and Frederic Wittman, Miroslava Benes and Francesco Passanti, Leila Kinney and Paul Summit, Mitchell L. and Ellen H. Silver, and Aaron Ockman.

CAROL OCKMAN AND KENNETH E. SILVER

SARAH BERNHARDT'S HANDKERCHIEF

Sarah Bernhardt, at least her memory, is alive and well and living in New York. Her handkerchief belongs to Cherry Jones, the 2005 Tony Award–winning best actress in John Patrick Shanley's drama Doubt. She has graciously lent it to our exhibition. The handkerchief was given to her by the great American actress Julie Harris, who received it from the first lady of the American theater, Helen Hayes. Whether Hayes got it directly from Bernhardt, as some think, or from the renowned Shakespearean actress Julia Marlowe is open to question.[1] What matters to the luminous sorority of actresses who have passed it down from one to the other for several generations is the physical connection to the first modern star in the West. To possess Bernhardt's handkerchief—to touch something that she has touched—makes her tangible as only the most personal objects can.

Reminiscing about the opening night of Christopher Isherwood's I Am a Camera (1951), when she received the handkerchief from Helen Hayes, Julie Harris said, "She was giving it to me as a talisman for my career . . . and saying that . . . [w]hen you see a wonderful performance by a young actress or actor, you have to give it on."[2] In fact, Harris gave it on twice. The first time was to Susan Strasberg on the opening night of Frances Goodrich and Albert Hackett's The Diary of Anne Frank (1955), and the second—since Strasberg died in 1999 without relinquishing it—thirty-eight years later to Cherry Jones on the opening night of Nora Ephron's Imaginary Friends (1993).[3] Like the best traditions, the transmission of the Bernhardt handkerchief is as much about renewal as the safeguarding of posterity. The performance that can happen only once, that can never be exactly repeated, is the essence of live theater. Each time a gifted actress makes her entrance, theater is reborn, and forever changed. For the women who have had the privilege of owning it, Bernhardt's handkerchief is not only a direct link to her and to her genius but also an assertion of their own distinctive talent. Embroidered with the name "Sarah" on one of its edges, this modest square of fabric embodies the continuity of brilliant theatrical performance.

CAROL OCKMAN AND KENNETH E. SILVER

1. In 1953 the Washington Post reported that Bernhardt gave the handkerchief to Hayes: "Unlike the legendary case of the older actress jealous of the younger one, here we have the mutual respect of two topflight artists. In fact, a handkerchief Sarah Bernhardt once gave Miss Hayes, she has passed along to the newcomer." Richard L. Coe, "Julie's Here in Two Roles This Week," Washington Post, March 8, 1953, L1. Julie Harris confirms this. In a letter to Susan Strasberg on stationery headed "Julie Harris" (cat. 184), the actress wrote:

December 11, 1955
Dear dear Susie, I can only say that you are beautiful to me—and your shining face kept reminding me of the picture of Anne Frank on the back of her book that I read several years ago—every breath you took seemed to me to come out of that lovely face.

The handkerchief I send to you was given

me three years ago or so—on the night the producers of "I Am a Camera" put my name in lights on the Empire. Miss Helen Hayes gave it to me. It was given to her daughter Mary—I enclose its history. It first belonged to the Great Sarah Bernhardt and I have treasured it because it not only belonged to her and must have touched her hand—but because it is a token of faith—how wonderful to know that others believe in you. The tradition of the handkerchief is wonderful; it is passed on for luck and happiness. I believe in you Susie, as you will one day believe in another and will give them [crossed out] her or him Miss Bernhardt's handkerchief. You are a beautiful actress and I pray the token brings you happiness and growth and all that you wish for.
With love always, Julie
The reference to Hayes's daughter is just one of the many loose threads in the history of the

handkerchief. Harris reiterates that she received it from Hayes in an interview in 2001: "Helen Hayes came back after the performance and she had a little envelope. Inside the envelope was a letter saying that this handkerchief had been given to her from Sarah Bernhardt on one of her farewell tours in America." Harris interviewed in the documentary Broadway Legends (2001; directed by John Erman and Joyce Van Patten). But Time magazine thought the handkerchief had traveled a somewhat different path to Harris: "Helen Hayes has solemnly passed on to her the handkerchief that Sarah Bernhardt gave to Julia Marlowe—sure symbol of her succession as first lady of the American theater." "A Fiery Particle," Time, November 28, 1955.

2. Harris interview in Broadway Legends.

3. Conversations with John Erman, May 2, 2005, and Cherry Jones, January 27, 2005.

THÉROIGNE

LA TOSCA

FROUFROU

PELLÉAS et MÉLISANDE

LE PASSANT

THEODORA

LA VIERGE D'AVILA

FOEDORA

LA DAME AUX CAMÉLIAS

L'AIGLON

Carol Ockman and Kenneth E. Silver

Introduction

THE MYTHIC SARAH BERNHARDT

By the dawn of the twentieth century, Sarah Bernhardt's fans were sending one another colored postcards of the star in her best-known roles. Having collected images of the actress as Marguerite Gautier (the consumptive courtesan with a heart of gold in La dame aux camélias), Floria Tosca (the impassioned prima donna done wrong), and Theodora (the calculating circus performer turned Byzantine empress), her devotees would then need seven more cards: Théroigne de Méricourt, Frou Frou, Zanetto, Teresa of Ávila, Pelléas, Fédora, and the Duke of Reichstadt. Once they had the entire group of ten, they could put them together for a supersize bonus—Bernhardt again as the Duke, her most famous breeches role (fig. 1).

Like the giant that emerges from the completed puzzle, Bernhardt was larger than life. Myths about her persist to this day. Her menagerie of wild animals was legendary, as were her well-publicized shenanigans (fig. 2). And everyone seems to remember that she slept in a coffin and performed Hamlet with a wooden leg. Neither is exactly true, but, like all myths, they have some basis in fact. The actress did have herself photographed in a coffin as a publicity stunt, and her leg was amputated late in her career (although it seems she did not wear a prosthesis). No matter how one thinks about it, her life was exceptional.

The daughter of a courtesan, Bernhardt was born in Paris in 1844, where early on she was introduced to some of the most influential aristocrats in Europe. Through her mother's connections, she entered the Conservatoire; admission to the elite acting school enabled her to join the company of the Comédie Française, the most revered theater in France. No sooner had she been elevated to the pinnacle of this artistic pantheon than she up and left for the fame and fortune of popular theaters and international tours. Notoriously promiscuous, Bernhardt had a son out of wedlock years before her short-lived marriage to a mediocre actor who was addicted to morphine.

As if these facts were not sensational enough, Bernhardt's mother was a Jew. For the actress, this was both a blessing and a curse. In biblical roles such as Photine, the heroine of Edmond Rostand's *La samaritaine* (fig. 3), she turned her Semitic exoticism into an alluring attribute. In the poster by Alphonse Mucha for the play, the Hebrew inscription "Jahweh" appears behind Bernhardt's head, while "Shaddai," another Hebrew word for God, accompanies the inset figure. Playing to the public's appetite for beautiful Jewesses redeemed by their conversion to Christianity, Bernhardt in the role of the Samaritan woman adheres to a faith resembling pre-rabbinical Judaism. Almost Jewish, but not quite, Photine is a sort of surrogate for Bernhardt and her equivocal religious identity. In spite of her

fig. 3 **Alphonse Mucha (Czech, 1860–1939), *La samaritaine*, 1897. Color lithograph, 68 1/8 x 23 in. (173 x 58.4 cm). Collection of Mr. Albert Malum and Ms. Jacqueline Morris, New York**

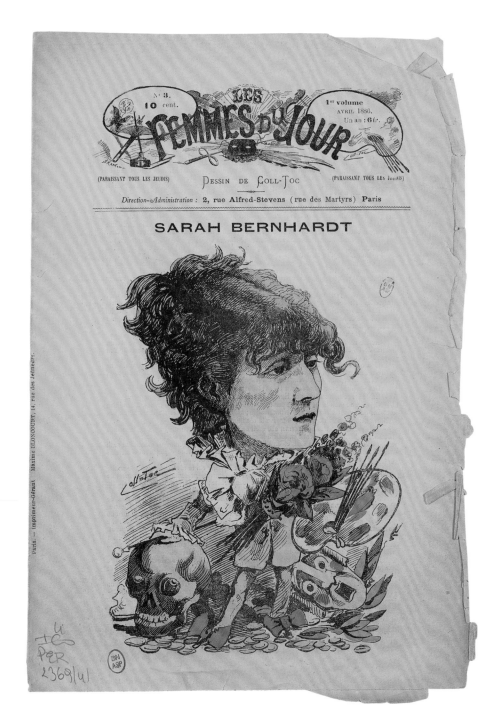

fig. 6 Henri de la Blanchère
(French, 1821–1880),
Rachel as Phèdre (Act II,
Scene 5), 1846, printed
1859. Albumen print,
7 1/2 x 5 1/2 in. (19 x 14
cm). Collections de la
Comédie Française, Paris

fig. 5 Sir Joshua Reynolds
(British, 1723–1792),
*Sarah Siddons as the Tragic
Muse*, 1784. Oil on
canvas, 94 1/4 x 58 1/8 in.
(239.4 x 147.6 cm).
The Huntington Library,
Art Collections, and
Botanical Gardens,
San Marino, California

birth, Bernhardt was baptized and raised a Catholic—a fact that did little to shield her from anti-Semitic attack. In a caricature by Coll-Toc (fig. 4), she is surrounded by a profusion of attributes relating to her careers as actress and as part-time painter. What at first glance appears a benign homage to an attractive, accomplished celebrity is undercut by a prominent allusion to Bernhardt's supposed Jewish avarice: she stands on a carpet of gold coins. The sinister mood is exacerbated by the mask of tragedy to her left and the cigarette-smoking skull, against which she leans, to her right.

Bernhardt was not the first actress to be denigrated as a Jew. The illustrious French tragedienne Rachel, for instance, was maliciously caricatured a quarter-century earlier. But whether Jewish or not, actresses by the late eighteenth century were so much a part of public life that they were inevitable subjects for scandal-mongering journalists as well as the most sought-after painters. Such was the renown of the English star Sarah Siddons that Thomas Gainsborough and Joshua Reynolds each plied his art in her service (fig. 5).[1] In addition to sitting for the noted academic artists Jean-Léon Gérôme and Eugène-Emmanuel Amaury-Duval, Rachel was one of the first actresses to be photographed (fig. 6).[2] Her example was significant for Bernhardt, who used photography on an unprecedented scale

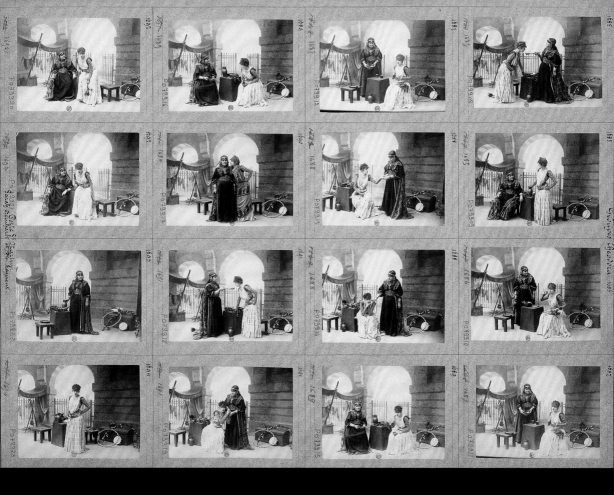

fig. 7a   Paul Nadar (French, 1856–1939), Sarah Bernhardt as Théodora with Fortune Teller, c. 1884. Albumen prints mounted on board, 21 7/8 x 28 5/8 in. (55.5 x 72.8 cm). Bibliothèque Nationale de France, Département des Estampes, Paris

opposite:

fig. 7b   Paul Nadar (French, 1856–1939), Sarah Bernhardt as Jeanne d'Arc, 1894. Gelatin silver prints mounted on board, 28 1/2 x 21 7/8 in. (72.5 x 55.5 cm). Bibliothèque Nationale de France, Département des Estampes, Paris

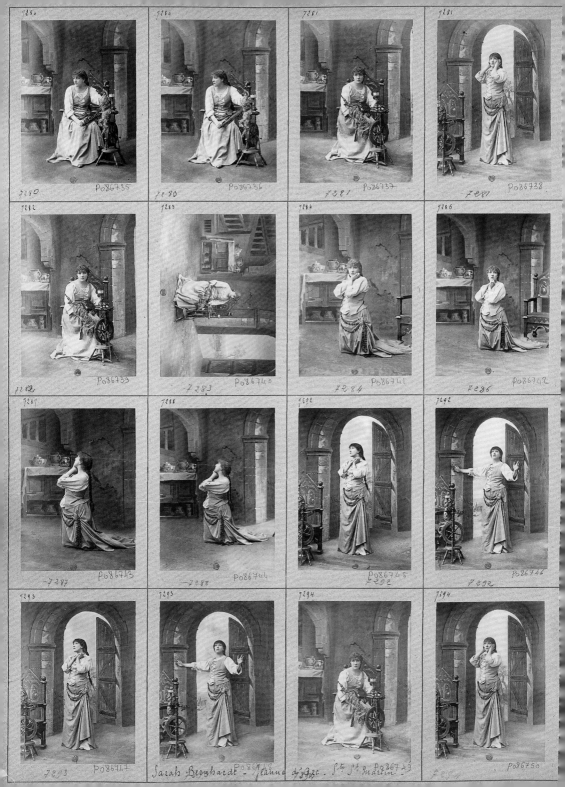

fig. 8   Édouard Lièvre (French, 1829–1886), Sarah Bernhardt's standing mirror with her motto, "Quand même," n.d. Wood with mounted brass and silver "Quand même" shield, gilt bronze mounts, inlaid enamel panels, mirrored glass, 9 x 4 x 2 ft. (274.5 x 122 x 61 cm). Ariodante, Paris

fig. 9   Belt with buckle inscribed "Sarah Bernhardt," n.d. Metal ornament on velvet, approx. 30 in. (76.2 cm). Musée Carnavalet—Histoire de Paris (OM 3403)

to spread her reputation around the world. The photographic studio of Nadar père et fils, which specialized in celebrity portraits, constructed elaborate sample boards of Bernhardt pictures (fig. 7). From these inventories of the actress in her theatrical roles and in her daily life, the Nadars would reproduce prints on demand.

Although an indispensable precursor for Bernhardt, Rachel was an actress of an utterly different kind. Her cerebral acting style—noble and self-contained, as the critics describe it—could not have been more removed from Bernhardt's highly emotional, physically expressive manner. Bernhardt emoted in this fashion on so many stages for so many years that the restrained, introspective pathos of her younger Italian rival Eleonora Duse came as a welcome relief to George Bernard Shaw and Anton Chekhov, among others.

As with Bernhardt's acting, so with her taste. If it is possible to describe a piece of furniture as flamboyant, it would have to be the nine-foot-high mahogany-framed standing mirror that the actress commissioned for her home from Édouard Lièvre (fig. 8). A major illustration of late-nineteenth-century neo-Renaissance style, it is an amalgam of Albertian architectural motifs, Della Robbia–inspired enameled terra-cottas, metallic finials, grotteschi, and rosettes. An ornate escutcheon over the long arched central mirror bears the actress's monogram and a banner spelling out her motto, "Quand même" ("No matter what," "Against all odds," "Through it all"), self-referential marks that we find in a large quantity of objects she owned. If this initialing of everything in sight was a bourgeois aping of aristocratic self-assertion, then the indigo velvet belt with her name in bold brass capital letters is pure period showmanship (fig. 9). The elaborate historicizing taste of her domestic decor—by turns Old Testament, Egyptian, Byzantine, medieval, and Orientalizing—was matched, if not exceeded, in her theatrical productions, over which she often exercised complete aesthetic control. The costumes for Théodora and Cléopâtre are among the richest and most thoroughly researched in fin-de-siècle stage design. Setting off the lavishly bejeweled clothing (fig. 10) are sumptuous accessories that include Theodora's double-eagle crown, studded with real amethysts, opals, and turquoises, and Cleopatra's golden pectoral, adorned with beads, semiprecious stones, and miniature royal portraits (figs. 11 and 12).

fig. 10 Théophile Thomas
(French, 1846–1916),
Tunic costume for
Euphratas in *Théodora*,
1884 and 1902. Fabric
with gilt thread, pearls,
semiprecious stones,
56 3/4 x 15 in. (144 x
38 cm). Bibliothèque
Nationale de France,
Département des Arts
du Spectacle, Paris

fig. 11   Double-eagle crown
          for *Théodora*, 1902. Velour
          and metal inset with
          opals, amethysts, and
          turquoise, 5 7/8 x 13 3/8 x
          7 1/2 in. (15 x 34 x 19 cm).
          Mutuelle Nationale
          des Artistes, Couilly-Pont-
          aux-Dames, France

fig. 12   Pectoral for Cléopâtre,
1890. Metal, pearls,
beads, sequins, gold
thread. Bibliothèque
Nationale de France,
Département des Arts
du Spectacle, Paris

fig. 13 Human skull given and inscribed by Victor Hugo to Sarah Bernhardt, n.d. 7 x 6 in. (17.8 x 15.2 cm). Victoria and Albert Museum, London (S117-1981)

Bernhardt's extravagant aesthetic extended to the late-nineteenth-century obsession with death and sexuality. Not only did she die for love onstage, she loved to surround and adorn herself with macabre objects (fig. 13). She cherished the human skull, given to her by Victor Hugo, which he had inscribed with a verse written in honor of her performance in his historical drama *Hernani*:

Skeleton, what have you done with your soul?
Lamp, what have you done with your flame?
Empty cage, what have you done with
The beautiful bird that used to sing?
Volcano, what have you done with your lava?
Slave, what have you done with your master?[3]

fig. 14 Alphonse Mucha (Czech, 1860–1939) and Georges Fouquet (French, 1860–1957), *Snake Bracelet*, 1899. Metal, 6 in. (15.2 cm). Sakai City Government, Japan

The astonishing snake bracelet designed for Bernhardt by Mucha and Georges Fouquet—one of the greatest pieces of Art Nouveau jewelry produced (fig. 14)—recalls her self-inflicted death by asp in *Cléopâtre*. Even Bernhardt's preternaturally sinuous body was described as serpentine, as it is in Dudley Hardy's mood piece, a diminutive painting in cool blues, greens, and grays, offset by blinding whites (fig. 16).

Hardy's is only one of many painted portraits of Bernhardt. Interestingly, her claim to avant-gardism in the visual arts rests not with traditional media (painting, sculpture, and drawing) but with advertising. The most memorable pictures of Bernhardt are reproducible, from the photographs by the Nadars, to Henri de Toulouse-Lautrec's lithographs, to Mucha's life-size posters. Bernhardt's instinct for publicity led her beyond the unique object to the realm of the mass-produced. Her savvy recognition of how a designer of exceptional talent could advance her career was groundbreaking. It leads us all the way to Andy Warhol, who as a

commercial artist made several line drawings of her, based on photographs, and later included her silk-screen portrait, based on Napoleon Sarony's photograph, in his series *Ten Portraits of Jews of the Twentieth Century* (fig. 15). In light of Bernhardt's embrace of new media, it is not surprising that she had her voice recorded by Thomas Alva Edison or that she was the first major legitimate actress to star in movies (figs. 17 and 18).

This expert manipulator of new media demands a multimedia approach. The exhibition *Sarah Bernhardt: The Art of High Drama* showcases paintings, sculptures, drawings, photographs, posters, costumes, jewelry, furniture, sound recordings, movies, advertising, and ephemera. For us as art historians, the quality of objects always comes first; the challenge here was to find the best work in all media without reducing Bernhardt's aesthetic of excess to a tidy demonstration of good taste. Equally demanding were the questions posed by celebrity itself and how it blurs the line between fact and fiction. Our exhibition argues that a "real" Bernhardt is inextricable from her show business persona, just as her biography is inseparable from the myths. Sarah Bernhardt as performer is our point of departure. We document her principal roles and the entrepreneurial zeal with which she forged the link between classical theater and boulevard entertainment. Her lavish stage productions, her carefully orchestrated self-presentation, and her claustrophobic domestic interiors constitute an unmistakable style *Bernhardt*, as the exhibition amply demonstrates. Bernhardt was also a working artist who achieved substantial

fig. 17 Sarah Bernhardt listen-
ing to a phonograph
recording of her voice
at the Bettini studio
(Lieutenant Giovanni
Bettini), New York

recognition in the Salons and art galleries of her day; the show includes a number of excellent pieces of her sculpture. The actress's career circled the globe, with performances in Britain, the Continent, the Americas, Africa, Australia, and the Pacific, but the United States was her second home. The time she spent in America figures importantly in the exhibition.

As scholars who have been working on French art and culture for many years, we are a part of revolutions in our field. This exhibition has provided the occasion for the kind of collaboration of which most scholars only dream. It has given us a platform to explore and realize interests we have shared since we met our first week in graduate school. *Sarah Bernhardt: The Art of High Drama* represents our long-standing commitment to social history in its many forms, including women's studies and gender, ethnic, and queer studies, as well as the interdisciplinary research these necessitate. Scholarship on popular culture, media, history of photography, and theater history, together with French and U.S. cultural studies, has informed this endeavor. *Sarah Bernhardt: The Art of High Drama* is intended as a contribution to the history of popular culture, at a time when its influence has never been greater. In the catalogue, Carol Ockman's essay "Was She Magnificent? Sarah Bernhardt's Reach" treats the subject of Bernhardt and mass culture as a compelling addition to the well-established emphasis on Bernhardt as a classical actress. In "Sarah Bernhardt and the Theatrics of French Nationalism (from Roland's Daughter to Napoleon's Son)," Kenneth E. Silver considers Bernhardt's art and life in the context of French politics and national identity. The actress's singular position as an avatar of taste in European visual culture is the focus of Janis Bergman-Carton's essay, "'A Vision of a Stained Glass Sarah': Bernhardt and the Decorative Arts." And Karen Levitov surveys the extraordinary range of contemporary opinions about Bernhardt by some of her most famous peers, including Mark Twain, Ellen Terry, Sigmund Freud, and Colette. A photographic essay chronicles Bernhardt's frequent tours in the United States and features pictures of the star at Niagara Falls, at San Quentin prison, and with Harry Houdini in New York. A chronology prepared by Suzanne Schwarz Zuber concludes the catalogue.

Welcome to the Sarah Bernhardt show.

fig. 18 Robert Kastor (French, active late 19th–early 20th centuries), *Au Cinématographie: La dame aux camélias*, 1911. Poster for the film directed by André Calmettes and Henri Pouctal, starring Sarah Bernhardt (Cinémathèque Française, 1912), 63 x 47 1/4 in. (160 x 120 cm). Collection of Mr. and Mrs. Jack Rennert, New York

BERNHARDT STYLE

Vallet (French, 1856–before 1934), Kid gloves from Sarah Bernhardt's personal wardrobe, c. 1910. Leather with multicolored and gold thread, 14 x 6 in. (35 x 15 cm). Musée Galliera, Musée de la Mode de la Ville de Paris (GAL 1983.26.1 AB)

René Lalique (French, 1860–1945), *Eagle Pendant with Chain*, from Sarah Bernhardt's personal wardrobe, 1898–1900. Gold, ruby, pearls, emaille; pendant 2 3/8 x 3 in. (6 x 7.5 cm). Musée des Arts Décoratifs, Paris

Feathered fan, from Sarah Bernhardt's personal wardrobe, c. 1905. Feathers, silver pailettes, mother-of-pearl, 9 7/8 x 14 1/4 in. (25 x 36 cm). Musée Galliera, Musée de la Mode de la Ville de Paris (GAL 2003.17.2)

Purse for Gismonda, 1896.
Fabric with gilt thread,
pearls, amethysts, 10 5/8
x 17 3/8 in. (27 x 45 cm).
Mutuelle Nationale des
Artistes, Couilly-Pont-
aux-Dames, France

Purse for an unidentified
role of Sarah Bernhardt's,
n.d. Velvet, approx. 6 1/4
x 6 1/4 in. (16 x 16 cm).
Bibliothèque Nationale de
France, Département des
Arts du Spectacle, Paris

Théophile Thomas
(French, 1846–1916),
Capelet for Théodora,
1884 and 1902. Fabric
with gilt thread,
gilt buttons, colored
stones, pearls, 15 3/8 x
31 1/2 in. (39 x 80 cm).
Bibliothèque Nationale
de France, Département
des Arts du Spectacle,
Paris

Théophile Thomas
(French, 1846–1916),
Cape for Théodora, c. 1884.
Fabric embroidered
with silk thread, glass
beads. Bibliothèque
Nationale de France,
Département des Arts
du Spectacle, Paris. For
information about crown,
see page 11

Carol Ockman

WAS SHE MAGNIFICENT?

Sarah Bernhardt's Reach

By her extraordinary power of swooning she filled the arms of the world.
—Jean Cocteau on Sarah Bernhardt, *Portraits-souvenirs*

Some forty minutes into Billy Wilder's film *The Seven Year Itch* (1955), "The Girl" (Marilyn Monroe) is in the apartment of Richard Sherman (Tom Ewell) showing him how she does her Dazzledent toothpaste commercial for television. "I had onions at lunch. I had garlic dressing at dinner. But he'll never know," she proclaims, "because I stay kissing sweet, the new Dazzledent way." She pauses to flash her inimitable smile, and continues, in a tone of wonderment: "Every time I show my teeth on television, I'm appearing before more people than Sarah Bernhardt appeared before in her whole career. It's something to think about. . . . I wish I were old enough to have seen Sarah Bernhardt. Was she magnificent?" (fig. 1).

Monroe's breathless homage compares her character's fledgling career in TV commercials with Bernhardt's lengthy career as a stage actress. It summons up Bernhardt's mythic quality: the rarefied realm where the classical tragedienne dwells is as Olympian as the modern world of advertising Marilyn inhabits is crass and materialistic. Of course, neither Monroe nor the character she plays (she was not yet thirty when she made the film, playing twenty-two) could have seen Bernhardt live. She died in Paris in 1923.[1] By the mid-1950s, Sarah Bernhardt was recent enough to be recollected and far enough away to be half forgotten.

But Monroe's evocation brings her back to life. At the same time, it poses the question: How do we remember Bernhardt? Over the course of a career that saw the birth of mass culture and mass consumption, Bernhardt became a star on a scale no one had seen before. As a result, we know her from photographs, paintings, posters, sculpture, movies, sound recordings, advertisements, caricatures, newspapers, magazines, and souvenirs.[2]

Although Monroe and Bernhardt might seem an unlikely pairing, in fact they both owe their stardom to the mechanisms of media-based celebrity. Bernhardt was the biggest star of all time; if Monroe's character feels the need to refer to her predecessor, it is because she aspires to be nothing less.

Her Double Life

"The Girl" in *The Seven Year Itch* gives voice to a series of oppositions that are integral to Bernhardt's modernity. Although she was known as the most famous stage actress of all time, her fame ultimately rests on reproduced imagery, including movies; if she was the embodiment of high art, she was also the avatar of mass culture; whereas she epitomized European culture in the American imagination, she was embraced among Americans as one of their own. And there are other dualities. Bernhardt was born a Jew but baptized and raised a Catholic. She was considered the most feminine of actresses yet celebrated for her male roles (including Hamlet and Lorenzaccio). She was attacked as promiscuous, but she always defended the sanctity of motherhood. A famous lover of men both on and off the stage, she also had lesbian relationships. Although she was blessed with superhuman energy, she was often sickly, even on the verge of death, and lived as an amputee for the last eight years of her life.

Bernhardt herself reveled in such paradoxes. When she published her memoirs in 1907, she titled them, aptly and suggestively, *Ma double vie*—My Double Life. But if readers expected juicy gossip, private confessions, and betrayals of her contemporaries, they must have been disappointed. Despite Bernhardt's winning self-irony, the memoirs are scripted to present the star in a flattering light. The author willfully leaves certain biographical elements shrouded in mystery. On the first page of the book, for example, she refers to her absent father, who abandoned her mother right after Sarah's birth, as being "in China." She makes no mention of her illegitimate (and only) son, Maurice, until well into the book, and even then does not allude to the circumstances of his birth. And Bernhardt rehearses again and again the commonplaces of her persona: her sickliness and imminent death ("I began to vomit blood. . . . The chief doctor found me stretched out in my bed drained, and seemingly dead"); her unruly hair ("This isn't hair; it's a mop!"); her unfashionable thinness ("I'm so slim that I can't get wet; I pass between the raindrops").[3]

In this constant play between hyperbole and omission, Bernhardt's "double life" raises questions about the real and the invented that we might ask about celebrities at any time or place. Calling her life double is a way for her to tell us that things are not always what they seem. When she admits to "the exaggeration that I have always brought to everything," she intimates that a real Bernhardt does not exist; she herself is always role-playing.[4] In the age of mass culture that was being born, the vast publicity machine whose task was to disgorge ever more and newer information about celebrities exploited Bernhardt's larger-than-life persona, delighting in the confusion between the "real" and the theatrical that she helped to reinvent continuously.

What appears to have been an instinctive understanding of mass media and mass marketing was key to Bernhardt's success. Her ability to turn even the most negative publicity to her advantage had few rivals then, and has few now. Let me admit at the outset that this is where my own fascination with Sarah Bernhardt begins. There is something instructive in the fact that a woman who was subject to constant disparagement could not only laugh in the face of her critics but laugh all the way to the bank. Bourgeois women were automatically tainted the minute they stepped into the workplace.[5] Earning money, being independent, having multiple careers made Bernhardt suspect from the start. Yet along with her rampant sexuality and skewed religious affiliations, these transgressions of female propriety had the ironic effect of making her more rather than less appealing to a mass audience. Bernhardt embodied the contradictions of her age and made them exciting.

Over the years I have come to think of Bernhardt as an Energizer battery, able to process all the energy around and within her, positive and negative, and to keep going. Her ability to repeat and vary her distinctive yet imitable style of acting is an almost uncanny simulation of modern industrial production. She understood repetition as inherently powerful. Much as her motto, "Quand même," variously translated "No matter what," "Against all odds," and "Through it all," was emblazoned on her stationery (fig. 2), her tea service, and her furniture, Bernhardt stamped her image wherever she went. Repetition meant both surefire and ongoing success. When Marilyn Monroe's character in *The Seven Year Itch* contrasts her mass-media commercialism to Bernhardt's exalted theatrical stature, what she fails to realize is that Sarah Bernhardt was not solely the last great stage actress of the nineteenth century but the world's first movie star as well. Indeed, film would be her passport to immortality. Without the technologies afforded by mass production—photographs, posters, sound recordings, and movies—we might not "remember" Bernhardt at all.

Portraits of a Star

If I had been Bernhardt, I would have chosen to be remembered in the suite of images made by the pioneering photographer Nadar (Gaspard-Félix Tournachon) when she was only twenty (figs. 3–5). Among the most famous portraits in the history of photography, they show Bernhardt's youthful figure, swathed in

fig. 2 **Stationery with Sarah Bernhardt's motto, "Quand même" (note dated 1903). Mutuelle Nationale des Artistes, Couilly-Pont-aux-Dames, France**

fig. 5 Félix Nadar (French,
1820–1910), Sarah
Bernhardt, c. 1860.
Albumen print, 8 1/2 x
6 3/8 in. (21.6 x
16.3 cm). Bibliothèque
Nationale de France,
Département
des Estampes, Paris

opposite:

fig. 3 Félix Nadar (French,
1820–1910), Sarah
Bernhardt, c. 1860.
Albumen print, 8 5/8 x
6 3/8 in. (21.8 x
16.3 cm). Bibliothèque
Nationale de France,
Département
des Estampes, Paris

fig. 4 Félix Nadar (French,
1820–1910), Sarah
Bernhardt, c. 1860.
Albumen print, 8 7/8 x
6 7/8 in. (22.5 x
17.5 cm). Bibliothèque
Nationale de France,
Département
des Estampes, Paris

a voluminous white burnoose or black velvet. Leaving only her head, neck, and left shoulder exposed, the lush cascades of drapery that envelop her small body under-score both innocence and sensuality. As she leans against a half-column, her sole adornment a small cameo pendant at her ear, Bernhardt in these pictures conveys all the attributes of the tragic actress—elegance, decorum, taste, nobility, dignity, and grace—or, rather, those of the great actress to come. When Bernhardt sat for Nadar, she had as yet no reputation; her earlier debut at the Comédie Française in Paris in 1862 was inauspicious. She did not make a real name for herself until the late 1860s at the Théâtre de l'Odéon, several years after these photographs were taken. Yet the promise of her youth and beauty is so indelibly captured through pose and light that these artful images might well stand for everything Bernhardt became. Nadar's photographs of her, like his other portraits of actresses and models, are at the same time titillating. We can easily imagine the loosely wrapped drapery coming undone, making literal the sexual availability of the model and would-be actress.

Bernhardt's extraordinary life rendered her the paragon of the nineteenth-century demimondaine. She was the daughter and niece of courtesans. Her mother, Youle van Hard (fig. 6), whose origins are reported as either Dutch or German Jewish, introduced her daughter to aristocratic patrons, such as the Duc de Morny (illegitimate half brother of Napoleon III), who encouraged her to audition for the Comédie Française.[6] According to Bernhardt, her father was a lawyer from Le Havre; he ensured her education at a convent school but neither married her mother nor featured much in his daughter's life. Bernhardt herself had numerous sexual partners. Around the time she sat for Nadar, she gave birth to a son, Maurice, who was conceived out of wedlock with the dashing Prince Charles de Ligne of Belgium (see Silver essay, fig. 11). The liaison with the debonair Belgian prince gave way to others: among those reported to have been her lovers are Albert Edward, Prince of Wales; an elegant young Hussar count, Émile de Kératry; Charles Haas, Marcel Proust's primary model for Charles Swann; her costars Jean Mounet-Sully and Lou Tellegen; the literary giant Victor Hugo; the writers Jean Richepin and Jules Lemaître; and painter friends and teachers Gustave Doré, Alfred Stevens, Georges Clairin, and Louise Abbéma (fig. 7).[7] Although she made a passionate marriage to a second-rate actor, Jacques (born Aristides) Damala, with whom she costarred, they were together only a year (fig. 8).

It fell to Clairin, who would become her longtime friend, to crystallize Bernhardt's full-blown sensuality in an eight-foot-tall oil portrait (fig. 9). Painted in 1876, when the actress's fame first reached its zenith, this over-life-size, over-the-top picture establishes the visual tropes of Bernhardt's persona: the soon-to-be-fashionable thin body with its serpentine pose; the racy chic of her corsetless gowns, inspired by lingerie, which contributed to the success of *La dame aux camélias* (*The Lady of the Camellias*) several years later (fig. 10); the passionate love for birds and wild animals, feathers and furs, which here become attributes of the hypersexualized actress. Against a dark ground, clad entirely in white, and propped

fig. 6 Sarah Bernhardt with her mother and her sister Régine, 1860s. Postcard, 5 1/2 x 3 1/2 in. (13.9 x 9 cm). Bibliothèque Nationale de France, Département des Arts du Spectacle, Paris

fig. 7   Sarah Bernhardt with friends at Belle-Isle, 1895 or after. Gelatin silver print, 5 1/4 x 7 1/4 in. (13.3 x 18.4 cm). Museum of the City of New York, Theater Collection, Gift of Mrs. Joseph Verner Reed (75.120.39)

fig. 8   Chalot & Co., Paris (French, active 1879–1884), Jacques Damala, n.d. Gelatin silver print cabinet card, 6 1/2 x 4 1/4 in. (16.5 x 10.8 cm). Performing Arts Collection, Harry Ransom Humanities Research Center, University of Texas at Austin

up by a pillow, the sitter lounges on a deep-red velvet divan. Bernhardt's body, cinched into one of her signature form-fitting gowns, is a continuous spiral, starting at the head and accumulating twists and turns as it moves from her silhouette to the lengthy train of her dress to the svelte wolfhound—her canine double—curled at her feet. The portrait was not much liked when it was painted. Émile Zola, with whom Bernhardt would later be allied in the crusade to exonerate Captain Alfred Dreyfus, was one of many to comment disparagingly: "I know that Mlle Sarah Bernhardt passes for the thinnest person in France, but that is no reason to drape her on a settee so that there's no body under her peignoir."[8] Yet the portrait is forward-looking. The sinuosity of the ensemble anticipates the whiplash curves of the Art Nouveau creators, including Alphonse Mucha and René Lalique, whom Bernhardt would patronize in the late 1890s.

The Triumph of the Feminine

The serpentine line became shorthand for Bernhardt's form. As Proust's and Bernhardt's intimate Reynaldo Hahn put it: "The spiral has always been Sarah's artistic formula. In all her gestures, one . . . finds the principle of the spiral."[9] Its predominance is closely linked to her use of her body onstage, and it is the rule in how she is depicted. We see it in her twisting torso viewed from the back in Clairin's oil painting of her as Doña Maria de Neubourg from Hugo's *Ruy Blas* (fig. 11); it is apparent in Bernhardt's splayed limbs, when, as Theodora, Empress of Byzantium, she blocks the door with her exceedingly long arms and legs in Paul Nadar's photograph (fig. 12). And it is most evident in her celebrated gyrating demise as Marguerite Gautier in *La dame aux camélias* (fig. 13). Her extremely

Clairin.
1876

SARAH BERNHARDT.

THE "Falk" STUDIOS

1895

496
GEORGE STREET
SYDNEY

COPYRIGHT.

fig. 11   Georges Jules Victor
Clairin (French, 1843–
1919), Sarah Bernhardt as
Doña Maria de Neubourg
in Victor Hugo's "Ruy Blas,"
1879. Oil on canvas,
21 5/8 x 12 5/8 in. (54.9 x
32.1 cm). Collections de
la Comédie Française,
Paris (1236)

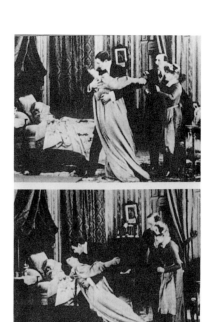

fig. 12 Paul Nadar (French, 1856–1939), Sarah Bernhardt as Théodora, c. 1884. Albumen print on card, 13 1/4 x 7 11/16 in. (33.7 x 19.4 cm). Harvard Theatre Collection, Houghton Library, Cambridge, Massachusetts

fig. 13 Three film stills of the death spiral from La dame aux camélias (Cinémathèque Française, 1912), directed by André Calmettes and Henri Pouctal

fig. 14   **W. & D. Downey (British,
active 1863–1910s), Sarah
Bernhardt as Izéyl, 1903.
Albumen print cabinet
card, 6 9/16 x 4 5/16 in.
(16.5 x 10.8 cm). Gift of
the Copenhagen Theatre
Museum, 1978;
Harvard Theatre
Collection, Houghton
Library, Cambridge,
Massachusetts**

fig. 15   **W. & D. Downey (British,
active 1863–1910s), Sarah
Bernhardt as Adrienne
Lecouvreur, c. 1880.
Albumen print cabinet
card, 6 5/8 x 4 5/16 in.
(16.8 x 10.8 cm). Bequest
of Evert Jansen Wendell,
1918; Harvard Theatre
Collection, Houghton
Library, Cambridge,
Massachusetts**

SARA BERNHARDT.

SARONY,   COPYRIGHT, 1891, BY NAPOLEON SARONY.   37 Union Sq. N. Y.

fig. 16 Napoleon Sarony (American, b. Canada, 1821–1896), *Sarah Bernhardt as Cléopâtre*, 1891. Albumen print cabinet card, 4 5/16 x 6 5/8 in. (10.8 x 16.8 cm). Bequest of Evert Jansen Wendell, 1910; Harvard Theatre Collection, Houghton Library, Cambridge, Massachusetts

physical style of acting revolutionized the performance of classical tragedy. To her teacher Joseph-Isidore Samson's instruction at the Comédie Française—"Support your speech with a simple gesture / Which must always precede the spoken word"—Bernhardt added the dictum that a descriptive glance must always precede gesture.[10] Izéyl's teary, beseeching eyes (fig. 14), the regally outstretched arms of Phaedra, and the sultry come-hither look of Adrienne Lecouvreur (fig. 15) announce through face and body the dramatic power of the verse.

Bernhardt's highly expressive style of acting was felt to be uniquely "feminine," in contrast to the *terribilità* of her illustrious precursor the great tragedienne Rachel (Élisa Félix; 1821–1858) (see Introduction, fig. 6). During Bernhardt's acclaimed London tour of 1879, the critic Tom Taylor characterized her as "by far the most feminine" Phaedra he had ever seen. He also observed that as Adrienne Lecouvreur, Bernhardt employed every facet of her talent to accentuate her femininity: "the wooing music of her sweet and silvery voice, the winning winding caresses of her lithe arms and slender figure, all the vocabulary of a loving woman's self-surrendering *abandon* in look, voice and action." Assessing a performance more than ten years later, the writer Anatole France remarked: "She did what no one had dared to do before her—she acted with her entire body. She put into her roles not only her whole soul, all her mind, and her physical grace, but also all her sexuality." If Rachel was understood to be cerebral—a chaste and untouchable deity— Bernhardt was that brand-new thing, a sex goddess. When she performed Cleopatra in the 1880s and early 1890s (fig. 16), a reporter for *The New York Times* observed that "good folk regarded her art as something forbidden, an alien evil. Young people did not tell their parents when they went to see her. . . . That scene in which the Serpent of Old Nile drew her coils round the throne of Marc Anthony, circling ever

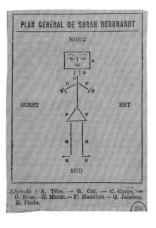

nearer with the venom of her wiles, was a revelation of things scarcely to be whispered."[11] If Bernhardt's physical style of acting was sometimes criticized, it was also a boon to foreign audiences, for it precluded the need for words during climactic scenes.[12]

Too Rich, Too Thin, Too Jewish

However dangerous it might be, Bernhardt's serpentine line was always more or less alluring. But her thinness could just as readily be turned against her. Rather than too much body, her critics often thought she had too little or none at all. Among the more curious images of the actress is "Le plan général de Sarah Bernhardt" (fig. 18), which diagrams her body like a map, or perhaps a military maneuver, duly labeled with points north (the region of her head), south (feet), east and west (arms and hands), and letters indicating the major body parts. Bernhardt's famously scrawny body, reduced here to straight-edge lines, is made geometry rather than flesh. "The General Plan" also suggests her vast reach, oriented as she is, like a landmass, toward all points on the globe.

The map recalls a family of images that ridicule Bernhardt's thinness.[13] Texts vie with pictures to document Bernhardt's excessively skinny body, including the

fig. 19 Alfred Le Petit (French, 1841–1909), "La poule aux oeufs d'or" ("The 'Tart' That Laid the Golden Eggs"), caricature of Sarah Bernhardt with Victorien Sardou, published in *Le grelot*, December 31, 1882. 12 3/4 x 11 1/8 in. (32.3 x 28.3 cm). Collection of Philippe Lechat, Paris

fig. 20 Alfred Le Petit (French, 1841–1909), Cover of *Les contemporains*, caricature, n.d. 11 3/4 x 15 3/4 in. (29.9 x 40 cm). Bibliothèque Nationale de France, Département des Arts du Spectacle, Paris

booklet "Too Thin or Skeletal Sara." She appears as anything from a skeleton to a variety of vegetables, insects, and birds, from mop to telegraph pole. Animate or inanimate, her body is unsexed and unsexy. Some caricatures of Bernhardt refer to more than one of her assorted perceived oddities. The mop and telegraph pole, for instance, emphasize also the unruly hair "of a blonde negress."[14] In the series of china plates, decorated with caricatures by Alfred Le Petit, of famous personalities as vegetables, Bernhardt features as "Le Salsifis," or salsify, otherwise known as oyster plant or vegetable oyster (fig. 17). The image of the desiccated stalk of a body, with long, thin leaves for hair and gnarled, branchlike fingers, is mitigated by the conclusion of the accompanying sonnet: "How can the salsify that is so thin / Contain such a great talent?"[15]

Still, it is the serpentine Bernhardt, and the association with the sensate and the sexual, that win out. Bernhardt's wispy figure transformed time and again into animate forms—airborne insect, big-beaked bird, hoofed panther. As disparate as these images may appear at first, they have something in common: they often have recognizably Semitic features. Caricatures by André Gill, Alfred Le Petit, Cabriol (Georges Lorin), and Coll-Toc all show Bernhardt in profile, with protruding nose and frizzy hair. In Le Petit's "The 'Tart' That Laid the Golden Eggs" ("La poule aux oeufs d'or"; fig. 19), Bernhardt's coiled torso, with its abbreviated wings, ends in chicken feet clad in black stockings (an allusion to prostitution). Under the watchful and approving eye of Victorien Sardou, her playwright and collaborator from the 1880s to the early 1900s, Bernhardt discharges from her flapping train a stream of golden eggs that collect in a group of already full baskets. Similarly, in Le Petit's caricature showing her as a well-fed bird with a cluster of moneybags hanging around her neck (fig. 20), Bernhardt's Semitic physiognomy is coupled with—what else?—an overweening love of gold. The caption seems to refer to the alacrity with which the actress would take the money and run at the end of the theatrical season: "Sarah, like the swallows, / Come May, flies off at full speed."[16]

Bernhardt's predecessor Rachel had been subjected to similar anti-Semitic attacks.[17] In Cham's (Amédé de Noé) undated "Andromache Abandoning Pyrrhus to Follow Barnum," Rachel nonchalantly strolls away from the Comédie Française on the arm of the American entrepreneur P. T. Barnum, who openly holds a big sack of money in his other hand. Marcelin's (Émile Planat) "The Great Tragedienne Begins Her 190th Season" (fig. 22) shows Rachel riding a chariot whose seat spells out "Caisse," or "Cashbox." In a manner quite different from Cham's, Marcelin underscores the specifically racial character of the entrepreneurial, grasping spirit equated with Jews, by showing Rachel and her herald with hooked noses, protruding fleshy lips, and convex brows.

This type of anti-Semitic vocabulary haunts Bernhardt in the late 1870s and early 1880s. The mud-slinging, anti-Semitic, and in every other way defiling biography *Les mémoires de Sarah Barnum* (1883), attributed to Marie Colombier, a disgruntled member of the actress's touring company, gives Bernhardt the surname of the incorrigible impresario who made the American careers of Jenny Lind and

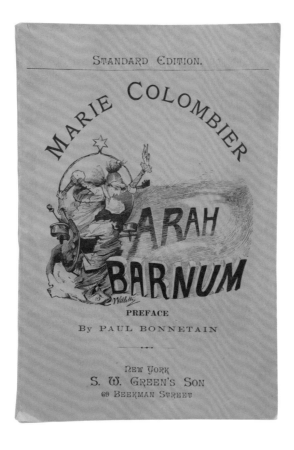

fig. 21 Marie Colombier (French, 1844–1910), *The Memoirs of Sarah Barnum*, 1884. Book, 7 5/8 x 5 x 1/2 in. (19.2 x 12.7 x 1.3 cm). Laurence Senelick Collection of Theatrical Imagery, West Medford, Massachusetts

fig. 22 Marcelin (Émile Planat) (French, 1830–1887), "The Great Tragedienne Begins Her 190th Season," caricature of Rachel published in *Le journal pour rire*, November 20, 1852. 17 3/8 x 12 5/8 in. (44 x 32 cm). Bibliothèque Nationale de France, Département des Estampes, Paris

Tom Thumb. As Marcelin did in his caricature of Rachel, Colombier repeatedly mentions Bernhardt's alleged cupidity. Léon-Adolphe Willette, who designed the cover of the book, exaggerates Bernhardt's nose and hair and, further, harnesses her springy energy in a carriage with a six-pointed star on top (fig. 21).[18] Although Willette and Le Petit went on to become the best-known anti-Semitic illustrators during the Dreyfus Affair, they did not portray Bernhardt at that time. One wonders why she suddenly found herself above the fray. At least part of the answer may lie in the fact that Bernhardt had become too useful as a symbol of France. To denigrate its greatest star was too high a price for the French to pay. In addition, after the early 1880s, she was frequently on tour abroad. If she was out of the spotlight in her homeland, she was its greatest sensation abroad.

Bernhardt's Jewishness did not always breed virulent anti-Semitism. The emphasis on her profile and wavy hair also distinguishes idealized images of her, such as Jules Bastien-Lepage's portrait, in which the actress caresses a statue of Apollo, god of poetry (see Bergman-Carton essay, fig. 24), or even the early profile photograph by Félix Nadar. Here these features recall the venerable tradition of *la belle juive*, the noble yet sensual Jewesses who populate the novels of Honoré de Balzac and Sir Walter Scott and the paintings of Eugène Delacroix and Théodore Chassériau.[19]

"Sarah Soon to Turn Man"

Bernhardt's unique style made her a trendsetter both on the stage and off. Not only did she capitalize on tight-fitting costumes that accentuated her willowy shape, she chose the richest of materials and embellished them with swags, chains, corsages, ruffles, furbelows, and boas (fig. 24). It is no accident that Henri Meilhac and Ludovic Halévy titled the play in which she debuted in 1880 *Frou Frou*, a term referring to "a rustling esp. of a woman's skirts" or "a showy or frilly ornamentation."[20] The star's personal wardrobe was equally extravagant. We often see her in a singular chinchilla coat, which she seems to have worn year-round, usually with an already stunning display of lace, satin, feathers, and jewels (see Bergman-Carton essay, fig. 8). Between seasons, she could be seen about town wearing a spectacular high-collared ermine capelet (fig. 23).

Strangely enough, the most feminine actress of her time also caused a sensation in breeches roles. Although it was common for actresses to play men in the nineteenth century—the American actress Charlotte Cushman, for one, was renowned for her portrayal of Romeo[21]—Bernhardt's excessive femininity gave her male impersonations a special thrill. It was a breeches role—the young Florentine troubadour in François Coppée's *Le passant* (*The Passerby*)—that first brought her critical acclaim, at the Odéon theater in 1869 (fig. 25). Between 1896,

fig. 23 Ermine capelet with high collar, c. 1898–1900. 33 1/2 x 26 3/4 in. (85 x 68 cm). Musée Galliera, Musée de la Mode de la Ville de Paris (GAL 1985.1.108)

Sarah Bernhardt.

when Bernhardt turned fifty-two, and 1900, she starred in three great male leads, in Alfred de Musset's *Lorenzaccio*, Shakespeare's *Hamlet* (fig. 26), and Edmond Rostand's *L'Aiglon*, in which she played the Duke of Reichstadt, Napoleon's son (see Silver essay, fig. 12). By the end of her life, she had eighteen breeches roles in her repertory, double the number of her early career.[22]

Bernhardt actually preferred men's roles. With the notable exception of Phaedra in Racine's play, she proclaimed that women's roles did not make "any great intellectual demand." Most women's parts were "mere play": "The characters are required to look pretty, to move gracefully, and to portray emotions natural to the average woman. Camille [the name in English of the protagonist of *La dame aux camélias*, and of the play itself[23]], with all her pathos and passion, is an easier study for a woman than L'Aiglon with his heroic aspirations."

In fact, the actress had a refreshing point of view about women and breeches roles:

A woman is better suited to play parts like L'Aiglon and Hamlet than a man. These roles portray youths of twenty or twenty-one with the minds of men of forty. A boy of twenty cannot understand the philosophy of Hamlet nor the

opposite:

fig. 24 Napoleon Sarony (American, b. Canada, 1821–1896), *Sarah Bernhardt in "Frou Frou,"* 1880. Albumen print on card, 6 11/16 x 4 5/8 in. (16.8 x 11.8 cm). Harvard Theatre Collection, Houghton Library, Cambridge, Massachusetts

fig. 25 W. & D. Downey (British, active 1863–1910s), *Sarah Bernhardt in "Le passant,"* 1869. Albumen print cabinet card, 6 1/2 x 4 3/8 in. (16.5 x 11 cm). Bibliothèque Nationale de France, Département des Arts du Spectacle, Paris

poetic enthusiasm of L'Aiglon. . . . An older man . . . does not look the boy, nor has he the ready adaptability of the woman who can combine the light carriage of youth with the mature thought of the man. The woman more readily looks the part, yet has the maturity of mind to grasp it.[24]

Bernhardt's performance as the young Aiglon may, ironically, have reignited the desire of many to see her again, well beyond age sixty, in the most celebrated female roles of her youth, especially Marguerite Gautier.[25] But it was Bernhardt in breeches who unleashed a riot of caricatures, including "Sarin Coquelhardt," in which the actress's name and body fuse with those of her distinguished male costar Constant Coquelin.[26] The front-page headline in a Boston paper of November 8, 1896, proclaimed "Sarah Soon to Turn Man." Here Bernhardt, in a glamorous gown, fences aggressively with her son; the image bespeaks not only her imminent sex change but also their rivalry over the Dreyfus Affair.

Bernhardt Fecit

As if her gender-bending were not galling enough, Bernhardt had a second career as a visible studio artist, regularly exhibiting sculpture at the Paris Salon from 1874 to 1891. She received an honorable mention for the monumental, if maudlin, *Après la tempête* (After the Storm; fig. 27) at the same Salon in which Georges Clairin's much-discussed portrait of her, and an oft-mentioned one by Louise Abbéma, hung. Bernhardt frequently had shows of her painting and sculpture in the cities where she was performing. Much as she flaunted her unconventionally skinny body in corsetless gowns, she gave a new twist to conventions of the woman artist's attire. Working in her studio in a white satin pants suit, designed by the sought-after couturier Charles Frederick Worth and accessorized by pumps with bows known as *noeuds de papillon*—butterfly bows (fig. 28)—Bernhardt feminized the then controversial masculine garb originally adopted by Rosa Bonheur, George Sand, and other female artists and writers. Yet she avoided self-consciously hyper-feminine representations at work of an earlier generation of women, including painters Elisabeth Vigée-Lebrun and Adelaïde Labille-Guiard.

The fact that Bernhardt blurred the line between masculine and feminine in her studio was not lost on the press. Her satin suit and beribboned slippers were a frequent focus of the caricatures made after she achieved recognition as a sculptor, and somewhat less as a painter, in the late 1870s. The attributes of her various careers—brush, palette, mallet, and calipers; lyre, plume, and tragic mask—often appear in these images. Stereotypes of Jewishness contribute to the presumed unnaturalness and decadence of woman as creative, as opposed to interpretative, artist. Cabriol's "L'Hydropathe Sarah Bernhardt" (fig. 29) boldly frames the diminutive figure of the actress in her studio outfit within a gigantic six-pointed star. The stark graphic presentation emphasizes other disturbing aspects: the masculine way she is sitting, splay-legged on a turned-around chair; the assertive full-frontal pose; the elongated face with unmistakably Semitic features; and the

opposite:

fig. 26   Lafayette (English, 1853–1923), Sarah Bernhardt as Hamlet, c. 1889. Gelatin silver print, 14 1/4 x 11 in. (36.2 x 27.9 cm). Gift of Frederick R. Koch, 1992; Harvard Theatre Collection, Houghton Library, Cambridge, Massachusetts

fig. 27   Sarah Bernhardt (French, 1844–1923), Après la tempête (After the Storm), 1876. Bronze

fig. 28 Melandri (French, active c. 1860s–80s), *Sarah Bernhardt Sculpting,* c. 1875. Albumen print cabinet card, 6 1/2 x 4 1/2 in. (16.5 x 11.4 cm). Bequest of Evert Jansen Wendell, 1918; Harvard Theatre Collection, Houghton Library, Cambridge, Massachusetts

fig. 29 Cabriol (Georges Lorin; French, dates unknown), *Sarah Bernhardt,* caricature printed as cover page of *Les hydropathes,* April 5, 1879. 11 x 9 in. (27.9 x 22.9 cm). Herbert D. and Ruth Schimmel Rare Book Purchase Fund, Jane Voorhees Zimmerli Museum, Rutgers, The State University of New Jersey, New Brunswick

top-heaviness of the image, produced by outsize head and frilly collar countering thin but forcefully positioned legs.[27] In one of André Gill's caricatures (fig. 30), Bernhardt again wears her stylish work clothes and further wields the implements of her arts; she has a bulging hooked nose and a serpentine form, and her leonine feet and tail suggest the sphinx. More baldly than any other, this caricature—chillingly invoking Jewishness, multiple occupations, and destructive sexual power— is a malevolent fusion of Bernhardt's perceived social transgressions.

À la Grande Artiste, l'Autre Grande Artiste

The centerpiece of the house Bernhardt had built for herself in 1875 near the Parc Monceau was a two-story atelier-salon. Documented in photographs, it is also the subject of the far-too-little-known watercolors of Marie-Désiré Bourgoin (fig. 31). Large and lush, one shows the otherwise empty room crammed with books and bibelots, while others show Bernhardt sculpting a reduced version of *After the Storm,* or painting her friend Louise Abbéma, who poses in exotic dress. Together with Georges Clairin and Gustave Doré, Abbéma helped decorate the new residence. She and Clairin were the most faithful chroniclers of Bernhardt's image and the central members of her self-appointed family.

fig. 30 André Gill (French, 1840–1885), *Sarah Bernhardt as a Sphinx*, caricature, published in *La lune rousse*, October 6, 1878, 25 x 18 1/8 in. (63.5 x 46 cm). Bibliothèque Nationale de France, Département des Arts du Spectacle, Paris

fig. 31 Marie-Désiré Bourgoin
(French, 1839–1912),
Sarah Bernhardt's Studio,
1879. Watercolor and
gouache over graphite
on paper, 26 11/16 x
20 7/8 in. (67.8 x 53.1 cm).
The Metropolitan
Museum of Art, New
York, Gift of Helen O.
Brice, 1942 (42.64.10)

In 1876, the same year that Clairin's portrait of Bernhardt appeared at the
Salon, Abbéma showed a large, much-discussed portrait of the actress.[28] At the next
Salon, Bernhardt returned the compliment by exhibiting a marble portrait bust
of Abbéma, who in turn displayed a sculpture for the only time in her life: a bronze
medallion of her heroine (fig. 33). Abbéma gives us an idealized yet deliberately
feminine portrait of Bernhardt, in which the chiseled profile is offset by curly fly-
away hair and profuse ruffles at the neck. That year, Bernhardt apparently made
a circular bronze portrait plaque of Abbéma (fig. 34). Remarkable for the depth of
its relief carving, the plaque by Bernhardt is alternately identified as a self-portrait
and a portrait of Abbéma. The appearance of the sitter, while arguably evoking

fig. 32 Louise Abbéma, n.d.
Photographic print,
6 7/8 x 4 7/8 in. (17.5 x
12.5 cm). Bibliothèque
Nationale de France,
Département
des Estampes, Paris

features shared by the two women, more convincingly points to Abbéma, whose physiognomic particularities—stepped nose, bony face, upswept but uncurly hair—and more tailored costume would constitute a very eccentric, indeed unprecedented, representation of Bernhardt. The countenance is markedly different from Bernhardt's unusual self-portrait in the form of an inkwell, in which she has a griffin's body, bat's wings, and a fish's tail (fig. 35). This work seems at once a rejoinder to those caricatures that emphasize her hybrid nature and an assertion of her transformative power.

The rich artistic dialogue, begun between the two women through the exchange of their portrait plaques, would continue for almost half a century.[29] The personal relationship between Bernhardt and Abbéma is as compelling as their artistic dialogue. Bow-tied and waistcoated, Louise Abbéma was the masculine foil to Bernhardt's carefully orchestrated femininity (fig. 32); even when Bernhardt flirted with transvestism, she continued to cultivate her female allure. In photographs where she and Abbéma merely seem to be hamming it up in front of the camera, like the one in which the tragedienne poses as an odalisque and her friend as a standing pasha, they knowingly invert heterosexual norms (fig. 36). Much as they asserted themselves as artists within the masculinized space of the Salon, they perform their intimate relationship for the camera as a playful transgression of

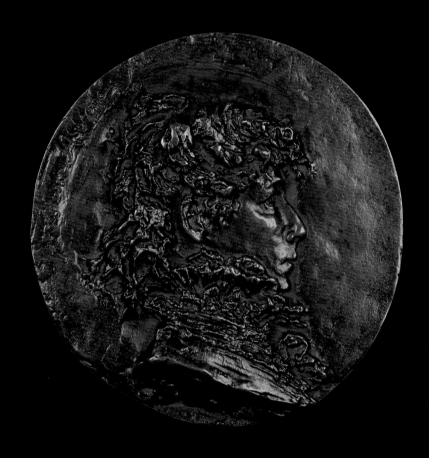

fig. 33 Louise Abbéma (French, 1858–1927), Plaque of Sarah Bernhardt, 1875. Bronze, diam. 4 1/8 in. (10.5 cm). Billy Rose Theatre Collection, The New York Public Library for the Performing Arts

fig. 34 Sarah Bernhardt (French, 1844–1923), Portrait of Louise Abbéma, 1875 (?), or Self-Portrait, 1878 (?). Bronze, 8 7/16 x 7 1/8 x 1 1/2 in. (21.1 x 18.1 x 3.8 cm). Museum of Fine Arts, Boston, Otis Norcross Fund and Gift of Robert A. Radloff and Ann Beha (1989.196)

fig. 35 Sarah Bernhardt (French,
1844–1923), Fantastic
Inkwell (Self-Portrait as a
Sphinx), 1880. Bronze,
12 1/2 x 7 1/2 x 9 in. (31.8 x
19.1 x 22.9 cm). Museum
of Fine Arts, Boston,
Helen and Alice Colburn
Fund (1973.551)

the typically feminized Orient.[30] Abbéma's masculine attire and passionate attachment to Bernhardt were enough to provoke a great deal of gossip in the first decade of their friendship. Evidently Abbéma owned an extensive series of photographs of Bernhardt in a variety of poses and costumes, which she displayed in albums in the salon area of her own studio. All of the photographs bore the same dedication: "To Louise Abbéma, the great artist, [from] Sarah Bernhardt, the other great artist" ("À Louise Abbéma, la grande artiste, Sarah Bernhardt, l'autre grande artiste").[31]

Dying Nightly

As to the story that Bernhardt slept in a coffin, a picture taken around 1880 by Melandri is the image that did most to spread the rumor (fig. 37). Fabricated and marketed by Bernhardt even before she had reached the midpoint of her life or her career (she was about thirty-five), the photograph conjures the performance of death as well as the real possibility of her imminent demise. To heighten the drama, her marble portrait bust of Abbéma (fig. 38) contemplates Bernhardt's "corpse," in a modern inversion of Rembrandt's painting *Aristotle with a Bust of Homer.* In this context Bernhardt's placement of the bust of Abbéma above her

fig. 36 Louise Abbéma as pasha and Sarah Bernhardt as odalisque, n.d. Cabinet card, 6 1/2 x 4 3/4 in. (16.4 x 12.1 cm). Bibliothèque Nationale de France, Département des Arts du Spectacle, Paris

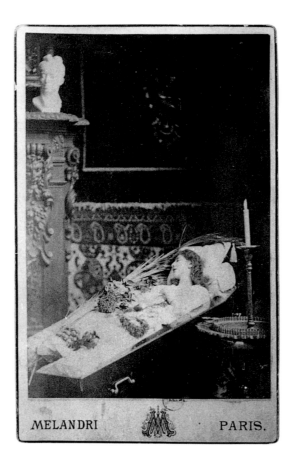

MELANDRI   PARIS.

coffin turns her companion into a guardian figure at the crossroads of mortality
and immortality, policing the threshold between life and death. The photograph
symbolizes their personal relationship as lovers and their shared identity,
struggling against prescriptive assumptions about women and about women artists
in particular. As such, it is disturbing that the upper portion of the photograph,
which shows the bust, is sometimes cropped when the image is reproduced.[32]
The two women's sweet revenge for this erasure is that they both lived long and
successful lives.

There may be no photograph associated with Bernhardt that tells us more
about her artistic and emotional trajectory. As suggested by the popularity of
such images as Henry Peach Robinson's famous photograph of a young woman
expiring, Fading Away (1858; Royal Photographic Society, London), John Everett
Millais's oil Ophelia (1850–51; Tate Gallery, London), and Bernhardt's own marble
relief of the same heroine (1881; Royal Danish Theatre, Copenhagen), death as
the ideal state of submissive womanhood was so pervasive a notion that many
could barely look at a sleeping woman without seeing her as already virtuously
dead. The photograph of Bernhardt also invokes the cult of invalidism and
early death that marked the real lives of nineteenth-century women and men.[33]

fig. 38   Sarah Bernhardt (French,
          1844–1923), Portrait Bust
          of Louise Abbéma, 1878.
          Marble, 16 1/2 x 10 5/8 x
          8 5/8 in. (42 x 27 x 22 cm).
          Musée d'Orsay, Paris
          (RF 3756)

As Bernhardt's own life story suggests, she was far from immune. Her memoirs, ending with her first American tour, of 1880–81, are riddled with references to her own suffering from, apparently, tuberculosis and neurasthenia. Her recollection of caring for her younger sister Régine as she was dying of tuberculosis is especially salient: "In front of the window was my coffin, where I frequently installed myself to learn my parts. Therefore when I took my sister to my home I found it quite natural to sleep every night in this little bed of white satin which was to be my last couch."[34]

Dating from around the same period, the coffin photograph may have yet another symbolic valence. In April 1880, Bernhardt resigned from the Comédie Française, where she had achieved the highest position of *sociétaire*. For the record, her decision to leave was prompted by her frustration at having to perform in a play she detested, Émile Augier's *L'aventurière* (*The Adventuress*). But more than avenging her honor, Bernhardt was intent on honoring a contract she had accepted without notifying the Comédie. The engagement at the Gaiety Theatre in London was a prelude to her first American tour. The photograph thus put a lid, as it were, on her career at the most prestigious theater in France.

The Distant Horizon

This denouement has all the earmarks of a liberation tale. Free to choose her own repertory and to be actress and manager of her own troupe for the first time, Bernhardt was at the helm of her career as she had not been before. The fact that within six months she was off touring the New World could only dramatize the sense of autonomy. Among the plays she performed in the United States and Canada—*Phèdre*, *Adrienne Lecouvreur*, *Hernani*, *Frou Frou*—was a new one, Alexandre Dumas fils's *La dame aux camélias*. It would become the most performed role of the North American tour, and of her entire career. Just on her first trip to America, she died sixty-five times as Marguerite Gautier (fig. 39).

The conclusion of Bernhardt's memoirs (she never wrote the second volume she intended) reveals how important was this sojourn. *My Double Life* closes with a description of her triumphant return home in the wake of her "great voyage": "I conclude the first volume of my souvenirs here, for this is really the first halting-place of my life, the real starting-point of my physical and moral being." After acknowledging how much she had matured in America and how much the promise of "the distant horizon" had meant to her, she ends her memoirs on an elated, death-defying note:

> My life, which I had at first expected to be very short, now seemed likely to be very very long; and it gave me great joy to think of the infernal displeasure that would cause my enemies.
> I resolved to live.
> I resolved to be the great artist that I wished to be.
> And, from the time of my return onward, I dedicated myself to my life.[35]

fig. 39   Napoleon Sarony
(American, b. Canada,
1821–1896), *Death
Scene from "La dame aux
camélias,"* 1880. Albumen
print cabinet card,
6 9/16 x 4 1/4 in. (16.5 x
10.8 cm). Bequest
of Evert Jansen Wendell,
1918; Harvard Theatre
Collection, Houghton
Library, Cambridge,
Massachusetts

Bernhardt's stirring ode to life is full of the theatrics we have come to associate
with the actress. Even when it is a question of life and death, she cannot resist the
delicious pleasure of annoying her rivals.

Paradoxically, her success at dying *released* her from expectations that she
would die young. As a classical tragedienne, Bernhardt must have had an uncanny
relationship to death. Her living depended on it. As she expired onstage, she would
often end by coughing up blood or falling into a dead faint. By the early 1880s,
her talent for dying was so remarked on that a final death agony was practically
mandatory. Rhapsodic critics insisted that she never died the same way twice. For
the next forty years, she died nightly, and sometimes two times a day, as Camille/
Marguerite Gautier, Phaedra, Doña Sol (in *Hernani*), Hamlet, Cleopatra, Tosca, and
a host of others (fig. 40).

To be sure, Bernhardt's thoroughly believable deaths are a tribute to her acting,
but they are far more than that. By dying nightly, Bernhardt performed, rather than
lived, the penance for her heroines' deviation from the straight and narrow—and
thus neatly dispensed with having to live it herself.[36] Bernhardt would die happily
in public for many years.

Reproduction and Immortality

The new life that Bernhardt invokes at the end of her memoirs differed indeed
from the life that preceded it. What most distinguished it from the old was the
actress's increasing involvement with mass culture. Once she was back in France,
she began a twenty-year collaboration with Victorien Sardou (see Levitov essay,
fig. 13), who wrote eight melodramas with her in mind, including *Théodora* (1884),
La Tosca (1887), and *Cléopâtre* (1890); they would be among her most famous roles.

Much better known today than the play, Giacomo Puccini's opera *Tosca*, which premiered in 1900, was so closely based on the work written for Bernhardt that the librettists, Luigi Illica and Giuseppe Giacosa, were sued, successfully, by Sardou for plagiarism. During the years that she worked with Sardou, Bernhardt sequentially rented the Théâtre de l'Ambigu (in the name of her seventeen-year-old son), bought an interest in the Théâtre de la Porte Saint-Martin, and in 1893 purchased outright the Théâtre de la Renaissance, where she was sole producer and director. In 1899, she took a twenty-five-year lease on the Théâtre de Paris, located on the place du Châtelet, which would later bear her name—Théâtre Sarah Bernhardt (now the Théâtre de la Ville).[37]

By the time she was in high gear, Bernhardt had become a one-woman dramatic enterprise—a virtual Sarah Bernhardt, Inc.—the success of her plays guaranteed through constant repetition and reproduction. One U.S. reviewer likened her repertory—in which, apart from wardrobe and makeup, the heroines were interchangeable—to Henry Ford's assembly line: "Year after year Victorien Sardou turned out a new vehicle for her talent, as they turn out motor-cars, all on the same lines, but each year's 'model' a slight mechanical improvement on the last."[38] No fan of the actress, George Bernard Shaw remarked much less favorably on this reproductive model:

Madame Bernhardt comes to us with a new play, in which she kills somebody with any weapon from a hairpin to a hatchet; intones a great deal of dialogue as a sample of what is called "the golden voice," to the great delight of our

fig. 41   Alphonse Mucha (Czech, 1860–1939), Gismonda, 1894. Color lithograph, 84 x 29 1/8 in. (213.4 x 74 cm). Collection of Mr. and Mrs. Jack Rennert, New York

fig. 42 Diadem for *La princesse lointaine*, c. 1895. Metal and pearls, 6 1/4 x 12 5/8 x 10 1/4 in. (16 x 32 x 26 cm). Bibliothèque Nationale de France, Musée et Bibliothèque de l'Opéra, Paris

curates, who all produce more or less golden voices by exactly the same trick; goes through her well-known feat of tearing a passion to tatters at the end of the second or fourth act. . . . This routine constitutes a permanent exhibition, which is refurbished every year with fresh scenery, fresh dialogue, and a fresh author, whilst remaining itself invariable.[39]

Bernhardt's turn to melodrama took her from the classical theaters of France to the more popular realm of the Grands Boulevards, and it was the publicity for these more popular houses that in turn brought her to Alphonse Mucha.[40] The Czech-born decorative pioneer of Art Nouveau owed his initial public recognition to the seven posters he made to advertise Bernhardt's theatrical roles. These are among the finest examples of fin-de-siècle graphic art. The internationally famous style Mucha became synonymous with the flowing organic lines, dreamy color, and abstracted patterns he defined in his first poster, of Bernhardt as Gismonda, from Sardou's play by that name (fig. 41). From 1895 to 1900, when he was under contract to the actress, Mucha also designed stage sets and costumes for her productions, including the diadem of jeweled lilies she wore as Mélisande in the third act of Rostand's La princesse lointaine (The Faraway Princess; figs. 42, 43). In Mucha's poster for a banquet honoring Bernhardt, the actress—frontal, hieratic, and crowned—

fig. 43 Reutlinger Studio (French, active 1850–1930), *La princesse lointaine*, c. 1895. Albumen print cabinet card, 6 1/2 x 4 1/4 in. (16.5 x 10.8 cm). Harvard Theatre Collection, Houghton Library, Cambridge, Massachusetts

fig. 44   Alphonse Mucha (Czech, 1860–1939), *Sarah Bernhardt*, 1896. Color lithograph, 26 1/4 x 19 in. (66.7 x 48.3 cm). Collection of Norma Canelas and William D. Roth, Winter Haven, Florida, and New York

fig. 45 Alphonse Mucha (Czech, 1860–1939), Studies for *La dame aux camélias* (designs for cover and interior of special program), 1896. Pencil and watercolor on paper, 11 x 18 1/8 in. (28 x 46 cm). Mucha Trust, London

following pages:

fig. 46 Alphonse Mucha (Czech, 1860–1939), *La dame aux camélias*, 1896. Color lithograph, 81 1/2 x 30 in. (207 x 76.2 cm). Collection of Mr. and Mrs. Joel Schur, Greenwich, Connecticut

fig. 47 Alphonse Mucha (Czech, 1860–1939), *Lorenzaccio*, 1896. Color lithograph, 80 1/2 x 29 7/8 in. (204 x 76 cm). Private collection, Maryland

fig. 48 Alphonse Mucha (Czech, 1860–1939), *La Tosca*, 1899. Color lithograph, 41 x 15 in. (104 x 38 cm). Posters Please, Inc., New York

fig. 49 Alphonse Mucha (Czech, 1860–1939), *Tragique histoire d'Hamlet*, 1899. Color lithograph, 81 1/2 x 30 1/4 in. (207 x 76.8 cm). Collection of Mr. and Mrs. Ivan Lendl, New York

looks every inch the Art Nouveau icon of a new Byzantium (fig. 44). Like her success, Mucha's depended on repetition and variation. The format of the *Gismonda* poster became the prototype for all the others: the title of the play at the top, the name of the theater where it was to be performed at the bottom, and between them, the single ethereal figure of Bernhardt *en rôle*, framed in an alcove and holding a prop—a palm for Gismonda, who carries it in the Easter procession of the play's last act; a camellia, as proffered by a deus ex machina hand, for Marguerite Gautier.

Adhering to the industrial model that Mucha originally conceived in 1895, each of his posters for Bernhardt is astonishingly fresh: *La dame aux camélias* and *Lorenzaccio* (1896), *La samaritaine* (1897), *La Tosca* and *Médée* (1898), and *Hamlet* (1899) (figs. 46–49; see also Bergman-Carton essay, fig. 5). Yet Mucha made extensive preparatory studies for his posters and for related Bernhardt projects, among them sketches for the costumes of Hamlet, drawings of the legs of the figure of Lorenzaccio, and sketches for a never realized program for *La dame aux camélias* (fig. 45).

Upper-class establishments such as the Comédie and the Opéra disdained illustrated posters. In appropriating the advertising strategies of the cabarets, Bernhardt allied herself with popular entertainment, as she did through her move to melodrama. By the 1890s, oversize-format posters were the norm. Mucha's, along with those of numerous competitors, were plastered all over the walls of Paris. So many *Gismonda* posters were torn down or purchased on the sly that Bernhardt ordered four thousand more to be sold at a later date. If she or her image was going to be commodified, as she had planned, she would be the one to profit from it.

The poster was celebrated by writers of the left and the bohemian community of Montmartre as a new, democratic form of art. For others its very accessibility made it an emblem of socialist and anti-establishment ferment. When one of the

LA TOSCA

DRAME EN CINQ ACTES ET SIX TABLEAUX DE M. VICTORIEN SARDOU

THÉATRE·SARAH·BERNHARDT

Mucha

TRAGIQUE HISTOIRE D'HAMLET
PRINCE DE DANEMARK
SARAH BERNHARDT

Mucha

THÉATRE SARAH BERNHARDT

foremost illustrators of the fin-de-siècle, Jules Chéret, portrayed Bernhardt advertising face powder (the brand name, La Diaphane, refers to its transparency), his audience would instantly recognize the negative associations of makeup with actresses and prostitutes (fig. 50). As a *chérette*, one of Chéret's archetypal glamour girls, Bernhardt could be a threatening figure of commercial upward mobility.[41]

Sadie Goes to Vaudeville

The tour de force of Bernhardt's savvy sense of supply and demand has to be her nine visits to America. Beginning in 1880, when she was thirty-six, and ending in 1918, when she was seventy-four, they spanned four decades. With one exception, the first tour of seven months, each lasted from eleven to sixteen months and extended to at least fifty cities and towns across the country. Several of these so-called American tours included stops in Canada and South America, while others extended to Europe and beyond, to Russia. On Bernhardt's world tour of 1891–93, two trips through the United States were part of an itinerary entailing both Americas; Samoa, Australia, and New Zealand; western Europe, Turkey, Greece, and Senegal. Bernhardt's first American farewell tour, organized by the Shubert brothers, took place in 1905–6 (fig. 51). It was followed by three more American farewell tours, in 1910–11, 1912–13, and 1916–18.[42] She traveled on her own train, "Le Sarah Bernhardt." This kind of reach, enhanced through repetition, was the stuff of mass marketing.

Bernhardt understood the need for paid publicity. But she also got plenty of it free. By the time she recognized the triumph of her characteristic "feminine" style and began to take advantage of it, so did others. Her emphatic gestural and emotional acting, together with her performance of female and male roles, made her a natural for impersonators. What has not been chronicled before, even by specialists of popular entertainment, is how far back the impersonations go. Anyone who has been called "Sarah Heartburn" might be interested to know that the minstrel William Henry Rice starred in a performance with that title at

fig. 51   **Map of Sarah Bernhardt tour route ("All Roads Lead to Texas"), 1905–6. 14.5 x 9 in. (36.8 x 22.9 cm). Museum of the City of New York, Theater Collection, Gift of Mrs. Walter Lowe Fairchild (40.18.170)**

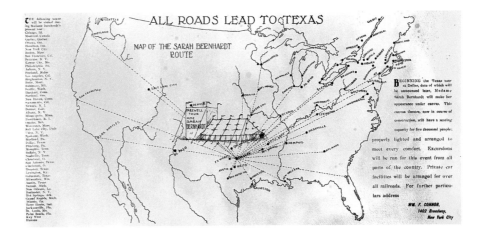

Philadelphia's Central Theatre in 1881. Even more unexpected, Bernhardt, who was performing *Adrienne Lecouvreur* and *Frou Frou* at the Chestnut Theatre at the same time, actually went to see her imitator. In the 1880s and 1890s, George Gale and Francis Leon of Haverly's Minstrels impersonated Bernhardt; some years later, so did British-born Marie Lloyd, whom T. S. Eliot called "the greatest music-hall artist of her time."[43] Female impersonators of Bernhardt such as Rice, Gale, and Leon all played in blackface and did diverse ethnic characters as well. Using alternative identities to camouflage their origins was a common strategy of assimilation for many immigrants. The superb poster of Leon as Sarah Bernhardt once had another half showing him as "Creole Rose" (fig. 52). Minstrelsy's best-paid performer in the 1880s, born Patrick Francis Glassey in Ireland, Francis Leon was so celebrated for his perfect femininity that he copyrighted himself "The Only Leon," to distinguish himself from a slew of imitators.[44]

Bernhardt was the first big-name star to cross over from legitimate theater to vaudeville. Between the mid-1890s and the end of World War I, a wave of famous stage actors followed suit. During her first season, 1912–13, vaudeville was at its height. A playbill for Bernhardt's tour those years boasted of vaudeville's having secured the services of the world's premier tragedienne:

fig. 52 "The Only Leon" as Sarah Bernhardt, n.d. Poster, 18 x 10 in. (45.7 x 25.4 cm). Harvard Theatre Collection, Houghton Library, Cambridge, Massachusetts

> The announcement that vaudeville would present the world's greatest actress, Madame Sarah Bernhardt . . . brought first an echo of universal surprise and then a flow of appreciation . . . if any vaudeville manager had had the temerity to think of her at all, she would have been considered an impossibility. As well attempt tempting Paderewski to compose ragtime, or persuade Rodin to model "sand statuary" in Atlantic City.[45]

When we consider that over the years she appeared on bills with La Napierkowska, a Polish wriggle dancer; W. C. Fields as a juggler, dressed in a tramp's outfit; three separate sets of performers posing as classical statuary; a cockatoo imitating a cornet; a soft-shoe team; Jack Benny playing the syncopated violin; and Warren Weems, advertised as "the merry blackface performer," Bernhardt's roots in the classical theater seem far away, to say the least.[46]

Much the same could be said of her American tour of 1905–6, when Bernhardt found herself in the middle of a war between the Syndicate, the theatrical trust that monopolized bookings in legitimate theaters and opera houses, and her sponsors, the Shubert brothers, who set themselves up in competition. When the Syndicate forbade her to appear in any of its theaters, she and the Shuberts sought other venues. During this tour, the world's most famous tragic actress played convention halls, circus tents (fig. 53), skating rinks, a combined swimming pool–auditorium, a boathouse, a former stable, and the dining room of the Hotel Royal Poinciana in Palm Beach. She played to sold-out houses even though she performed only in French. The more discerning members of her audience could follow along with the authorized English editions of the plays, copyrighted by

fig. 53 Henry Clogenson (American, active 19th– early 20th centuries), *Sarah Bernhardt in Front of Circus Tent, Dallas, Texas, 1906.* Inscribed to Louise Abbéma: "Voilà la tente dans laquelle j'ai jouée. Ah! Que je regrette que tu n'ais pas vu cela!" (Here is the tent in which I performed. Oh how I wish you could have seen this!) Gelatin silver print, 9 1/8 x 11 3/4 in. (25 x 30 cm). Bibliothèque Nationale de France, Département des Estampes, Paris

fig. 54 Printed play text in English: *The Bernhardt Edition: La Tosca,* published by Fred Rullman, n.d. 10 1/4 x 6 7/8 in. (26 x 17.5 cm). Harvard Theatre Collection, Houghton Library, Cambridge, Massachusetts

the actress (fig. 54). Bernhardt had an extraordinary capacity to bring classical theater and European culture to a mass public, whether in a circus tent in Kansas or at the Metropolitan Opera House in New York.

Viewed from the traditional hierarchical point of view, in which legitimate theater is at the top, Bernhardt's career—from the Comédie Française to the boulevard and the music hall, to vaudeville and film—is a startling example of downward mobility. But from today's point of view, her incremental embrace of new forms of popular entertainment and new technologies is prescient.[47] The actress's decision to star in movies was consistent with her desire to disseminate her image as broadly as possible. For this, and for the simple desire to work and thus be alive, she kept going.

She Looks No More Than Twenty-five

Bernhardt's heightened consciousness of death induced an appetite for life so great that it may well explain the perpetual youth many critics continued to find in her acting when she was well into her sixties and seventies. One press clipping captioned "She Grows Younger with Her Years" confronted "Bernhardt at 18" with "Bernhardt a Grandmother and Past 50," and at first glance they are identical profiles. She "looks no more than twenty-five," she is "never a minute older than her heart—which, everyone knows, is 17": these typify the laudatory comments made when she performed *L'Aiglon* at age sixty-six in a London music hall. Such willing disbelief must have been a comfort, but it could not keep at bay the more withering assessments of her late performances. "The tremendous old woman was nothing so much as a wounded lioness," wrote a detractor who saw Bernhardt play Marguerite Gautier in 1916. Another remarked with obvious distaste that "despite her luminous reputation," she was "almost grotesque."[48] Such criticism not withstanding, the fact that a woman approaching seventy could still arch her entire body backward was hardly unimpressive. What might appear at best gimmicky, and at worst a desperate attempt to maintain her popularity, indicates the enduring force of her classical training.[49]

Bernhardt had to contend with more than the challenge of aging. In 1915 her right leg was amputated above the knee, as a result of complications from the improper treatment of an earlier injury. Contrary to popular belief, she never performed Hamlet with a wooden leg. She categorically refused to wear a prosthesis, because it was cumbersome, and similarly rejected crutches and wheelchair. Instead, she ordered a litter, narrow enough to slide easily into a car or elevator (see Silver essay, fig. 17).[50] She had the wood painted white and the sides carved and gilded in Louis XV style. Until her death in 1923, she had herself carried in public. She gave up *Hamlet* but continued to perform one-acts, old and new.

How Bernhardt finessed her disability is apparent in descriptions by her contemporaries. An anonymous author observed: "As one crosses a ford by stepping from stone to stone, she is able to go, if she wants to, from chair back to sideboard, from balustrade to bank in a garden. Of course, no one in the audience will be aware . . . of the subterfuges which her skill makes use of, for her talent as a speaker is without equal." It is hard to think of Bernhardt's amputation without considering World War I and her wartime repertory, which included the one-act *Du théâtre au champ d'honneur* (From the Theater to the Field of Honor). About this play, a critic remarked: "When she stands before her judges as Jeanne d'Arc or dies gloriously as Queen Cleopatra, one forgets her accident. And as the gallant dying soldier on 'The Field of Honor,' she need not walk."[51]

Media response to the amputation reveals the worst aspects of celebrity as commodity and fetish. A film magnate offered Bernhardt a well-paying contract to let him advertise his movie as her first legless performance. P. T. Barnum cabled an offer of ten thousand dollars to display her severed leg. According to Boston's *Sunday Herald*, Bernhardt responded at once to the showman's offer: "If it is my left leg you want, see the doctors; but if it's the right leg, you must see my manager in New York."[52]

The lure of vaudeville for Bernhardt must have been at least in part financial—she commanded the exorbitant fee of seven thousand dollars per week, a sum twice that paid to any other performer on the scene, and also greater than anyone made on the legitimate stage. After the amputation, vaudeville must have been all the more attractive: brief appearances requiring little movement suited the star best. Film, which allowed for interruption, meant that she could make the five-reel, sixty-minute movie *Jeanne Doré* without having to walk (see illustration in Chronology). Yet even with the heavy makeup for which she was known, it was hard

fig. 55   Sarah Bernhardt wearing dark glasses, filming *La voyante* (The Fortune-teller), 1923. Gelatin silver print, 6 3/4 x 9 1/8 in. (17.1 x 23.1 cm). Bibliothèque Nationale de France, Département des Arts du Spectacle, Paris

to camouflage Bernhardt's age in her late films, such as *La voyante* (The Fortune-teller), which she was making at the time of her death (fig. 55).[53] Moreover, Bernhardt's style of acting, which had revolutionized classical tragedy in the 1870s, was increasingly outmoded. Henrik Ibsen's naturalism and actors like Eleonora Duse were now the fashion; even Bernhardt performed in an Ibsen play, *The Lady from the Sea*, in 1906.

How long Bernhardt successfully managed to repeat herself remains a matter of opinion. One enthusiast commented in 1907: "It is remarkable that after being dead so often and in so great a number of parts, Madame Sarah Bernhardt at this stage in her artistic career, can still find new devices in herself and show us a way of dying that we did not know before." But at times that seriousness could implode and collapse into comedy. A critic with a New York paper in 1912 reported that Bernhardt's deaths "by self-administered poison . . . totaled well over 10,000; she had jumped into the scenic artist's Seine 7,000 times, had sent 5,000 bullets into her head with a revolver; stabbed herself as frequently as all her other 'deaths' put together."[54]

Queen of Camp

In her now classic essay "Notes on Camp," Susan Sontag relegated Bernhardt's films to the scrap heap.[55] "Many of the objects prized by Camp taste are old-fashioned, out-of-date, *démodé*," Sontag asserted, before musing: "Maybe Method Acting (James Dean, Rod Steiger, Warren Beatty) will seem as Camp some day . . . as Sarah

fig. 56 Eva Le Gallienne as
L'Aiglon (with Ethel
Barrymore), 1934. Gelatin
silver print, 8 x 10 in.
(20.3 x 25.4 cm). Museum
of the City of New York,
Theater Collection,
Gift of Mr. and Mrs.
Spencer Merriam Berger
(50.178.679)

Bernhardt's does, in the films she made at the end of her career." Much as she was
for Marilyn Monroe's character in *The Seven Year Itch*, the original Bernhardt
was irretrievable for the critic. Because she summoned Bernhardt the film actress
"in the process of aging or deterioration," Sontag was unable to imagine her as the
paragon of turn-of-the-century aesthetics. Elsewhere, for instance, the critic had
nothing but praise for "the thin, flowing sexless bodies in Art Nouveau prints and
posters," but she failed to acknowledge that Bernhardt was the model for and pro-
genitor of this style.[56]

Sontag was right when she claimed that Bernhardt was out-of-date in her
films. She was wrong, however, when she asserted that camp's imitative impulse—
its victory of "style" over "content," "aesthetics" over "morality," "irony" over
"tragedy"—lacks the capacity for social critique. Sontag appeared not to recognize
either the potential for political radicalism that camp, homosexual camp in
particular, represents or the possibility that there might be a category applicable
to Bernhardt, something akin to lesbian camp. (If the photograph of Bernhardt
and Abbéma as odalisque and pasha isn't lesbian camp, I don't know what is.)

Old-fashioned as Sontag may have found her style, Bernhardt's reproduction
of self was a completely engaged act, even a form of avant-gardism. By using
mass culture to replicate herself, Bernhardt made her name synonymous with the
actress in the West. Stardom as we know it today cannot be understood without
her example. We may take it as a given that celebrities are to be photographed,

featured in magazines, quoted as newsworthy, subjected to biographical inquiry, used to sell products, and generally worshipped in our culture. But that wasn't the case before Bernhardt. With her, stardom became an international language, a shared experience of emotional identification brought about by mass-produced media, especially photography and film. There is even a potent irony at work here. Bernhardt died before the advent of talking films, and thus it is impossible for us to experience her greatest gift fully: her voice. The poor quality of early sound recordings gives little idea of what Victor Hugo called her *voix d'or*—her golden voice. Although she is known to have spoken her lines while making a film version of *La dame aux camélias* in 1911–12, we have to make do with pantomime and subtitles. As a result, the mute image of Bernhardt is how we remember her.[57]

Hollywood Legend

Bernhardt established the template for show business icons as we know them. She launched the vogue for fashionable vamps like Theda Bara, née Theodosia Goodman, who starred in the film *Cleopatra* in 1917, when Bernhardt was playing the role in a one-act in vaudeville. When the great comedienne Fanny Brice spoofed Bara in "I'm Bad," or when Bobby Vernon, one of the original Keystone Kops, cross-dressed as Cleopatra, they were parodying Bernhardt too.[58] Brice reserved her darts for Bernhardt alone in the song "Sadie Salome," Sadie being a nickname for Sarah and *Salome* the infamous Oscar Wilde play that he wrote with Bernhardt in mind but that she never performed.[59] In fact, only if we know that Brice was imitating Bernhardt can we understand Barbra Streisand in *Funny Girl* fifty years later. When she belts out "I'm the Greatest Star," and the lyric "I'm a natural cougher" with exaggerated throat-clearing, she is parodying Bernhardt as the consumptive Marguerite in *La dame aux camélias*. Bernhardt lived on as well in stage performances of L'Aiglon by such fabled actresses as Maude Adams and Eva Le Gallienne (figs. 56, 57). And lest we forget, there is Bernhardt's enormous legacy for opera, stand-up comedy, and drag.[60] The experience of our great-grandparents seeing Sarah Bernhardt live survives in a lexicon of phrases, pronounced to whining children, especially girls, when they are being overly dramatic: "Who do you think you are, Sarah Bernhardt?" and "You're a regular Sarah Heartburn" are repeated to this day.

The number of evocations of Bernhardt in Hollywood films testifies to her reach. *Babes on Broadway*, a typically lush Metro-Goldwyn-Mayer production directed by Busby Berkeley in 1941, features Judy Garland and Mickey Rooney as starry-eyed young actors. In the scene paying homage to the golden age of New York theater, Garland, gotten up in the stretchy Aiglon bodysuit in which Bernhardt was much photographed, and a short blond wig, recites the hero's speech on the plain of Wagram (fig. 58). No amount of declamatory zeal can disguise the dismal French accent, yet all the bad French in the world can't threaten Bernhardt's place in the canon. In the duo's first song-and-dance routine in the movie, when Rooney croons: "When you're arising, start . . . exercising daily . . . bend and touch the

fig. 57 Napoleon Sarony Studio, *Maude Adams as L'Aiglon*, c. 1901. Gelatin silver print, 5 1/4 x 3 3/4 in. (13.3 x 9.5 cm). Museum of the City of New York, Theater Collection

floor fifty times or more," Garland's retort, "A fine start to be a Bernhardt,"
gives voice to the indisputable ambition of countless actors before and since. The
number of references to Bernhardt by actors in other Hollywood films confirms
her influence. These include John Barrymore in Howard Hawks's *Twentieth Century*
(1934), Joseph Cotten in William Dieterle's *Portrait of Jennie* (1948), Jane Powell in
Robert Z. Leonard's *Nancy Goes to Rio* (1950), Julie Andrews in Robert Wise's *Star!*
(1968), and Nicole Kidman in Baz Luhrmann's *Moulin Rouge!* (2001).[61]

Bernhardt's specter features most conspicuously in a musical comedy, one
of the few theatrical forms in which she never plied her craft. The plot of Charles
Walters's *The Barkleys of Broadway* (1949), with a screenplay by Betty Comden and
Adolph Green, revolves around Bernhardt's stature as the consummate French
artiste. Aspiring to move beyond the song-and-dance act she and movie husband
Fred Astaire have perfected on Broadway, the character played by Ginger Rogers,
enticed by the title role in a serious drama called *The Young Sarah* (fig. 59), succumbs
to the wiles of French playwright and director Jacques Barredout (Jacques François).
Unbeknownst to Rogers, her dramatic success depends on Astaire's coaching her
by phone, devilishly impersonating Barredout's distinctive French accent. Rogers,
like Garland in *Babes on Broadway*, attempts to replicate Bernhardt, here reciting
"The Marseillaise" as her audition piece for the Conservatoire, with a French accent
even less convincing than that of Garland (who was originally cast to play the role).
When Rogers discovers the hoax, she returns to both Astaire and Broadway in a
smash-hit song-and-dance extravaganza where Manhattan dazzlingly replaces the

fig. 58 Judy Garland in *Babes on
Broadway* (MGM, 1941),
directed by Busby
Berkeley. Academy of
Motion Picture Arts and
Sciences, Beverly Hills,
California

fig. 59 Ginger Rogers in The Barkleys of Broadway (MGM, 1949), directed by Charles Walters

Parisian setting of *The Young Sarah*. Her lesson—also the moral of *The Barkleys of Broadway*—is that Fred and musical comedy are as good as, maybe better than, classical drama. Bernhardt is the foil for Rogers's recognition of her own talent as an equally golden-throated but home-grown hoofer, even though she does not realize that Bernhardt made this same voyage from high to popular entertainment.

So when Marilyn Monroe, after comparing her Dazzledent commercial with Sarah Bernhardt on the stage, asks the question "Was she magnificent?" the answer is a resounding "Yes!"

Jeanne Darc

Sarah Bernhardt

IMP. DRAEGER & LESIEUR...PARIS.   NOUVᵉˢ AFFICHES ARTISTIQUES ... G. DE MALHERBE & H.A. CELLOT RUE N-D DES CHAMPS.84   VERDOUX DUCOURTIOUX & HUILLARD SC.

Kenneth E. Silver

SARAH BERNHARDT AND THE THEATRICS OF FRENCH NATIONALISM

From Roland's Daughter to Napoleon's Son

fig. 1 Eugène Grasset (French, 1841–1917), *Sarah Bernhardt as Jeanne d'Arc* (second version), 1894. Poster, 47 1/4 x 31 1/2 in. (120 x 80 cm). Bibliothèque Nationale de France, Département des Estampes, Paris

What Becomes a Legend Most?

Sarah Bernhardt was not just the most famous actress in the world for more than half a century, she was also the world's most famous Frenchwoman. "France without Sarah Bernhardt would be like France without the stirring memory of Napoleon," wrote an American admirer in 1917.[1] Three years earlier, the French playwright Henri Lavedan compared her to the promoter of the Suez Canal: "Alongside [Ferdinand] de Lesseps, Mme Sarah Bernhardt, of truly national character and an unalloyed patriot, merits the title Great Frenchman."[2] She remained a touchstone for Frenchness more than two decades after her death. On the centennial of her birth—soon after the liberation of Paris from Nazi occupation—French national radio attached a plaque to the building at 3 rue de l'École de Médecine:

> 25 October 1844
> Here was born
> Sarah Bernhardt
> Glory of our Theater

This plaque has been affixed on October 25, 1944, under the auspices of the French radio service, which on this day carried the name of Sarah Bernhardt around the world, where Sarah Bernhardt carried on high the name of France.[3]

Since it is not at all certain that Bernhardt was born anywhere near this building in the Sixth Arrondissement—her place of birth has been given as either 125 or 265 rue du Faubourg-Saint-Honoré, in the Eighth Arrondissement; 22 rue de la Michodière, in the Second; or, according to one source, somewhere in the Twelfth—we might conclude that facts are perhaps irrelevant when it comes to legends.[4]

Bernhardt herself thought so. As an actress, she was acutely aware of the differences between reality and illusion, and between dull recitation and powerful theater: "On occasion I have tried, along with the dramatist, to force the audience to return to the truth and to destroy the legendary aspect of certain characters whose true nature modern historians have revealed; but the audience has not followed me. I soon came to the realization that legend always triumphs over historical fact. . . . Jesus, Joan of Arc, Shakespeare, the Virgin Mary, Mohammed, and Napoléon . . . have all entered into legend."[5] The distinction Bernhardt draws between truth (or history) and legend is one that every celebrity comes to know. It is the distinction, not only between private life and what the public sees, but also between the uninspiring and the exemplary: "We do not want Joan of Arc to be a crude strapping peasant woman. . . . In legend she remains a frail being, led by a divine spirit. Her girl's arm, holding up the heavy standard, is supported by an invisible angel. The beyond is reflected in her child's eyes from which the warriors draw their strength and courage. It is thus that we wish her to be. And the legend remains triumphant."[6] There may have been something self-serving in her insistence on Joan of Arc's frailty, since the role would become identified with the famously skinny Bernhardt.

Although it is evident from Paul Nadar's photograph (fig. 2) that she had filled out a bit by 1890, when she premiered in Jules Barbier's *Jeanne d'Arc* at the Théâtre de la Porte Saint-Martin, her Maid of Orléans appears all tensile strength and youthful élan (Bernhardt was forty-five). She has an especially otherworldly gaze in Eugène Grasset's medievalizing poster for the production (fig. 1), and seems very well dressed for a simple peasant girl.[7] Her splendid cuirass (fig. 3), of white leather embroidered with brilliantly colored fleurs-de-lis and featuring a central mandorla of the Virgin and Child (preserved in the collection of the Bibliothèque Nationale, Paris), testifies to the care that the actress, who asked her friend Félix Duquesnel to produce *Jeanne d'Arc* for her, took with the visual design of her plays. After seeing Bernhardt as Joan of Arc, the novelist Anatole France wrote that "she bears upon her face that afterglow of stained glass which the visitations of the saints had left [on her],"[8] and commented on Bernhardt's special capacity to embody myth: "She is at the same time a vision of an ideal life and an exquisite archaism: she is the legend animated."[9]

fig. 2 Paul Nadar (French, 1856–1939), *Sarah Bernhardt as Jeanne d'Arc*, 1890. Albumen print cabinet card, 6 9/16 x 4 5/16 in. (16.5 x 10.8 cm). Harvard Theatre Collection, Houghton Library, Cambridge, Massachusetts

fig. 3 Théophile Thomas (French, 1846–1916), Jeanne d'Arc cuirass with bag, 1890. White leather with multicolored embroidery, metal, 34 1/4 x 22 7/8 in. (87 x 58 cm). Bibliothèque Nationale de France, Département des Arts du Spectacle, Paris

The Horrible Moment of Awakening

Sarah Bernhardt's first foray into the realm of legendary national portrayal took place fifteen years earlier. In 1875 at the Comédie Française, she was cast in the title role of *La fille de Roland* (Roland's Daughter; fig. 4), Viscount Henri de Bornier's "sequel" to the Carolingian epic poem *La chanson de Roland* (The Song of Roland). As Berthe, she played the surviving daughter of Charlemagne's beloved nephew, the very model of a First Crusade knight who had valiantly fought and died in battle against the Saracens. Bernhardt found the versification somewhat flat but the play enveloped in a "great patriotic" atmosphere.[10] *La fille de Roland* was a huge success, and she knew why: "It was a short time after the terrible war of 1870. The play contained frequent allusions to it. And, thanks to the chauvinism of the public, it had a greater success than the work itself merited."[11] The "terrible" Franco-Prussian War, which ended in defeat and national humiliation, and the uprising of the Commune take up several chapters of her autobiography, *Ma double vie* (My Double Life), published in 1907. Like many of her compatriots, Bernhardt was powerfully marked by the events of 1870–71: "Ah! The horrible moment of awakening!" she exclaims in her memoir. "The Emperor of France had to give his sword to the Emperor of Prussia. Nothing can wipe out the memory of that cry of pain and rage uttered by the whole nation!"[12]

Bernhardt had just achieved her first great success, in a breeches role, in François Coppée's *Le passant* (The Passerby), at the Théâtre de l'Odéon, when war was declared. Almost immediately she jumped into real, not fictive, action: during the siege of Paris she established a military hospital—what the French call an *ambulance*—at the Odéon. The soldiers' beds were in the lobby and those of the officers in the theater buffet. When the bombardment became too intense she moved the sick and dying into the basement, but rising water and rats forced her to find other quarters. As if announcing a theatrical event, a poster informed that the Odéon hospital, "created and directed by Mlle Sarah Bernhardt," would move to the rue Taitbout (fig. 5). After the war, she was awarded a medal for her efforts on behalf of her country.[13]

Bernhardt's patriotic fervor was shaped by the particularities of her political outlook. She was a centrist republican with leftist leanings and a predilection for Bonapartism. Even beyond the widespread and enduring French taste for a strong national leader in the anti-Bourbon, post-Revolutionary mold, her attachment to the Napoleonic heritage is not surprising: she had direct links to Emperor Napoleon III (also called Louis-Napoleon), a man she knew personally and liked.[14] Bernhardt had performed at the Tuileries palace for him and the Empress Eugénie with the Théâtre du Gymnase company in 1864 and with the Odéon company, in Le passant, the year before Louis-Napoleon's abdication. But her connections went further back, to those entertained at the salons of the van Hard sisters— Bernhardt's mother, Youle, and her aunt Rosine—well-known and highly placed courtesans of the July Monarchy and Second Empire. These connections included Napoleon III's doctor, Baron Hippolyte Larrey (whose father had been physician to Napoleon Bonaparte), and the illegitimate half brother of the emperor, the rich and influential Duc de Morny, who facilitated young Sarah's entrance into the Conservatoire, the exclusive theater school of the Comédie Française.[15]

Bernhardt's ties to the Bonapartes in no way limited her sympathies, probably because her links were, apparently, more sentimental than ideological. Referring to the Franco-Prussian War, she singles out "[Patrice] MacMahon's sublime but impotent struggle as he was pushed back to Sedan."[16] Although this same French general would brutally put down the uprising of the Commune the next year, she was not deterred from understanding, and justifying, the brutalities of the Communards, especially the women. She writes with feeling: "What suffering these desolate mothers, these frightened sisters, these worried fiancées endured! How excusable were their revolts in the Commune, even their murderous folly!"[17] And although neither pacifist nor antinationalist, she was a fervent antimilitarist: "I hate war! It exasperates me, it makes me shudder all over. . . . Let everyone be a soldier in the moment of danger, yes, a thousand times yes! That everyone should arm himself for the defense of his country, and that one should kill to defend one-self and one's own, makes sense. But that there are still, in these modern times, young men whose only dream is to kill other people in order to make themselves a career—that passes the bounds of comprehension!"[18]

Catholic and Jew

In addition to being an interpreter of national figures, a centrist republican, and a great French patriot, Sarah Bernhardt was a Jew. Or was she? She was born of a Jewish mother, and as Carol Ockman and others have shown, she was subject

fig. 5   Poster for a clinic run by Sarah Bernhardt at the Théâtre de l'Odéon in Paris, 1871

SARA BERNHARDT.

Otrony PUBLISHING COMPANY,
11 E. SIXTEENTH STREET,
NEW YORK.

fig. 6   Napoleon Sarony
(American, b. Canada,
1821–1896), *Sarah
Bernhardt as Léah*, n.d.
Collodion print cabinet
card, 6 9/16 x 4 1/4 in.
(16.5 x 10.8 cm). Bequest
of Robert P. Bowler, 1919;
Harvard Theatre
Collection, Houghton
Library, Cambridge,
Massachusetts

fig. 7 André Gill (French, 1840–1885), Sarah Bernhardt as Chimera, caricature, c. 1880. Oil on panel, 24 x 16 1/2 in. (61 x 42 cm). Mutuelle Nationale des Artistes, Couilly-Pont-aux-Dames, France

to vicious anti-Semitic attack for much of the 1870s. But she considered herself Catholic, or at least she did most of the time. In her autobiography, she recounts a meeting in New York with a "female reporter, with short hair and a mannish tailored skirt," who asked her: "Are you JewishCatholicProtestantMuslimBuddhist-Zoroastrian or a deist?" To which Bernhardt replied: "I am Catholic, Mademoiselle!" "Roman or Orthodox?" the reporter inquired. At this, Bernhardt relates, "I leapt up. She was really too annoying!"[19] When Bernhardt was condemned as immoral by French clergy in Montreal, during a visit in 1898, she asserted: "I am not a Jewess but a Christian and a Frenchwoman. . . . The early portion of my youth was passed in the convent of Grandschamps [sic] in Versailles."[20] Of course, this was true: she was baptized as a child, educated in a convent school, and raised a Catholic (a rosary presented to her by the pope at Castel Gandolfo is now in the Laurence Senelick collection; fig. 8). She went so far as to credit her sense of drama to her Christian upbringing. "It is to the church and only the church that I owe my being in the theater," she affirmed in 1890. "Even as a child my imagination was struck by ecclesiastical chants, the contemplative attitudes of the congregation, the mystical qualities of the ceremonies, the solemn silence with which one listened to the priest."[21]

Bernhardt's public proclamations of her religious identity were, however, equivocal. Just after the Franco-Prussian War, in which she had behaved so patriotically, her Jewishness seemed an asset. "I am a Jewess but not a German," she wrote to a Parisian newspaper in response to allegations of her Germanic origins: "I am French, absolutely French," she avowed. "If I have a foreign accent . . . it is cosmopolitan but not Teutonic. I am a daughter of the great Jewish race, and my somewhat uncultivated language is the outcome of our enforced wanderings."[22] And although the first chapters of her autobiography firmly root her young life in a Catholic environment and skirt the issue of her immediate family's faith, she nonetheless confesses at least marginally to Jewish ancestry much later: "I lodged my grandmother in an old-age home. . . . My grandmother was Israelite and strictly and faithfully observed the laws of her religion."[23]

Proust's Bernhardt

"Her religion," Bernhardt says of her grandmother's faith, distancing both herself and her mother from Judaism. This continual slipping in and out of her Jewish skin might be said to characterize the behavior of many Belle Époque Frenchmen and Frenchwomen of Jewish or intermarried families, especially in the bourgeoisie. Among these is Bernhardt's acquaintance Marcel Proust. In an often cited letter to his friend Count Robert de Montesquiou, who had made denigrating remarks about Jews at a party both attended, Proust wrote rather obsequiously: "Dear Sir, Yesterday I did not answer the question you put to me about the Jews. For this very simple reason: though I am Catholic like my father and my brother, my mother is Jewish. I am sure you understand that this is reason enough to refrain from such discussions."[24] If Bernhardt and Proust shared the complicated heritage of mixed Jewish and Catholic backgrounds, they came from very different worlds. Proust's was unimpeachably respectable: his cultivated mother, Jeanne Weil, came from a wealthy family of industrialists and financiers; his father, Adrien Proust, from a family of provincial shopkeepers, was among France's most celebrated physicians. Bernhardt's was the opposite: a courtesan for a mother, and a father who was a shadowy figure at best. Bernhardt's father never married Youle van Hard, and he seems to have disappeared from his daughter's life almost immediately after her birth. Although one of Bernhardt's biographers, the notoriously unreliable Louis Verneuil, claims that her father was from a "recognized Christian family" of Le Havre, there is no evidence to back up this claim or any other concerning her paternity.[25]

Despite their differences, Bernhardt and Proust used the same narrative strategy for positioning themselves as Gentiles within French culture by dwelling on their Christian upbringing. By the end of the second chapter of her memoirs, Bernhardt has told us that her "very devout" uncle Faure, who joined the Carthusian order upon the death of his wife, insisted that young Sarah be sent to convent school at Versailles.[26] This is followed in the next three chapters by an extended account of her Christian education. By the second chapter of *Du côté de*

fig. 8   **Rosary given to Sarah Bernhardt by Pope Leo XIII at Castel Gandolfo, n.d. Silver and wood beads, silver cross with feathers; beads: 26 1/2 in. (67.3 cm), pendant: 4 x 3 1/4 in. (10.2 x 8.3 cm). Laurence Senelick Collection of Theatrical Imagery, West Medford, Massachusetts**

chez Swann (Swann's Way), the first book of the monumental À la recherche du temps perdu (In Search of Lost Time), Marcel, the narrator, is in the small town of Combray, where he accompanies his parents to Mass: "How I loved our church, and how clearly I can see it still!"[27] But Marcel-the-narrator is not identical with Marcel Proust—which allows Proust to remake the world as he sees fit.[28] Thus, the rich and well-connected Jews of his mother's real-life Parisian family become the comfortable and well-connected—but now Gentile—provincial relatives of Recherche (thereby eliminating, in fiction, the problem posed by the Orthodox Jewish law of matrilineal descent, that is, that the Jewish faith is passed down through the mother, not the father). But hasn't Bernhardt already revealed her discovery of this same procedure, about the triumph of legend over historical fact? Didn't she tellingly entitle her memoirs Ma double vie—My Double Life?

Bernhardt and Proust moved in some of the same social circles, and they shared three significant friends: Reynaldo Hahn, Robert de Montesquiou, and Charles Haas. Hahn, a composer of art songs, was Proust's contemporary; his Venezuelan mother was a Catholic, and his father was a German Jew. He was also extremely close to Bernhardt and would write one of the more interesting biographies of the actress.[29] Montesquiou, of ancient French lineage, was the most celebrated aesthete of fin-de-siècle France.[30] A writer and connoisseur, he had been Bernhardt's intimate in the 1870s, and it was at a party he gave in her honor at his house in Neuilly that Proust first met the actress. Haas, a handsome and cultured man-about-town, was purportedly one of Bernhardt's lovers: in Ma double vie, she mentions that he was at her apartment on the rue Auber the night it was gutted by fire. Haas, who was briefly the inspector general for French historical monuments, was a friend of the Prince of Wales and one of the few Jewish members of the exclusive Jockey Club and the Cercle de la Rue Royale.

The group of friends would find their way into Proust's monumental oeuvre. His most important character, the Jewish socialite Charles Swann, was modeled on Haas;[31] Robert de Montesquiou was the principal model for the homosexual aristocrat Baron de Charlus; and Bernhardt was the model for Berma, the great actress about whose art Marcel has a profound realization over the course of the saga. Although Bernhardt and Proust knew each other but slightly, the people who connected them were crucial in both their lives, as well as in the life of French culture at the turn of the century.

The historical Sarah Bernhardt also appears intermittently throughout Recherche. She is referred to first in Du côté de chez Swann, when the young Marcel develops a fascination for actors and actresses: "I classified the most distinguished in order of talent: Sarah Bernhardt, Berma, [Jeanne-Julia] Bartet, Madeleine Brohan, Jeanne Samary."[32] The list camouflages, amid four real players of the Théâtre Français, his fictional Berma, after her real-life model, Bernhardt. This doubling of the virtual and the real is a characteristic Proustian strategy. A variation on the "two Marcels," it allows historical fact and legend to be held in suspension so that they may enrich and undermine each other. Thus when, in À l'ombre des *jeunes filles en fleurs* (Within a Budding Grove), Marcel tells the esteemed writer Bergotte that he has been to see Berma in Jean Racine's *Phèdre* (fig. 9), we get a superb appreciation of the audacious theatricality of Bernhardt's acting style in her most famous classical role: "He told me that in the scene in which she stood with her arm raised to the level of her shoulder . . . she had managed to suggest, with great nobility of art, certain classical figures. . . . Yes, she's really charming, that little sixth-century Phaedra, the rigidity of the arm, the lick of hair 'frozen into marble,' yes, you know, it's wonderful of her to have discovered all that. There is a great deal more antiquity in it than in most of the books they're labeling 'antique' this year."[33] Yet in *Recherche's* previous volume, *Du côté de chez Swann*, Proust allows himself to take a jab at the actress by way of the fatuous Dr. Cottard, who comments, when he is invited to the theater by Madame Verdurin: "To be sure, we're far too near the stage, and one is beginning to get sick of Sarah Bernhardt. . . . She's what they call the Golden Voice, isn't she? They say she sets the house on fire. That's an odd expression, ain't it?"[34]

The Dreyfus Affair

Real and imaginary Marcels, real and imaginary Bernhardts! All this complicated finessing of reality and fiction was rather beside the point for the two "real" ones during the Dreyfus Affair, because of the Jewish faith of their mothers' families. Both came out in favor of Alfred Dreyfus and of his defender Émile Zola. Proust referred to himself as "the first of the Dreyfusards" because he had managed to obtain the signature of Anatole France for the "Manifesto of the Intellectuals," in support of Zola, which was published the day after "J'accuse," his open letter denouncing the injustice against Dreyfus, appeared in the newspaper *L'aurore*.[35] That same day Bernhardt sent her friend Zola the following letter (fig. 10).

> Cher Grand Maître,
>
> Allow me to speak of the inexpressible emotion I felt when I read your cry for justice. As a woman I have no influence. But I am anguished, haunted by the situation, and the beautiful words you wrote yesterday brought tremendous relief to my great suffering.
>
> I thought of writing to thank [Auguste] Scheurer-Koestner [vice-president of the Senate, and an ardent Dreyfusard] but knowing that everything that admirable man does is considered criminally suspect, I thought that if an *artiste*—what am I saying?—an *actress* was known to admire his courageous deeds, that discovery would be used to crush him. To you whom I have loved so long, I say thank you with all the strength of a melancholy instinct which cries out to me: "It's a crime! A crime!"[36]

Even Bernhardt's real support of Dreyfus and Zola has been turned into legend. It has been claimed, for instance, that the actress was present at the degradation of Captain Dreyfus at the École Militaire on the morning of January 5, 1895:

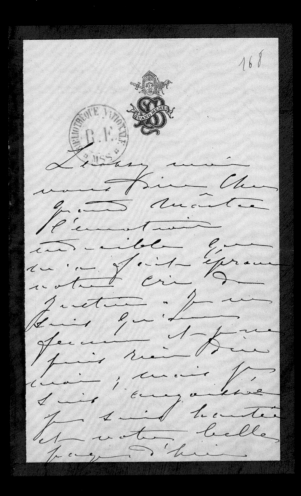

"Crowds had started to gather in the 'piercing cold' outside the ornate iron gates. . . . Nearby, undoubtedly attracting the most attention, Sarah Bernhardt waited with another group of notables under the elaborate stone reliefs of mythological figures that ran across the building's eighteenth-century walls."[37] There is no evidence of which I am aware for placing Bernhardt at the scene, but there is a cited source: the ever-mythologizing Louis Verneuil, who claimed even more astonishingly that "Zola had never paid any attention to the Dreyfus Case.[38] The clear, lucid, and irrefutable manner in which Sarah expounded the facts was a revelation to him. The very next day he saw Scheurer-Koestner, and three days later his mind was made up. Interrupting all other activities, he would now have only one object—to free the innocent man."[39] Not only did Verneuil think that Bernhardt had invented Dreyfusardism, but he also seems to have launched the idea, repeated so often that it passes for fact, that Bernhardt confronted a lynch mob alongside Zola the day after "J'accuse" was published: "About six in the evening, a furious crowd marched up to the Rue de Bruxelles shouting 'Death to Zola!' and besieging the novelist's little house. The police had to be called in great haste. Suddenly a window opened on the second floor, and Sarah Bernhardt appeared. She had come to congratulate Zola on his courageous campaign, which she had initiated two months earlier."[40] Needless to say, having Bernhardt on the scene makes better theater than her congratulating him by mail, even though, as we just saw, that is what she did.

But perhaps it is the fiction rather than the reality—the *theater*—of the Dreyfus Affair that lets us glimpse most poignantly the shared triumphs and agonies of Bernhardt and Proust. For, apart from the specific references to Bernhardt and Berma in *À la recherche du temps perdu*, there is a sense in which the story of Charles Swann and his family is Bernhardt's story, or Bernhardt's *and* Proust's stories. Swann, after all, has risen about as high in French culture as one can for a Jew, or a partial Jew (that's what he is, like Bernhardt and Proust). With money, cultivation, wit, and all the right friends in society, Swann is even an intimate of Basin and Oriane, the Duke and Duchess de Guermantes, the most aristocratic, alluring, mythic French couple, in Marcel's view. The Proust–Weil clan had also risen this high, as, in a somewhat louche rendition, had the van Hard–Bernhardts (we might say that when Charles Swann falls in love with and marries the courtesan Odette de Crécy, he has crossed over from the dull respectability of Proust's family to the demimondaine glamour of Bernhardt's).

Proust has more in store for his half-Jew than arriving at the social pinnacle. Swann becomes a hero during the Dreyfus Affair, even a kind of martyr. Discovering his Jewish roots, he emerges, to the great displeasure of his intimates from the Faubourg Saint-Germain, as a vocal Dreyfusard, grows an enormous "Jewish" nose, and falls fatally ill with cancer. The result for his family? Ever greater social advancement. His widow, Odette, is free to remarry, and thus their daughter, Gilberte, becomes first Mademoiselle de Forcheville (thereby losing her odd, un-French name, Swann) and then, after her marriage, the Marquise de Saint-Loup, cousin to the Guermantes, who "as a rule . . . concealed her origins."[41] In Albertine

fig. 11 Napoleon Sarony (American, b. Canada, 1821–1896), *Maurice Bernhardt as a Young Man*, n.d. Gelatin silver print. Billy Rose Theatre Collection, The New York Public Library for the Performing Arts

disparue (*The Fugitive*), Marcel and his mother discuss this modern-day miracle whereby Jews are transformed by their intermarriage with families of *la vieille France*:

> [Mother:] And yet, can you imagine for a moment what old Swann—not that you ever knew him, of course—would have felt if he could have known that he would one day have a great-grandchild in whose veins the blood of old mother Moser who used to say: "Ponchour Mezieurs" [that is, with an Alsatian/Yiddish accent] would mingle with the blood of the Duc de Guise!
>
> [Marcel:] But you know, Mamma, it's much more surprising than that . . . because [Swann] married a whore.[42]

The Bernhardt story is just as surprising, only it is true: The Jewish courtesan Youle van Hard, friend of the Duc de Morny, has a child out of wedlock, who becomes the most famous actress in the world and who in turn gives birth out of wedlock to a son, Maurice (fig. 11), whom she conceived with Prince Charles de Ligne of Belgium. And just as the fictional Gilberte rejects the Jewish blood of funny old mother Moser, so the real Maurice Bernhardt, who marries a Polish princess, Maria Jablonowska, rejects his portion of Jewish blood and becomes both an anti-Semite and an outspoken anti-Dreyfusard. One of Maurice's daughters,

Lysiane, recounts a violent argument between her father and her grandmother Sarah: "The luncheon was proceeding gaily when suddenly the name of Dreyfus was mentioned. . . . My grandmother poured me out another bumper of white wine, then, at a remark by my father . . . she broke her plate in two. Her son (my father) took offence at this and got up and began to pull my mother away from the table by her hand. Then my grandmother broke my plate on [the actor Édouard] Geoffroy's arm and Geoffroy became purple with fury. . . . The whole party scattered with screams of rage."[43] Things apparently turned so bad that Maurice fled with his family from Paris to Monte Carlo, "and for many painful months Maurice and Sarah were not on speaking terms."[44] Was it her now contentious relationship to her beloved son that so anguished and haunted Bernhardt, as she wrote to Zola about the Dreyfus Affair?

Reconciling Differences: The Eaglet

> The first night of L'Aiglon . . . was a battle . . . because in that year, 1900, the Dreyfus case was raging, and the play, like everything else, had become a party question. That is to say, there was a party of Nationalists who were ready to praise or damn the play, and a party of Dreyfusards who were prepared to do the contrary to whatever the Nationalists did. Both parties were swept off their feet. Sarah conquered them in the first act. I never witnessed a more authentic triumph on the stage. I never saw before an audience which was prepared to be hostile so suddenly and completely vanquished.[45]

L'Aiglon, the Eaglet (fig. 12), instantaneously joined Phaedra, and Marguerite Gautier in La dame aux camélias (The Lady of the Camellias), as one of Sarah Bernhardt's signature roles. Playing a young man of seventeen when she was fifty-five, just as she had played the young Saint Joan at forty-five, undoubtedly helped the actress create a theatrical sensation, but so did the play's author and its subject. This was Edmond Rostand's successor to his colossal triumph Cyrano de Bergerac, of two years earlier; now he was creating a star vehicle for his good friend Bernhardt. Drawn from French history, like its predecessor, L'Aiglon is the story of the final days in the life of Napoleon Bonaparte's only surviving heir, his son Franz, the Duke of Reichstadt. It is set at the Viennese court, where, after the exile and death of his father, Franz is held in luxurious, aristocratic captivity by his mother, the Archduchess Maria Louisa of Austria, and her father, Emperor Francis I, and by Prince Metternich, the Austrian chancellor.

Rostand himself was a Dreyfusard and insisted at every opportunity that L'Aiglon was not intended as a political statement: "Good God! It's not a cause that I attack or defend . . . and this is nothing other than the story of an unfortunate child."[46] Although it had the surprising effect of acting as a reconciliation piece for a France torn apart by "the Affair," its potential as a nationalist vehicle is obvious. The plot, which is stretched extremely thin over the course of its six long acts in

fig. 12   Hand-tinted postcard
of Sarah Bernhardt as
L'Aiglon, c. 1900. 3 3/8 x
5 3/8 in. (8.7 x 13.7 cm).
Bibliothèque Nationale
de France, Département
des Arts du Spectacle,
Paris

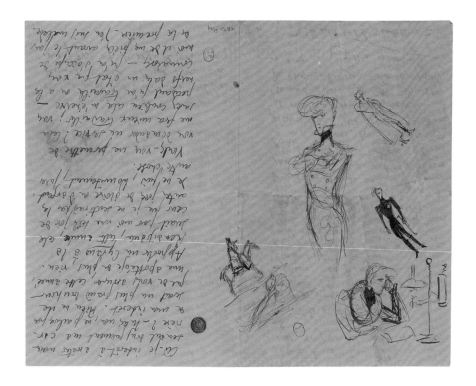

fig. 13 Edmond Rostand
(French, 1868–1918),
Letter from Edmond
Rostand to Sarah
Bernhardt with sketches
for L'Aiglon, late 1899.
Bibliothèque Nationale
de France, Département
des Arts du Spectacle,
Paris

verse, involves the attempt on the part of the Eaglet's supporters—including one
of his father's loyal old officers, Flambeau—to rally Napoleon II to return to France
and seize the throne. Sensitive and weak, the Duke of Reichstadt is unequal to
the task. The most famous scene in the play has him at the site of the Battle
of Wagram, impotently invoking the ghosts of his father's glorious and bloodied
troops. But the Duke's predicament allowed the author—and thus his French
audience—to wallow in hours' worth of Napoleon worship and national self-pity.
Partisans on both sides of the Dreyfus Affair could unite in their lament,
reaffirming their shared francité (Frenchness) despite the celebrated case that was
calling into question nearly every tenet of French identity.

Sarah and Franz were tailor-made for each other, beginning with the costume
that the designer Paul Poiret may have had a hand in creating, but which, to judge
from the sketches Rostand sent to Bernhardt (fig. 13), seems to have originated with
L'Aiglon's author.[47] An all-white uniform of cotton jersey fabric, with bold, dark
contrasting collar and sash, and a line of gold buttons running down the front (in
slenderizing contrast to the double row suggested in Rostand's sketch), it allowed
the once wraithlike star to regain her svelte ligne. But the role of Napoleon II was
perfect for Bernhardt in more important ways. It represented the fulfillment of
a number of the nationalist themes that had helped define her career and persona
from the beginning. Having already impersonated the trumped-up Carolingian
heroine Berthe, Roland's daughter, as well as the legendary daughter of the nation,
Joan of Arc, she could now resuscitate the short-lived, mostly forgotten son of

France's greatest modern warrior. Left-leaning Bonapartist that she was, Bernhardt now had the opportunity to "conquer" and "vanquish" the audience with her lyrical tributes to Napoleon Bonaparte as the progeny of 1789. This interchange from the play's third act, between Franz and the Austrian chancellor, sympathetically evokes Napoleon's seizure of power and the Revolution as spiritual grandparents— "grandsire" and "granddam"—of the Duke.

> DUKE OF REICHSTADT: Upon my father's side
> I am related closely, Sire, to Freedom.
> METTERNICH: Yes, the Duke's grandsire was the eighteenth Brumaire!
> DUKE OF REICHSTADT: Yes, and the Revolution was my granddam![48]

Buttressed by the star's performance, the evocative power of the play consisted in its ability to distract the audience from the current internecine strife. It also served to redirect nationalist energies toward the same defeat that, as Bernhardt knew so well, had meant the success of that other less-than-scintillating verse drama *La fille de Roland*: the Franco-Prussian War. Perhaps without realizing it, this is what the critic Patrick Besnier means when he says that "*L'Aiglon* is in fact a long *lamento*, a meditation on defeat and death."[49] The "revenge" for 1870—both for the generalized national humiliation and for the specific loss of the provinces of Alsace and Lorraine—reverberates throughout the play. Not only is the enemy Germanic—the Austrian court is a none-too-subtle allusion to the Prussian—but French taste is repeatedly lauded at the expense of the supposedly crude sensibility of Franz's captors. Flambeau tells the Duke that his brother is an upholsterer in Paris, so he knows of what he speaks: "They try to imitate us here; but Lord! They've got a curious kind of Louis-Quinze! . . . Just look how finicky this wood-work is." By comparison, he directs Franz's attention to the room's tapestry: "What taste! What mystery! It sings. It laughs. . . . Why? Don't you know? Why, these are Gobelins!" Then Flambeau brings home his point: "How plain it is that cunning craftsmen made them. This taste, this elegance swears with the rest—And you my Lord, were also made in France!"[50]

"Made in France," just like the star of L'Aiglon, the most celebrated actress in the world. What gave the role its special piquancy for the French was the super-imposition of legendary performer and legendary character; it should be recalled that Franz's father, Napoleon, was among the historical figures Bernhardt singled out in her discussion of the power of legend in theatrical representation. Of course, the greatest stars always confront us with this epistemological problem: Is it the actor or the acted that compels us? In the strange game of substitutions that characterizes all realist drama, L'Aiglon might be said to fetishize French national loss: instead of Napoleon we get his son, instead of the Eagle we get the Eaglet, instead of the Dreyfus Affair we get the story of Napoleon II's captivity and demise (itself a displacement of the Franco-Prussian defeat). And instead of the young Franz, Duke of Reichstadt, we get the late-middle-aged Sarah Bernhardt.

fig. 14 Emmanuel Coulange-
Lautrec (French,
1824–1898), L'Aiglon
quinquina apéritif P. Serve,
1900. Poster, 59 x
49 1/4 in. (150 x 125 cm).
Bibliothèque Forney,
Paris (BF NO 198523)

It is both the power and the futility of substitutions—of *fetishism*—that Rostand's play asserts. And who better, in the midst of the Dreyfus Affair, to embody the double-edged sword of make-believe than the star who had burned bright for so long in the theatrical firmament, the Divine Sarah? Every time Franz asks about his father's legacy or his own potential for glory, it might as well be the aging Bernhardt talking about herself: "But where's the proof that France still feels herself my Father's widow?" the Duke, in the second act, asks, about French national feeling for Napoleon; to which Flambeau replies: "Their love for you, my Lord? Why that's immortal!" and proceeds to take from his person various articles—a pair of suspenders, a snuff box, a handkerchief, a colored print, a pipe, a cockade, a medal, an egg cup, a tumbler, a plate, a necktie, playing cards, an almanac, a knife, and a napkin ring—each of which bears a portrait of Franz.[51] Flambeau wants the Duke to understand that it is these "trivial fancy goods" that prove, by their very ordinariness and ubiquity, the immortal love of France for the Bonapartes.

But wasn't this just the sort of proof that had long been offered by France, and the world, of their immortal love for Bernhardt—the endless photographs, pamphlets, and souvenir booklets? Indeed, with L'Aiglon, Bernhardt memorabilia achieved a spectacular new level of cultural penetration. As if in uncanny imitation of the play itself, all these objects featured the actress not in her real-life attire but in her costume and makeup for the Duke of Reichstadt. They include photographs in which he/she is doubled, tripled, even quintupled; statuettes; buttons and cuff links (a pair of which belonged at one time to the playwright Moss Hart; fig. 15); and advertisements. Competing quinine aperitifs featured the image of Bernhardt in the role of the Duke of Reichstadt in their ads. The poster for L'Aiglon quinine (fig. 14) shows Bernhardt as Franz, with the improbable addition of Cyrano de Bergerac raising his sword behind a rock; the poster for Michaud shows Bernhardt as Franz enjoying a drink amid a gaggle of contemporary celebrities. Since Rostand wrote the play expressly for Bernhardt, who was closely involved in its creation, it seems likely that author and star had at least an inkling of the kinds of cultural displacements L'Aiglon might elicit. They must have sensed how charged the confusion between legendary star and star-crossed legend could be.

If *La fille de Roland* and *Jeanne d'Arc* had helped establish Bernhardt as the foremost interpreter of French national heroines, L'Aiglon confirmed her as the one-and-only authentic theatrical incarnation of France.[52] In the years after L'Aiglon, she had another chance to play La Pucelle, in Émile Moreau's *Le procès de Jeanne d'Arc* (*The Trial of Joan of Arc*), nearly two decades after she had first played the saint. In rapid succession, in 1902 and 1904, she took the title role of the French Revolutionary heroine in *Théroigne de Méricourt*, by Paul Hervieu,[53] and the role of Marie-Antoinette in Henri Lavedan and Georges Lenotre's *Varennes!*[54] Bernhardt had no problem playing such politically disparate characters. "If he is a republican, he must uphold with warmth and conviction royalist theories," she wrote of the obligation of the actor to his métier, "and if he is a conservative, anarchist theories,

fig. 15 **Cuff links depicting Sarah Bernhardt as Franz, Duke of Reichstadt, in L'Aiglon, 1900 or after. Gold, each 1/2 in. (1.25 cm). Museum of the City of New York, Theater Collection**

if such is the wish of the playwright."[55] She did not really have to worry about playwrights' wishes, since she herself already was an object of national veneration: "Sarah Bernhardt Day" was observed on December 9, 1896, in Paris. It began with a lunch at the Grand Hôtel, for which Alphonse Mucha designed the menus (fig. 16), and at which tributes were offered. Later that day, a production, "The Apotheosis of Sarah Bernhardt," was staged at the Théâtre de la Renaissance, in which Bernhardt performed scenes from *Phèdre* and *Rome vaincue* (*Rome Vanquished*), and five poets read sonnets in her honor. In 1914, Bernhardt was made a Chevalier of the Legion of Honor.

What She Represented: Bernhardt and *la Grande Guerre*

"You haven't seen what Sarah Bernhardt said in the papers: 'France will go on to the end. If necessary the French will let themselves be killed to the last man.' That I do not doubt," Baron de Charlus says near the end of *Le temps retrouvé* (*Time Regained*), the culminating novel of *À la recherche du temps perdu*, "but I ask myself to what extent *Madame Sarah Bernhardt* is qualified to speak in the name of France."[56] It is the middle of the Great War. Charlus here appears to be speaking for the novel's author, who, a number of pages later, as Marcel-the-narrator, confides to the reader: "The idea of a popular art, like that of a patriotic art, if not actually dangerous seemed to me ridiculous."[57] That Proust saw fit to take a parting shot at the diva—and even to call into question her right to speak for the nation— testifies to his aversion for chauvinist rhetoric, and also to Bernhardt's stature in wartime France.

During the last decade of her life, Bernhardt showed her compatriots and the world, as she had in 1870, what bravery and vigor looked like. By a strange twist of fate, on February 22, 1915, she joined the ranks of the *mutilés de guerre*. That day, because of gangrene resulting from an injury she had sustained years before, she had her right leg amputated. The courageous Dr. Denucé successfully operated on the seventy-year-old star, in Bordeaux, after several other surgeons declined to take the risk. Back in Paris by autumn, Bernhardt wasted no time in making her contribution to the war effort. She performed in a specially written one-act play: "This was *Les Cathédrales* by Eugène Morand . . . in which various actresses, symbolizing the chief cathedrals of France, recited heroic couplets about the Patrie, La Gloire, the recovery of Alsace-Lorraine and further sentiments calculated to wring tears and cheers from a wartime audience."[58] Bernhardt played the role of Strasbourg cathedral—a particular object of veneration, because it was in the "captured province" of Alsace—and brought the audience to its feet with her exhortation: "Pleure, pleure, Allemagne! L'Aigle allemande est tombé dans le Rhin!" ("Weep, weep, Germany! The German Eagle has fallen into the Rhine!") This was the type of thing for which Marcel expresses such disdain in *Time Regained*, and no one did it as well as Bernhardt, or as widely.

In early 1916, she went to the Front—to Rheims, along the Marne, to the Argonne, and close to Verdun—where she performed various patriotic pieces for

fig. 16   Alphonse Mucha (Czech, 1860–1939), Menu for La journée Sarah Bernhardt (Sarah Bernhardt Day), 1896

fig. 17   Sarah Bernhardt as
amputee on the front
in her sedan chair,
published in Literary
Digest, c. 1916–17.
Bibliothèque Nationale
de France, Département
des Arts du Spectacle,
Paris

the poilus. This meant that she had to be carried to the makeshift stages and jerry-rigged theaters on her specially designed sedan chair (fig. 17), and one can only imagine how moving it must have been for the soldiers to see la grande Sarah share their ordeal, at least temporarily. She also starred in a propaganda film that enjoyed enormous success in France and abroad, her sole film made expressly for the screen (that is, not an adaptation of a stage play): Mères françaises (Mothers of France), directed by Louis Mercanton. Bernhardt plays Madame d'Urbex, wife of a provincial squire whose son, a lieutenant, dies in her arms at the Front, to which she has made her way against all odds.[59]

At the end of the year, Bernhardt embarked on her final American tour, which would last almost two years, and during which she would appear in, among other productions, a one-act play that she may have written herself (although she claimed that it was the work of a French soldier): Du théâtre au champ d'honneur (From the Theater to the Field of Honor).[60] The play, about a young actor who enlists in the army and dies at the Front defending the tricolore against the Germans, featured the one-legged seventy-two-year-old actress in the role of the twenty-year-old hero, Marc Bertrand. Proust's disdain notwithstanding, it was apparently Bernhardt's finest hour—at least according to Nashville's Tennessean. Here is what the paper's theater critic had to say about the evening program of February 8, 1917, which included Bernhardt in a comic interlude, Rosalie; in the death scenes from Cléopâtre and La dame aux camélias; and in Du théâtre au champ d'honneur:

No wonder men are willing to die upon the field of battle. No wonder France is giving her very heart in the struggle which she feels is for her honor and existence. For last night, Sarah Bernhardt, the divine, showed the spirit of France itself to an audience here which packed the Vendome theater to the walls; and when as the dying soldier she clasped her tri-color about her form and the orchestra burst forth in the "Marseillaise" as the curtain fell, the audience rose to its feet and encored her in what was probably the greatest ovation ever given an actor or actress in this city.

For it was France there before them. France, the youthful and joyous of old, now bleeding to death in No Man's Land, yet with the "drapeau" saved. Only one who has heard it on the field of battle could have put the expression that Bernhardt did into that dying invocation "Vive la France!" That was when the house rose to its feet and men shouted and men cried.

About the entire evening there was something that made one feel a tinge of the pathetic. It may have been the three death scenes which Bernhardt so vividly portrayed; it may have been her years and the feeling of what her life, now drawing to its inevitable close, must have held; or it may have been the deeper feeling of what she represented, the transparency of the tragedies which she gave, the mortal agony of her France.[61]

For it was France there before them: Sarah Bernhardt had brilliantly managed to incarnate a series of national heroes, from Roland's daughter to Joan of Arc and the Duke of Reichstadt. But this was her greatest triumph—now aged and battered, the once skinny daughter of a Jewish courtesan as France herself. Had she been sent by her government to rally Americans to the French cause? There is no record of it. But less than two months after the performance that made men in Nashville shout and cry, the United States joined the Allies in the Great War.

DIVA
SARAH·BERNHARDT
·MEA·INSPIRATRIX
·A·DIOTIMA
TOVS·MES·DÉSIRS·TOVS
MES·VOVLOIRS·ME
VIENNENT·D'ELLE
XV·IVIN·MCMVII

Janis Bergman-Carton

"A VISION OF A STAINED GLASS SARAH"

Bernhardt and the Decorative Arts

fig. 1 Walter Spindler (French, 1878–1940), Sarah Bernhardt Invoking Diotima (Homage to Sarah Bernhardt), 1908. Watercolor and crayon on paper, 7 1/8 x 9 1/2 in. (18.1 x 24.1 cm). Collection of Robert A. Zehil, Monte Carlo

I shall never forget the first time I saw Sarah Bernhardt. A reluctant, protesting, child martyr, I was being dragged through the Louvre by a French governess bound and bent upon giving my infant American mind a correct leaning toward art. At the foot of a broad stairway whose majestic upward sweep, even to my infant eye, was splendidly noble, Mademoiselle seized my elbow. "Look, American child," she hissed, "C'est Sarah!" and, floating down the stairs, I beheld a vision in a bluey-green gown, clinging and long, and trimmed with wide bands of deep colored golden fox fur. The eyes of the woman, her hair and the tawny fur she wore all had the same look of the deep red gold as she approached the "American child" whose eyes were glued upon the vision silhouetted against the background of that epic in marble, the Winged Victory. . . . From that day to this I never see the "Winged Victory" . . . without a vision of a stained glass Sarah.

—Helen Ten Broeck, 1917

The supernatural quality of Helen Ten Broeck's remembrance is not unusual within the Bernhardt lore. Nor is the conflation of categories, Bernhardt as actress and as work of art. More uncommon is the doubleness of the visual memory, the "vision of a stained glass Sarah" silhouetted "against the background of that epic in marble, the Winged Victory." By itself, the image of a "stained glass Sarah"

fig. 2 Réne Lalique (French, 1860–1945), Brooch dedicated to Sarah Bernhardt and given to the Comédie Française by André Malraux, 1896. 5 1/8 x 5 3/4 in. (13 x 14.5 cm). Collections de la Comédie Française, Paris. Malraux probably gave this brooch to the Comédie on Sarah Bernhardt Day (December 9)

fig. 3 Sarah Bernhardt (French, 1844–1923), Algae, 1900. Bronze, 4 x 19 1/4 (10 x 49 cm). Mutuelle Nationale des Artistes, Couilly-Pont-aux-Dames, France

conjures the actress's palette, the "bluey-green" and "tawny" golds that dominate Walter Spindler's watercolor homage, for example (fig. 1). It summons the showy visuality of Bernhardt's clothing, the vivid colors, jewels, and sumptuous fabrics she chose to ornament her trademark silhouette. It also invokes Bernhardt's engagement with the decorative arts, a field revitalized and diversified in the nineteenth century, coincident with her own rise to stardom. While that engagement provides the broad framework for this essay, it is the dialectic in Ten Broeck's recollection that is its focus: Bernhardt's simultaneous identification with one of history's greatest Hellenistic sculptures, the *Nike of Samothrace*, or the *Winged Victory* as it is also known, and a lovely, more human-scale piece of decorative glass. The comparison of Bernhardt to these artworks underscores the monumental and enduring quality of her performances onstage and in life. Her capacity to embody them both, concurrently, underlines the variability of her image and how publicly it oscillated between the categories of "art" and "decoration."

Bernhardt's paintings and sculptures, with which she began experimenting in the early 1870s, represent more straightforward examples of her forays into the visual arts.[1] Her relationship to the decorative arts is more elusive, in part because the category itself is so broad and fluid.[2] The variety of Bernhardt's roles here is a case in point. In the realm of the decorative arts, she operated as patron, artist, consumer, and even work of art. She contributed to the evolution of Art Nouveau jewelry, commissioning and collecting bracelets, brooches (fig. 2), hair clips, and necklaces from such brilliant designers as René Lalique. She produced small decorative bronzes (fig. 3), some of which were displayed at the Universal Exposition of 1900 in Paris. Her habits as a consumer in the decoration of her homes figure in portraits by Marie-Désiré Bourgoin (see Ockman essay, fig. 31) and Graham Robertson (fig. 4), among others; Bernhardt's lavish expenditures on furniture, tapestries, carpets, and works of art are well documented in illustrated magazines of the period. She also was patron and subject of luminous theater posters such as that for *Gismonda* (see Ockman essay, fig. 41)—images that helped catapult the artist Alphonse Mucha to fame, extended the sphere of her own iconic presence, and promoted the aesthetic of sumptuous color and organic linearity by which Art Nouveau design is best known (fig. 5).[3]

Even the historical trajectory of Sarah Bernhardt's career shares traits with that of the decorative arts. Both claim early associations with elite institutions that are subsequently complicated by ties to reproductive technologies and commodity culture. Bernhardt began her career with the venerable Comédie Française, the theater considered one of France's most esteemed and tradition-bound venues of official culture.[4] She broke her contract with the company in 1880 to refashion herself as an independent agent, and the decision dogged her for the remainder of her life. Some regarded the turn toward touring companies and boulevard theaters, and the greater riches and fame they promised, as entrepreneurial greed, not the artistic freedom she claimed.[5] It was the mark of a *cabotine* playing to the degraded tastes of an increasingly powerful bourgeois clientele.

fig. 4 Walford Graham Robertson (British, 1866–1948), *The Actress Sarah Bernhardt in Her Salon*, 1889. Oil on panel, 17 1/4 x 12 in. (44.3 x 30.5 cm). Private collection, Paris

fig. 5   Alphonse Mucha (Czech, 1860–1939), *Médée*, 1898. Color lithograph, 81 x 30 in. (206 x 76.2 cm). Laura Gold, Park South Gallery at Carnegie Hall, New York

fig. 6   Georges de Feure
(French, 1868–1943),
Poster for *Le journal
des ventes*, printed by
Lemercier, Paris, 1898.
Color lithograph on
paper, 25 1/4 x 19 1/2 in.
(64 x 49.5 cm). Musée
de la Publicité, Paris

The modern decorative arts also had roots in ancien régime institutions. They originated with a culture of objects made by hand for a primarily aristocratic elite. Yet in the nineteenth century, they, too, were shadowed by ties to vulgar taste and bourgeois materialism, specifically the growing demand for mass-produced bibelots. Here I am comparing a woman, Sarah Bernhardt, to an artistic genre, the decorative arts, not because I accept the simile as sound, but to make the point that the same comparison informed many fin-de-siècle discourses of art and decoration.[6] It is suggested, for example, in an Art Nouveau poster by Georges de Feure for the *Journal des ventes* (fig. 6) that juxtaposes a fashionable Parisienne and a decorative art object. They are interchangeably enticing visual spectacles—a motif common in late-nineteenth-century journalistic illustration and poster culture. Feure's work foretells the reliance of twentieth-century advertising on illusory female types with blank expressions onto which any fantasy can be projected. But even real women, like Bernhardt, used, and were used by, this discourse that superimposed women, decoration, and commerce. Among the more intriguing examples are a lithographic portrait by Paul Berthon (fig. 7) and Alphonse Mucha's poster for *La samaritaine* (see Introduction, fig. 3). In these depictions, Bernhardt's features are generalized to produce an image that is at once Bernhardt and a decorative typological double.

The category of the "decorative arts," an umbrella term, facilitates that kind of fluidity. The phrase "decorative arts" refers to objects that are functional but not without aesthetic significance, objects that are not designated "fine arts" and that have some use-value in interior design or the decoration of one's person. It encompasses ceramics, metalwork, furniture, jewelry, textiles, glass, porcelain, silver, enamel. By the middle of the nineteenth century, the discourse of the decorative arts was inflected more and more by its identification with bourgeois consumerism and machine technology, by-products of the Industrial Revolution. Although debates over the hierarchy of "fine" and "applied" arts, and their respective vulnerabilities to the influence of commerce, certainly predate the nineteenth century, they intensified as social and technological changes prompted those living with the consequences of the Industrial Revolution to assess its benefits against its liabilities.[7]

Regular reminders of art's association with industry in the nineteenth century appeared in the context of the Universal Exposition, or World's Fair, the primary laboratory and catalyst for design and manufacturing reform. London's Crystal Palace exhibition of 1851 and the Paris World's Fair of 1855 were the earliest of these government-sponsored expositions where national rivalries in technology, fine arts, and industrial design took center stage. These expositions were the century's most opulent theaters of the spectacle of consumption and the principal forums of debate over boundaries between aesthetic standards and economic demands.

Multiple national and regional decorative arts movements were born of such debate in the 1800s in cities including New York and Glasgow, Munich and Madrid.

fig. 7 Paul Berthon (French, 1872–1909), *Sarah Bernhardt as Mélisande in "La princesse lointaine,"* 1901. Color lithograph on paper, 25 3/4 x 19 3/4 in. (65.3 x 50.2 cm). Victoria and Albert Museum, London (E 133-1981)

Although their impact on the "fine arts" of painting, sculpture, and architecture was pronounced, they continue to reside in the margins of histories of modern art. The modern art marketplace belongs to a dealer–gallery system whose profitability, ironically, remains bound to sustaining the illusion of art's distance from commerce and to championing misunderstood genius.[8] Because the decorative arts are hard to separate from at least some commercial context and typically are the product of collaboration, they occupy a secondary space in the visual arts hierarchy.

Britain's Arts and Crafts Movement and Belgium's Libre Esthétique rank among the most influential in decorative arts reform. Part socialist critique, part utopian quest, they challenged the valuation of fine over applied arts as a product of the class system and sought to improve the quality of modern life by redressing the shoddiness of machine-made objects and the vulgarization of material culture.[9]

While these movements were founded in reaction against official art institutions, the craft initiative in France—the one with which Bernhardt would have been most familiar early in her artistic career—actually was rooted in official culture. It was propelled less by artists than by manufacturers and entrepreneurs who were concerned with economic protectionism and national pride. Despite the efforts of figures like Edmond and Jules de Goncourt to restore France's former eminence within the aristocratic luxury trades, the greatest innovation in decorative arts design and production took place elsewhere, in England, Belgium, and even the United States. France did lead in the late nineteenth century in retailing and advertising, but that achievement was tainted by its association with the commercialization of art.[10] The identification of fashionable women with the decorative arts in the fin de siècle, increasingly, functioned as a strategy to evade that onus.

Bernhardt's own first sustained engagement with the decorative arts was evident in the realm of her personal wardrobe. Her impulse to decorate herself, to present herself as a work of art, even before she had the income or clout to do so, is clear from the generous photographic record she left (figs. 9, 10), and in the letters and memoirs of contemporaries. Recalling their first meeting in 1866, Félix Duquesnel, associate director of the Théâtre de l'Odéon, wrote: "She was dressed in a tunic of light-colored crepe de chine with iridescent embroidery, a Chinese cut that left her bare arms and shoulders lightly veiled with lace. . . . On her head sat a coolie hat of finely woven straw hung all around with bells that trembled at the slightest movement. . . . Artistry emanated from her entire being."[11] Bernhardt's cultivated memorability as an unmistakable sight is also the subject of a letter by the playwright Octave Feuillet: "Unlike any of the other actresses, she comes to rehearsals all dressed up . . . velvet from head to foot. Velvet dress, velvet jacket, a black lace scarf draped over her shoulders and a little high collar . . . with her hair all frizzed out."[12]

Bernhardt's play with clothing throughout her career ranged from the baroque spectacle of her close-fitting, full-length chinchilla coat (fig. 8) to the Art Nouveau sinuosity of the low-waisted, body-hugging dresses she wore beneath, fashions she

fig. 8 Reutlinger Studio (French, active 1850–1930), Sarah Bernhardt in Personal Wardrobe, n.d. Photographic print, 4 3/4 x 6 1/2 in. (12 x 16.5 cm). Bibliothèque Nationale de France, Département des Estampes, Paris

MADAME SARAH BERNHARDT.

W. & D. DOWNEY
PHOTOGRAPHERS
COPYRIGHT
57 & 61, EBURY STREET.
LONDON, S.W.

Paris

fig. 9 **W. & D. Downey (British, active 1863–1910s),** *Sarah Bernhardt in Personal Wardrobe,* 1902. Albumen print cabinet card, 6 1/2 x 4 1/4 in. (16.6 x 10.8 cm). Bibliothèque Nationale de France, Département des Arts du Spectacle, Paris

fig. 10 **Otto (French, active c. 1892–1917),** *Sarah Bernhardt in Personal Wardrobe,* 1893. Albumen print cabinet card, 6 1/2 x 4 1/4 in. (16.6 x 10.8 cm). Bibliothèque Nationale de France, Département des Arts du Spectacle, Paris

fig. 11 **W. & D. Downey (British active 1863–1910s), Sarah Bernhardt as Théodora, c. 1884. Albumen print cabinet card, 6 9/16 x 4 1/4 in. (16.5 x 10.8 cm). Bequest of Evert Jansen Wendell, 1918; Harvard Theatre Collection, Houghton Library, Cambridge, Massachusetts**

refined to flaunt, rather than downplay, her painfully thin torso and the untamed curliness of her shoulder-length hair. The trademark silhouette she cultivated in life was translated into artistic facsimiles, most markedly in the vernaculars of photography and caricature (see Ockman essay, pp. 29–38). In ways that anticipate the tenets of modern brand identification, her one-of-a-kind body, the undulating line around which her clothing was designed and her poses affected, generated an industry of infinitely reproducible doubles.

Bernhardt's brilliant instincts about visuality and repetition were honed in Baron Haussmann's Paris. She grew up during the city's transfiguration, around its boulevards, fashion houses, and seductive window displays.[13] In this environment, she assimilated the advantage of becoming a unique and sought-after sight, whether onstage in a dazzling costume (fig. 11), posing for photographers in her unusual homes (fig. 12), or capitalizing on the timing of other high-profile cultural spectacles. An 1889 article in *Le Figaro* reports that tourists came to Paris that year to see the country's two most memorable silhouettes: the centerpiece of the Universal Exposition, the Eiffel Tower; and France's most internationally renowned ambassador, Sarah Bernhardt.[14]

The reproduction and dissemination of the Bernhardt silhouette made it fair game for satirists such as Henri Demare. A caricatural pastiche (fig. 13) of 1883 gathers several of her most characteristic images with others invented to invoke notorious episodes or gossip drawn from the Bernhardt lore. Despite the reduced scale of the "original" in this collection of quotations, the actress's aura is aggrandized by the reiterative and retrospective quality of the caricature's recycling.

QUELQUES CHAPITRES DE SA VIE *(A suivre)*

Moreover, while many flocked to the spectacle of the actual Bernhardt, in the flesh, most people experienced her "as a facsimile," just this way.

Bernhardt's invention and choreography of facsimiles of herself—her assemblage of artful patterns of self-referential images, in what might be called an "image bank"—was one of her most creative enterprises. The impulse to generate and bank images dates back to her early years at the Paris Conservatoire, and the striking Nadar photographs of the actress as ingénue. The possibilities grew in proportion to her fame, income, and independence, and in relation to technological advances in photography and the mass-circulation illustrated press. By the late 1870s, she had produced a veritable industry of Bernhardt images that in many ways made possible her decision to walk away from the Comédie Française and become, essentially, an independent agent.

The image bank consists of unorthodox publicity stills, postcards of her eclectically appointed homes (fig. 14), iconic posters of her silhouette, and, as her earning power grew, a plethora of decorative objects that adorned her and her residences. From pieces of pottery and bronze plaques bearing her features (figs. 15, 16) to decorative objects inscribed with the motto by which she claimed to live her life, "Quand même" ("No matter what"; figs. 17, 18, 20), these decorative art objects were photographed and described in magazine pieces documenting the excesses and eccentricities associated with "La Bernhardt." "Over the top," "extravagant"—such descriptions dominate most characterizations of Bernhardt's homes, by journalists and close friends alike. One friend affectionately compared her boulevard Péreire home to a "show window in a second-hand furniture shop: priceless objects and rubbish all mixed up in happy confusion."[15]

opposite:

fig. 13   Henri Demare (French, 1846–1888), *Sarah Bernhardt with Louise Abbéma*, caricature, published in *Le grelot*, February 18, 1883. 19 1/8 x 15 1/2 in. (48.5 x 39.5 cm). Bibliothèque Nationale de France, Département des Arts du Spectacle, Paris

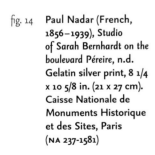

fig. 14   Paul Nadar (French, 1856–1939), *Studio of Sarah Bernhardt on the boulevard Péreire*, n.d. Gelatin silver print, 8 1/4 x 10 5/8 in. (21 x 27 cm). Caisse Nationale de Monuments Historique et des Sites, Paris (NA 237-1581)

fig. 15 Paul François Berthoud
(French, 1870–1939),
Jardinière of Sarah
Bernhardt, 1905.
Bronze, 15 x 20 x 10 in.
(38.1 x 50.8 x 25.4 cm).
Collection of Raphael
Benjamin Sinai, London

fig. 16 René Lalique (French,
1860–1945), Portrait
Medal of Sarah Bernhardt,
1896. Silver, diam.
4 1/8 in. (10.5 cm).
The Jewish Museum,
New York; Purchase:
Miriam and Milton
Handler Endowment
Fund, 1998-112

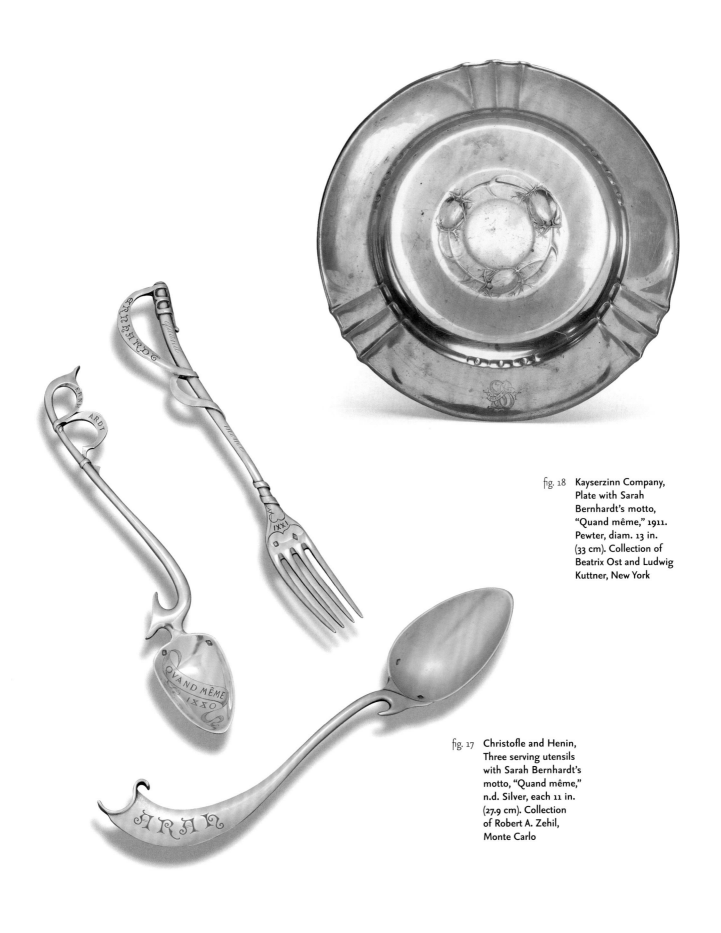

fig. 18 Kayserzinn Company, Plate with Sarah Bernhardt's motto, "Quand même," 1911. Pewter, diam. 13 in. (33 cm). Collection of Beatrix Ost and Ludwig Kuttner, New York

fig. 17 Christofle and Henin, Three serving utensils with Sarah Bernhardt's motto, "Quand même," n.d. Silver, each 11 in. (27.9 cm). Collection of Robert A. Zehil, Monte Carlo

The image bank also served Bernhardt's own engagement with the dialectic of art and decoration; it was an inexhaustible and flexible source of Bernhardt facsimiles available for exhibition in print-shop windows, on street kiosks, or in the illustrated press. A volume she published in 1879 represents a particularly elaborate and creative use to which she put her catalogue of stories and images. *Dans les nuages: Impressions d'une chaise* (In the Clouds: Impressions of a Chair; fig. 19) was itself a decorative object, a book illustrated with drawings, mostly of Bernhardt, by Georges Clairin. The story was a thinly disguised fictionalization of the recent and much-publicized hot-air balloon trip Bernhardt had made with Clairin and the nephew of an ardent balloonist named Eugène Godard.[16] The adventure—described in Demare's caricatural pastiche as well (fig. 13)—is narrated by a humble straw chair that has always dreamed of travel and high places.[17] Through a series of coincidences, the chair ends up tied precariously to a hot-air balloon in which the famous actress Doña Sol (Bernhardt's most acclaimed recent role, in Victor Hugo's *Hernani*) and her companion Clairin float over Paris until they are grounded by a storm. Although the chair finds Doña Sol alternately mesmerizing and appalling, he is elated at story's conclusion to be welcomed into the entourage of her Parc Monceau home, on the rue Fortuny. The hôtel, which Bernhardt had lately built and decorated, became one of Paris's "most distinctive sights." Its interior provides the stage for the story's denouement, the fulfillment of the chair's dreams, as he is brought to rest in "a huge room full of carpets, potted plants, and bric-a-brac."[18]

The loose plotline of *Dans les nuages* is a vehicle through which Bernhardt replays highlights from her recent history of provocative gestures and images. These include her real-life adventure *dans les nuages*; her most celebrated sculpture, *Après la tempête* (After the Storm; see Ockman essay, fig. 27); and her supposed penchant for the morbid and the eccentric—the photograph of her in a coffin (see Ockman essay, fig. 37 and pp. 51–55); the bat motif running through her interior design and her personal wardrobe (fig. 21); and the bizarre hybridity of her bronze *Self-Portrait as a Sphinx* (see Ockman essay, fig. 35), produced shortly after *Dans les nuages*.[19]

The book also makes pointed reference, in the text and in two of Clairin's illustrations, to one of Bernhardt's most provocative costumes and photographic facsimiles, the famous "atelier ensemble" on which she collaborated with the couturier Charles Frederick Worth. Bernhardt commissioned a series of photographs by Melandri of herself as visual artist *en travesti*, in white silk pants, overblouse, and neck ruffle, that caused a stir in 1878.[20] The composition and cropping of one in particular (see Ockman essay, fig. 28 and pp. 43–44) showcases Bernhardt's self-aware play—her identity as actress, artist, and work of art. She poses, in the decorative and androgynous costume of "the artist," adjacent to her own sculpted self-representation. The sculpture, seen in profile, and slightly elevated to the right of her actual head, is compositionally implied to be the mirrored reflection of the actress, whose pose and gesture further substantiate that relationship. Her spinal twist is a hinge between the stabilizing verticality of her own straightened right arm and leg, and their echoes in the decorative carving of the stool legs.

fig. 19 **Title page from *Dans les nuages: Impressions d'une chaise* (In the Clouds: Impressions of a Chair) by Sarah Bernhardt, 1878. Illustrations by Georges Clairin. 12 x 9 in. (30.5 x 22.9 cm). The Metropolitan Museum of Art, New York, The Elisha Whittelsey Collection, The Elisha Whittelsey Fund, 1963 (63.602)**

fig. 20 Edmond Rostand
(French, 1868–1918),
La princesse lointaine
(book given by
Edmond Rostand to
Sarah Bernhardt),
1911. Moroccan leather-
bound book with
metal filigree and semi-
precious stones. Private
collection, New York

fig. 21 Otto (French, active
c. 1892–1917), Sarah
Bernhardt in Personal
Wardrobe (Bat Hat), 1880
Albumen print cabinet
card, 6 1/2 x 4 3/16 in.
(16.4 x 10.7 cm).
Harvard Theatre
Collection, Houghton
Library, Cambridge,
Massachusetts

fig. 22   Illustration by Georges Jules Victor Clairin (French, 1843–1919) in *Dans les nuages: Impressions d'une chaise* (In the Clouds: Impressions of a Chair) by Sarah Bernhardt, 1878. 12 x 9 in. (30.5 x 22.9 cm). The Metropolitan Museum of Art, New York, The Elisha Whittelsey Collection, The Elisha Whittelsey Fund, 1963 (63.602)

The dialectic of Bernhardt as art and decoration (and as artist and actress) that registers in this photograph, and in several *Dans les nuages* illustrations (fig. 22), resonates elsewhere in the book—most intriguingly in its narrator, another Bernhardt facsimile. Many details of the narrator's life and ambition echo the Bernhardt mythology: the androgyny, the scare of invalidism, a child deprived of parental love, and the aspiration to exotic travel, to name a few.[21] Also interesting in this context is the casting of the narrator as a chair, a decorative object. The chair begins life, not just as one of many in a shop, but one that is damaged, its wood "still bleeding." Only the lucky circumstance of a gentleman's kindness makes possible the chair's distinction and fulfillment of lifelong dreams. This plot, especially its details of physical frailty and miraculous rescue, notably resembles the one Bernhardt disseminated about her early life.[22] In the end, through a combination of fate, ambition, and openness to risk and experience, both Bernhardt and chair are transfigured from the decorative to the artistic and rare.

The interplay in *Dans les nuages* between Bernhardt's self-representation and the decorative became an even more salient feature of her image bank once she was financially stable and in control of aesthetic and economic details of her life. It was then that she was able to undertake the spectacular and lucrative vehicles for which she is best known today, but it was also then that she was branded, in the eyes of her fiercest critics, more decorative commodity than artistic rarity. Onstage, those vehicles included *Fédora* and then *Théodora*, collaborations with Victorien Sardou that capitalized on the vogue for exotic spectacle and extravagant production values. Offstage, they included her homes and studios, a series of ever more ornately decorated, and regularly photographed, domestic interiors. The relationship between these theatrical and residential settings is implied in the comment of a friend who remarked that, to Bernhardt, a home represented just "one more set of scenery."[23]

From the late 1870s on, images and descriptions of her lavish residences appeared in magazine articles, in the pages of a handsome Art Nouveau booklet, *The Home of Sarah Bernhardt in Paris* (fig. 23), and even in a film, *Sarah Bernhardt à Belle Isle* (1912). By all accounts and photographic evidence, these spaces were eclectic and chaotic. Even more renowned than the rue Fortuny home, which takes center stage in *Dans les nuages*, was Bernhardt's last, and most lavish, Paris residence, on the boulevard Péreire. Purchased partly with vast earnings from her American and British tours, the house was, according to a *Figaro* reporter, "a fantastic jumble of Oriental carpets, animal skins, bizarre bronzes, Mexican idols, canvases on the easel, beribboned garlands of flowers, Egyptian vases, [and] encroaching plants, all lit by the glimmer of a fire."[24] Like the "picturesque jumble" of her previous homes, the decor was more hodgepodge than planned design. According to her granddaughter, Bernhardt "was more interested in the shape or the colour of a curio, than its origin, its antiquity, or its value." While some of her souvenirs were "precious or rare," her granddaughter found others "frankly hideous."[25]

Bernhardt's taste in interior decor seems to have represented, in its most exaggerated form, the very ethos of excess and random eclecticism that most nineteenth-century decorative arts reformers were devoted to eradicating. Given the immoderate expense on clothing, jewelry, furnishings, and unusual knickknacks—Mary Louise Roberts describes "a Veblenesque life of conspicuous consumption"—and the very public way in which Bernhardt flaunted them, it is not hard to understand why she was so regularly invoked to represent the symbiosis mentioned earlier.[26] She seems almost to have invited the kind of comparison Georges de Feure makes in his poster of 1898 (fig. 6) among fashionable Parisienne, expensive bibelot, and the economic subtext, commerce, that implicitly binds them.[27] The subject of Feure's poster, the admiring gaze of an expensively dressed shopper affixed to the unusual object elevated in her hands, was, as I have indicated, a common motif in Art Nouveau.

Although no real consensus exists about Art Nouveau's chronological parameters or valuation, most scholars agree that its fertile period dates to the last decade of the nineteenth century and first few years of the twentieth and that its most important impact was in architecture and the decorative arts.[28] Heralded for its promise of a universal visual language and condemned as insidious foreign plot, praised as the resurrection of refined, elite art and degraded as vulgar commerce, Art Nouveau occupies the same dialectical cultural space that Bernhardt traversed.[29] Her performances in French in cities around the world were seen as the transcendence of national boundaries and as further evidence of Jewish

fig. 23   The Home of Sarah
Bernhardt in Paris, after
1890. Booklet, 7 1/2 x
5 1/2 in. (19 x 14 cm).
Mutuelle Nationale des
Artistes, Couilly-Pont-
aux-Dames, France

overinfluence.[30] Her enlightened support of artists such as Lalique suggested an
understanding of ancien régime quality, at the same time that her public displays
of consumer excess dramatized better than any social critic could the clichéd
equation between female consumerism and the decorative.[31]

As I have suggested, Art Nouveau manifestations in France focused chiefly
on efforts to reclaim its former eminence in the aristocratic luxury trades. They
sought to make up ground lost to Glasgow, Brussels, Vienna, New York, and other
decorative arts centers, cities once regarded as provincial in their decorative arts
traditions. France's inability to compete in a field it historically had dominated
generated an antagonism toward Art Nouveau's foreign origins that only intensified
with late-nineteenth-century anti-Semitic discourse, and the Dreyfus Affair, which
gave it focus. A striking instance appears in a review by the critic Arsène Alexandre
on the occasion of the opening in 1895 of the decorative arts gallery and shop
for which the movement is named. Of Siegfried Bing's L'Art Nouveau, Alexandre
commented: "It all smelled of the lewd Englishman, the Jewess addicted to
morphine[,] or the cunning Belgian, or an agreeable mix of these three poisons."[32]
As Kenneth Silver writes, this comment is generally understood as a response
both to the large number of non-French designers that Bing showcased and to
Bing's German Jewish background.[33]

The invocation of "a Jewess" in relation to the Bing enterprise was not atypical
of anti-Semitic commentary of the fin de siècle. Bernhardt is mentioned several

fig. 24   Jules Bastien-Lepage
(French, 1848–1884),
Sarah Bernhardt, c. 1879.
Oil on canvas, 17 1/4 x 13
1/2 in. (43.8 x 34.3 cm).
Private collection

times in discussions of visits to L'Art Nouveau. The actress, whose mother was Jewish, was a frequent target of anti-Semitic commentary. Her association with the hybrid foreignness of the gallery/shop was one of many anti-Semitic clichés with which she was tarred. Others included her mania for travel, the lingering sign of "la juive errante"; her affinity for America, and the avarice it confirmed; and the decorative excesses and eccentricities of her homes that marked her as "a true daughter of Israel."[34]

The relationship between Bernhardt's habits of consumption and her engagement with the decorative arts also informed, and was informed by, other fin-de-siècle discourses of Art Nouveau. It evokes, for example, the burgeoning literature on home decor that celebrated the domestic as a sphere of power for the modern Frenchwoman. Debora Silverman has observed that Art Nouveau theorists and entrepreneurs promoted the decorated interior as a domain crucial to the well-being of the national psyche.[35] As patriotic act and fulfillment of a biological destiny, the modern Frenchwoman was expected to serve as guardian of that interior.[36] In addition to the economic boon of promoting home decor as a realm of female artistic self-expression, this rhetoric also articulated a tame, domestic alternative to "la nouvelle femme," the nontraditional, "masculine" woman choosing less conventional life paths made possible by recent changes in France's education, press, and divorce laws.[37]

Although Bernhardt generally evaded the "nouvelle femme" label, she did represent the kind of independence and self-sufficiency for which the stereotype stood.[38] Yet she also represented the cliché of obsessive self-adornment and a preoccupation with shopping that might be associated with the modern ideal of the female artist of the home. In this final section, I consider Bernhardt's play on and with these types, as it relates to the dialectic of art and decoration with which I began.

A sumptuous portrait of the actress by Jules Bastien-Lepage (fig. 24) offers a useful early example of this dialectic. Its juxtaposition of art object and woman anticipates Georges de Feure's Parisian shopper (fig. 6) in its subject's three-quarter-length format, decorative profile, and absorption with the work she holds carefully in her hands. Both images spotlight a single female figure and a decorative object, but while it is the imminent purchase that inspires the Parisienne, it is the transformative power of art that underlies Bernhardt's captivation.

Bastien-Lepage represents the actress and her creative powers, in a state usually reserved for the male artist or connoisseur.[39] He pays homage to the actress as decorative art, but also as contemplative artist. Her communion is not with an untitled, unattributed art commodity, but rather with a statuette of Orpheus, by Bastien-Lepage himself, a symbol of Bernhardt's artistry. One of the actress's most distinctive, transporting traits, her "golden voice," frequently was compared to Orpheus's lyre; the comparison is reinforced here in the dominant triangle of the composition, formed by the lines of Bernhardt's back, gaze, and raised left arm, and in the passages of gauzy, opalescent paint that connect her face, hands, and surrogate.

Bastien-Lepage's image is a gesture of respect. A related, written representation, from two years later, invokes that coupling for a very different effect. On the occasion of Bernhardt's first Russian tour, in 1881, a trip made soon after she broke her contract with the Comédie Française and began the more entrepreneurial phase of her career, a Moscow theater critic, S. Vasil'ev, described her as "very talented, but not an actress of genius. She gives us remarkably clear . . . palpable, almost chiseled types. They are splendid statuettes, which one would gladly place on one's mantelpiece. But a statuette is not a statue."[40]

The duality of Vasil'ev's image of Bernhardt, his differentiation between statue and statuette, recalls the passage with which this essay began. Whereas Helen Ten Broeck admired Bernhardt's capacity to be both "that epic in marble" and a decorative object, "a stained glass Sarah," Vasil'ev identifies her exclusively, and degradingly, with the statuette. As the diminutive, feminine suffix -ette suggests, and Vasil'ev confirms, "a statuette is not a statue."

By definition, a statuette is understood to be a small representation in the round of a figure, sculptured, molded, or cast in any of a number of materials. It often depicts a mythological figure, like Orpheus in Bastien-Lepage's sculpture, an allegorical personage or eminent person, or, in its later-nineteenth-century incarnations, a celebrity, like Bernhardt as the title character from Edmond Rostand's play L'Aiglon (see Silver essay, pp. 88–94) in L. Raphael's bronze (c. 1900; fig. 25). The statuette became a compromise for many nineteenth-century sculptors, in the face of changing technologies and growing demands for smaller, more affordable art better suited to domestic environments.

As was true for Bernhardt, the artistic and economic positions of the statuette were inextricably bound. They depended on various factors: the distribution of labor between artist and foundry; the number of reproductions permitted; the display venue and audience; the ranking of the artist involved. The valuation of a particular statuette resided in a constellation of circumstances that determined whether it would be regarded as bibelot or objet d'art, as something cheap and mass-produced or expensive and handcrafted, a decorative commodity or a rarity.

Vasil'ev's identification of the actress with the statuette implies her complicity in the commercialization and vulgarization of culture. It brands as a decorative commodity the newly independent Bernhardt—the actress who walked away from the life of a Comédie Française sociétaire in favor of control over roles she played and money she could earn. But Vasil'ev's image might also be used to recover Bernhardt's play on and with the statuette motif. It could underline her peerless value in the growing market for cheap celebrity images, whether photographs (fig. 8, 9), medallions (fig. 16), or statuettes (fig. 25) (see Ockman essay, esp. pp. 24–29).[41] It could be used to recover Bernhardt's fashioning of her own body as a type of statuette, with the form-fitting costumes and silhouette that made her irresistible to the caricaturist's sensibility. Her image bank, in a sense, depended on the very

fig. 25 L. Raphael, L'Aiglon Statuette, c. 1900. Bronze, 7 1/4 x 1 3/4 x 2 in. (18.4 x 4.5 x 5.1 cm). Laurence Senelick Collection of Theatrical Imagery, West Medford, Massachusetts

dialectic a statuette could embody: its reference simultaneously to a one-of-a-kind work of art and an infinitely reproducible commodity.

A photograph taken at her boulevard Péreire home (fig. 12) suggests the actress's play with the themes implied in the juxtaposition of statue and statuette. Its focus is the pillarlike figure of Bernhardt, who gazes down at a statuette she holds. Unlike the Orpheus in Bastien-Lepage's portrait, this statuette is indistinct and appears less important than the thought it triggers. Its small scale and the supporting role it assumes in the composition point our attention elsewhere. An extension of the line of Bernhardt's forearm, the statuette directs our eye to the mantelpiece, and a second, recognizable sculpted figure. It is an image of Mary Magdalene, framed by a mirror and set at an angle that points to her connection with the actress, a relationship reinforced by the rounded line of Bernhardt's sleeve, echoed in the nude saint's arching back.[42]

The figure of the actress has been associated with sin and temptation from the first years women were allowed on the stage.[43] But the inclusion of Mary Magdalene in the photograph in mirrored relation to Bernhardt's silhouette complicates our anticipation of the saint's embodiment of the polarity of sin and salvation. The composition is cropped and lit so that Bernhardt is its central and most stable element. Her Giottoesque form, in a loose-fitting aesthetic gown—a departure from the body-hugging fashions in which she usually was photographed—transfigures sinful self-display into saintly modesty. This tension illuminates Bernhardt's creative manipulation of the dialectic of statuette and statue: talent versus genius, miniature versus monument, decorative versus art, artistic consumer versus contemplative aesthete. It also makes explicit the quality at issue in each of these polarities, which is associated with the degraded term in each pair of opposites: female gender. Talent, the miniature, the decorative, and the artistic consumer are all gendered female, and the increasingly fluid category of the decorative in this period comes to signify the feminine itself.

One of Bernhardt's own decorative art objects, Algues (Algae), a small bronze she displayed at the Universal Exposition of 1900 (fig. 3), may represent her most creative play with the categories of art and decoration. Its silhouette resembles her own, or at least the caricatural abbreviations of her pencil-thin form. Algae conjures the interplay she cultivated between the long, tapering line of her body and the decorative flourish of her fanning train, "the style she invented," according to Reynaldo Hahn, "and continues to wear in spite of changing fashions, a form that clings to her legs and ends in a swirling out about the ankles."[44] What better example of Bernhardt's engagement with the decorative arts, and the questions underlying the dialectic of statue and statuette, than a sculpture of her own making that is at once art and artist, art and decoration, miniature and yet evocative of the monumental?

Karen Levitov

THE DIVINE SARAH AND THE INFERNAL SALLY

Bernhardt in the Words of Her Contemporaries

If we were to pile together everything that has been written about [Sarah Bernhardt] and were to sell it by the ton (at 150 rubles per ton), and if we were to dedicate the receipts from the sale to the "Society for the Protection of Animals," then—we swear by our quills!—we could at least give dinner and supper to the horses and dogs at [the fashionable restaurant] Olivier's, or at [that dump of a place] Tatar's.

—Anton Chekhov

The Russian writer and dramatist—whose naturalistic style was antithetical to Sarah Bernhardt's melodramatic theater—was appalled by the vast publicity that surrounded the fin-de-siècle French actress. However, Chekhov's satiric observation calls attention to the immense quantity of writing devoted to Bernhardt during her life. Critics and columnists fed the public's insatiable desire to know about this entrancing star of the stage, and well-known writers also fell under her spell. Oscar Wilde called her the "greatest tragic actress of any stage now living."[1] Henry James, writing about the London performances of the Comédie Française for an American journal, commented on "the extraordinary vogue of Mademoiselle Sarah Bernhardt": it would, he said, "require some ingenuity to give an idea of the intensity, the ecstasy, the insanity as some people would say, of curiosity and enthusiasm provoked by Mlle. Bernhardt."[2]

In the various viewpoints of her peers, Sarah Bernhardt's representation has vacillated between heavenly muse and earthly or even devilish creature. The actress was "The Divine Sarah," continually lauded for her eternal youthfulness, her golden voice, her classical declamatory delivery, her captivating aura, and her Catholic convent schooling. Simultaneously, she was "The Infernal Sally," harshly criticized for her insistence on acting when she was beyond a "respectable" age and for her shrill intonation, her overwrought acting style, her personal decadence, and, not least, her origin as the daughter of a Jewish courtesan.

Bernhardt contributed to the public frenzy around her, cultivating her image and directing her own publicity campaign, as well as publishing her memoirs. Although newspaper columnists and theater critics wrote most prolifically about her, many of her more famous contemporaries took it upon themselves to comment on her professional career and personal life. Henry James based a character in his novel *The Tragic Muse* on her and wrote about the actress in the press. To him, Bernhardt was "a child of her age—of her moment—and she has known how to profit by the idiosyncrasies of the time."[3] The playwright and novelist Alexandre Dumas *fils*, long a friend of Bernhardt's mother and an early supporter of young Sarah's career, summed up the effect of her infamous disposition: "She drives me mad when I am with her. She is all temperament and no heart;

fig. 2   Sarah Bernhardt, c. 1865–70. Ferrotype, 3 x 2 in. (7.6 x 5.1 cm). Musée Carnavalet—Histoire de Paris (PH 9023)

fig. 3 Georges Jules Victor Clairin (French, 1843–1919), Fan with portrait of Sarah Bernhardt and names of Bernhardt productions, 1881. Watercolor with tortoiseshell frame, 12 1/4 x 24 3/8 in. (31 x 62 cm). Musée Galliera, Musée de la Mode de la Ville de Paris (GAL 1989.254.1)

but when she is gone, how I work! How I can work!"[4] And Victor Hugo, in a letter to Bernhardt dated November 21, 1877, the first night she performed in his *Hernani* at the Théâtre Français, responded with great emotion. He sent Bernhardt a tear-shaped diamond on a chain bracelet as a symbolic gift, accompanied by a note: "Madame: You were great, and you were charming; you moved me—me the old warrior, and at a certain moment when the public cheered, enchanted and overcome by emotion, I wept. The tear which you drew from me belongs to you. I place it at your feet."[5]

The extraordinary response to Bernhardt in her time by her more noted fans and critics demonstrates her impact in the late nineteenth and early twentieth centuries across two continents. The quotations that follow show how Bernhardt was perceived as both remarkably otherworldly and distinctly corporeal and how these perceptions were based largely on nineteenth-century concepts of gender and ethnicity.

The Divine Sarah

Representations of women in art and literature have often shifted between saint and concubine; Sarah Bernhardt notably was seen as both. In the late nineteenth century, women who worked for a living—whether in the domestic sphere, in the fabric trades, or as servers and performers in café-bars, concert halls, and theaters—were associated with prostitution.[6] The backstage of the opera, for example, was a place where wealthy male patrons had access to young female dancers. This is seen in popular photographs as well as in Edgar Degas's numerous studies of dancers that often include well-dressed men seated in dressing rooms, waiting in the wings during recitals, or conversing backstage at the opera. These relationships were widely known to be sexual and territorial and that the opera, the theater, and other Parisian entertainments were in part venues for illicit pleasure-seeking.[7]

In addition to the questionable morality of Bernhardt's profession, the fact that her mother and an aunt were both courtesans extended this association to young

Sarah. Yet her talents as an actress eclipsed the impression of dubious morals, and she was most often held in the highest esteem, even called divine, by those who saw her perform. Mark Twain's famous observation positions Bernhardt above all others: "There are five kinds of actresses: bad actresses, fair actresses, good actresses, great actresses—and then there is Sarah Bernhardt."[8]

Oscar Wilde was another of Bernhardt's great devotees: "The three women I have most admired are Queen Victoria, Sarah Bernhardt, and Lillie Langtry. The first had great dignity, the second a lovely voice, and the third a perfect figure; I would have married any one of them with the greatest pleasure."[9] Wilde uses the metaphor of marriage to designate these three great personages not as desirable women, since he himself preferred men, but as archetypes of power, art, and beauty, respectively.

D. H. Lawrence similarly fell in love with Bernhardt, and warned of her powers, after seeing her perform in Dumas fils's *La dame aux camélias* (*The Lady of the Camellias*) at age sixty-three: "I could love such a woman myself, love her to madness; all for the pure wild passion of it. Take care about going to see Bernhardt. Unless you are very sound, do not go."[10] And the American stage actress Laurette Taylor declared, "She was the greatest . . . of all time. [She lived] when the theatre was so magnificent as to be almost unreal. In fact she was called 'the Magnificent.'"

While a few admirers spoke directly of Bernhardt's divine status, especially in regard to her voice and her eternal youthfulness, others alluded to the celestial aura about her. In 1894, the critic Henri Fouquier defined her greatness as "the mixture of the poetry of an impersonal, mythical being with an almost frightening precision of movement."[11] The French poet Théodore de Banville mythologized Bernhardt's youthful perfection: "She is the only actress that the sculptor has made expressly to practice the art of acting. . . . Moreover, she is so well-equipped to give the impression to poetry that, even when she is immobile and silent, one feels that her movement, like her voice, obeys a lyrical rhythm. A Greek statue, wishing to symbolize Poetry, would choose her for a model."[12] And the drama critic Francisque Sarcey, on seeing the forty-nine-year-old actress in Jean Racine's *Phèdre* in 1893, said, "It is strange, astounding, inexplicable, but nevertheless true that Madame Sarah Bernhardt is younger, more splendid and, let us face the fact, more beautiful than she has ever been, of a more artistic beauty, which gives one a thrill of admiration as at the sight of a beautiful statue."[13] In 1905, an article in the New York *Telegram* claimed that Bernhardt, then in her early sixties, "might be any age or no age at all . . . . [This] strange being [whose body] had ceased to be governed by the hampering laws of the flesh," was "something supernatural."[14]

Throughout her long life—she continued to act until her death at seventy-eight—Bernhardt garnered extensive praise for her *voix d'or*, or "golden voice," to which was frequently attributed godly characteristics. The biographer and critic Lytton Strachey venerated it: "The secret of that astounding utterance baffles the imagination. The words boomed and crashed with a superhuman resonance which shook the spirit of the hearer like a leaf in the wind. The *voix d'or* has often

fig. 4 Henri-Marie-Raymond de Toulouse-Lautrec (French, 1864–1901), *At the Théâtre de la Renaissance: Sarah Bernhardt in "Phèdre,"* 1893. Lithograph on Japan paper, 18 1/8 x 12 3/16 in. (46 x 31 cm). The Metropolitan Museum of Art, New York, Bequest of Scofield Thayer, 1982 (1984.1203.157)

been raved over; but in Sarah Bernhardt's voice there was more than gold: there was thunder and lightning; there was heaven and hell."[15] Jules Lemaître, critic and dramatist, also remarked on the "extraordinary purity" of her voice; it was, he said, "a stream of gold."[16]

Gertrude Stein's companion, Alice B. Toklas, was moved by the strength and power of that voice after seeing Bernhardt in *Phèdre* in Berkeley in 1906 (see pp. 152–153, fig. 6): "Evidently Bernhardt had had no rehearsals, nor had she studied the large stage. Her arms outstretched, with her piercing cry she backed forever toward the curtained door. She prolonged the cry, the golden voice continued. The audience was breathless. Finally she reached the curtain and disappeared. I had seen her in many of her poignant roles but was never more moved than then."[17]

Bernhardt's voice also made a lasting impact on Sigmund Freud. While in Paris in 1885–86, the father of psychoanalysis saw Bernhardt perform in Victorien Sardou's *Théodora* and remarked on her convincing delivery:

fig. 5 Rochlitz Studio, Sarah Bernhardt as Phèdre, after 1915. Tinted gelatin silver print, 11 1/8 x 7 1/4 in. (28.3 x 18.4 cm). Harvard Theatre Collection, Houghton Library, Cambridge, Massachusetts

I can't say anything good about the piece itself. . . . But how that Sarah plays! After the first words of her lovely, vibrant voice I felt I had known her for years. Nothing she could have said would have surprised me; I believed at once every-thing she said. . . . I have never seen a more comical figure than Sarah in the second act, where she appears in a simple dress, and yet one soon stops laugh-ing, for every inch of that little figure lives and bewitches. Then her flattering and imploring and embracing; it is incredible what postures she can assume and how every limb and joint acts with her. A curious being: I can imagine that she needn't be any different in life [from how she is] on the stage.[18]

In Freud's eyes, Bernhardt's complete embodiment of the role not only blurred the distinction between actress and character but also dissolved the psychological barrier between stage and audience. Freud was clearly smitten with her: "Yesterday my failure to write had another cause. My head was reeling; I had been to the Porte St. Martin theater to see Sarah Bernhardt."[19]

Writing about Bernhardt's performance in a breeches role in Miss G. Constant Lounsbury's *L'escarpolette* (The Swing), Mark Twain—typically deriding the crude-ness of Americans in contrast to the culture of France—claimed that her voice was alluring enough to transcend language: "I never appreciated to the full how uncouth our English language is until I heard the deliciously sweet, mellifluous French of Mme. Sarah Bernhardt here today. It sounded so beautiful that I felt I was going to understand it, but I didn't. Nevertheless I was made very happy by the sight of Mme. Bernhardt as a marvelous young and dazzling cavalier."[20] Others who may have been less enthusiastic about Bernhardt as an actress remained bewitched by her voice. In 1904, a New York theater critic wrote: "Sarah's name and fame rest upon one speciality—the power to electrify any crowded house of foreigners [i.e., Americans] by the simulations of a terrific cyclone of rage, agony, horror—that is the speciality in which she is expected to indulge. People wait

fig. 6 Leonetto Cappiello
(Italian, 1875–1942),
Cover of Le théâtre, 1903.
Color lithograph,
14 1/4 x 10 1/2 in. (36.2 x
26.7 cm). Posters
Please, Inc., New York

until 11 p.m. if necessary and sit through hours of her tedious 'liquid gold,' but they must be treated to it. It is their only use for Sarah Bernhardt."[21] The critic Desmond McCarthy, who wrote under the name "Affable Hawk" for London's *New Statesman*, poignantly conveyed the power of that "golden voice": "She might have acted in the dark and held us."[22]

In an extension of her divine embodiment, the Pre-Raphaelite painter Edward Burne-Jones—who had refused Bernhardt's commission of a painting of herself as Theodora—referred to her, if a bit ironically, as royalty:

fig. 7   William Nicholson
(British, 1872–1949),
Poster for the Grand
Théâtre de Génève,
1897. Wood-block print,
10 5/8 x 10 in. (27 x
25.5 cm). Bibliothèque
Nationale de France,
Département des Arts
du Spectacle, Paris

Tell me how long *She* stays and how long she is to be seen and worshipped in this new play—for go I must, although I shall be ill for a month after it.

Even if I were free tomorrow I don't think I could meet her at lunch. I cannot speak French even to a waiter and what could I say to her?

No, come with Her and gently interpret what She says to me and I will gape open-mouthed and be quite happy. . . . On no account is She to be bored or tired, but to have everything Her own lovely way and at a minute's notice.[23]

The writer Luce Dalrue characterized Bernhardt in 1897 as a "queen" and a "priestess outside the temple"; she saw in the actress "the fantastic evocation of a modern poster, suddenly gifted with life, a breathing illustration of some very old Fairy Tale book, illuminated with fine gems and gold."[24] Dalrue's description was written just when Art Nouveau posters of Bernhardt by Alphonse Mucha and other artists were being seen in the streets of Paris.

The English actress Ellen Terry attended Bernhardt's hundredth performance of Shakespeare's *Romeo and Juliet*; in a later article she conjured Bernhardt's ephemeral nature rather than her merely human qualities:

fig. 8 Napoleon Sarony (American, b. Canada, 1821–1896), *Sarah Bernhardt in "Ruy Blas,"* 1900. Gelatin silver print

How wonderful she looked in those days! She was as transparent as an azalea, only more so; like a cloud, only not so thick. Smoke from a burning paper describes her more nearly! She was hollow-eyed, almost consumptive-looking. Her body was not the prison of her soul, but its shadow. . . . On the stage she always seemed to me more a symbol, an ideal, an epitome than a *woman*. . . . She was always a miracle. . . . It was this extraordinary decorative and symbolic quality of Sarah's which made her transcend all personal and individual feeling on the stage. No one played a love-scene better, but it was a picture of love that she gave, a strange orchidaceous picture rather than a suggestion of the ordinary human passion, as felt by ordinary human people. She was exotic— well, what else could she be? One does not, at any rate one should not, quarrel with an exquisite tropical flower and call it unnatural because it is not a buttercup or a cowslip.[25]

Terry's laudation encapsulates some of the prevailing character traits that were attributed to Bernhardt at the time, as a woman, an actress, and a Jew. She is seen as feminine—delicate, decorative, and idealized—yet she exists also outside the realm of respectable womanhood—elusive, sickly, and exotic—characteristics associated in the late nineteenth century with actresses, prostitution, and Jewishness. In this incarnation, Bernhardt is the Divine Sarah, yet the suggestion is that beneath her allure is something distinctly aberrant.

The Infernal Sally

Mocking the journalists who incessantly gushed over Bernhardt's divinity, particularly in regard to her supposed agelessness, the theater critic George Jean

Nathan claimed that the overdone publicity turned the once Divine Sarah into an "Infernal Sally." In his parody of her, Nathan mimics articles written about the sixty-six-year-old Bernhardt:

> The Divine Sarah again has proved her divinity! The slender figure, alert . . . dominant, vigorous, full of sap, and verdant; the facial play of all the emotions that made her mobile features beautiful; and lastly the golden voice, with its rise and fall, its crescendo and its diminuendo, its soft and feline purr, giving place to the rasp of agony and the stress of anger, made curiosity mongers sit up and rub their eyes. Of age—not a vestige, not a symptom, not a suspicion. The horror of senility had passed her by. She frolicked and she coquetted; she posed in the cozy attitudes of lovely youth—she as the youngest thing on the stage—and they were all her juniors.[26]

Although Nathan acknowledges that Bernhardt is "still, and probably justly, acclaimed the most proficient actress of her time," he does not judge her divine: "Art may never age, but woman, alas! . . . Sarah Bernhardt, the world of my neighbors *per contra*, is—human."[27]

As frequently as she was called divine, Bernhardt was associated with base humanity, if not monstrosity. Henry James fictionalized Bernhardt in his novel *The Tragic Muse* as the character Miriam Rooth, "a kind of monster" who refuses to display the meekness and decency expected from a woman artist.[28] Bernhardt was overtly sexual yet also the ideal of pure femininity, even in her breeches roles. Her critics expounded on her "Oriental exoticism," supposed deviant sexuality, unusual thinness, monetary ambition, thirst for publicity, and grandiose ego, and even deemed her mad and consumptive.

Jean Cocteau used a monster analogy—qualified, however—when writing of Bernhardt in the film *Camille* (1912): "I recommend to those who cannot admit the existence of sacred monsters that they . . . see the film of Madame Sarah Bernhardt. . . . What actress will play the great amoureuses better than Sarah in this film? None. And when it is over, we find ourselves back in modern life, like the diver who returns to the surface after having come face to face with a giant devil fish in tropic seas."[29] Bernhardt's wavering reception as divine manifestation or monstrous being can be connected to her ambiguous religious status: when she was praised, her Catholicism was often mentioned, and when she was criticized, she was more often identified as Jewish. During Bernhardt's audition at the acting conservatory, the composer Daniel-François-Esprit Auber asked her whether she was Jewish. She said yes but that she had been baptized. "What a shame it would be," Auber responded, "if such a pretty child had not been baptized."[30] Yet François Bournand and Raphaël Viau, in their anti-Semitic book *Les femmes d'Israël* (1898), were not convinced that baptism had altered Bernhardt's innate and inescapable origin: "Whether initiated into the worship of God by Gemara [Talmud] or by catechism, Sarah Bernhardt is neither more nor less than a Jewess and nothing but a Jewess."[31] In 1902, William Dean Howells reported that while watching Bernhardt perform her "She Hamlet," he never forgot for a moment that it was a woman as the melancholy Dane, and that the woman was a Jewess, and the Jewess a French Jewess.[32]

Bernhardt's Jewish "exoticism" was used both as criticism, in anti-Semitic terms, and as praise, for her sensuality. Ernest Lys, writing about her performance as the Christian martyr in Jules Barbier's *Jeanne d'Arc*, said that Bernhardt's half-Jewish origin "gave her face the troublesome grace of the bohemian or gypsy" and linked her "to the Orient and to the primitive world."[33] The companion of the novelist Radclyffe Hall, Una Vincenzo, Lady Troubridge, commenting on Bernhardt in Edmond Rostand's *L'Aiglon*, did not mention her Jewishness directly, but inferred both her Oriental exoticism and her courtesan background, which she found appealing. Lady Troubridge expressed a longing, "how utterly in vain, for dark, mysterious narrow eyes, a high-bridged nose, a questing, haunted expression and an interesting past."[34]

In the nineteenth century, as mentioned earlier, Jewishness was often associated with disease, principally consumption, which Bernhardt was often mistakenly accused of having. In 1885, historian Anatole Leroy-Beaulieu associated the two

fig. 9 "Sarah Bernhardt—New York's Latest High Pressure Craze," caricature of Bernhardt's Farewell American Tour, 1905–6. 12 x 8 in. (30.5 x 20.3 cm). Billy Rose Theatre Collection, The New York Public Library for the Performing Arts

fig. 10 Émile Bertin (French, 1878–1957), Maquette for La sorcière, Act IV, 1903. Watercolor on paper, approx. 10 x 12 in. (25.4 x 30.5 cm). Bibliothèque Nationale de France, Département des Arts du Spectacle, Paris

most famous Jewish actresses of the nineteenth century—Bernhardt and her predecessor Rachel (Élisa Félix)—with illness: "Those lean actresses, the Rachels and Sarahs, who spit blood, and seem to have but the spark of life left, and yet who, when they have stepped upon the stage, put forth indomitable strength and energy. Life, with them, has hidden springs."[35]

One of Bernhardt's most scathing critics, her former friend the actress Marie Colombier, wrote a pseudo-memoir of her more famous colleague under the thinly veiled title Les mémoires de Sarah Barnum. In this account, Colombier describes "La Barnum" with anti-Semitic clichés that ally Jewishness with prostitution.[36] Among the characterizations that Colombier draws for Bernhardt: "commercial intelligence inherent to her race"; "lust for profit"; "instincts of a daughter of Israel"; "absence of morals characteristic of all the Barnums"; "disorder and . . . oriental laissez-faire."[37]

On Bernhardt's death, a writer for The Times of London suggested the image of the wandering Jew: "The actress did create . . . a new type—the embodiment of Oriental exoticism: the strange, chimaeric idol-woman: something not in nature, a nightmarish exaggeration, the supreme of artifice. This type and Sarah became one. She wandered all over the world with it, and no wonder that it became in the end somewhat travel-stained."[38]

Although Bernhardt was often identified by her Jewishness, she was just as often perceived as removed from defining categories because she played such a variety of roles. During the Dreyfus Affair, when anti-Semitic violence marred Parisian boulevards, poet and novelist Daniel Lesueur portrayed Bernhardt as a calming figure whose art placed her above the fray:

While in the street, Jewish windows are smashed, and in the Chamber, socialist noses are broken . . . Mme. Sarah Bernhardt practices in tranquility, with her divine poses, the rites of the cult of Beauty. In our somber era, our days of conflict and ugliness, she arises, luminous, on the threshold of an invisible temple . . . gathering the oracles of eternal Beauty in order to impart them to us. . . . Does she not stand outside of any race, any one time, any one civilization, like an incarnation of immortal love? The enigmatic smile of Cleopatra, of Theodora, of Joan of Arc has floated on her lips. One by one, their souls have animated her. Was she born in our century?[39]

A persistent theme in contemporary comments on Bernhardt is her highly seductive style of acting. As Anatole France described her performance: "She did what no one had dared to do before her—she acted with her entire body. She put into her roles not only her whole soul, all her mind, and her physical grace, but also her sexuality."[40] Willa Cather saw Bernhardt in Sardou's *La Tosca* in Omaha, far from the Paris stages. Although she never witnessed a performance by Bernhardt's younger rival Eleonora Duse, she read everything about both actresses in the New York papers. In her comparison of the two, Cather used deviant sexual terms for Bernhardt while elevating Duse to the level of deity: "Art is Bernhardt's dissipation, a sort of Bacchic orgy. It is Duse's consecration, her religion, her martyrdom."[41] For his part, D. H. Lawrence chose animal metaphors to sexualize Bernhardt after seeing her in *La dame aux camélias* at the Theatre Royal in Nottingham in 1906: "Oh, to see her, and to hear her, a wild creature, a gazelle with a beautiful panther's fascination and fury, sobbing, sighing like a deer sobs, wounded to death, and all the time with the sheen of silk, the glitter of diamonds. . . . She represents the primeval passion of woman, and she is fascinating to an extraordinary degree."[42]

Colette—who wrote stories about the demimonde of courtesans that also happened to be the world of Bernhardt's family—was enraptured by the physicality and material sumptuousness of the actress's performance: "A play with shields, with feathers, with torches, a play in which Sarah [was] girded with gallo-roman jewels, embroidered gold, opals, covered with Renaissance brocade, crowned with Merovingian beads, she glowed with anachronisms. . . . Only the physical magic lodged in my mind, as if Sarah Bernhardt, instead of interpreting a dramatic work, had come there to sing, to dance, or juggle knives."[43]

People were intrigued in particular by Bernhardt's extreme thinness, which was praised, criticized, and lampooned in the days before such a figure was fashionable. In the satirical journal *Puck* on Bernhardt's first American tour, a purported "Walt Whitman," referring to Bernhardt by the nickname Sadie, noted her exiguous physique:

Sadie!
Woman of vigorous aspirations and remarkable thinness!

I hail you. I, Walt Whitman, son of thunder, child of the ages,
I hail you.[44]

A harsher parody is given by American poet Henry Wadsworth Longfellow: "The Famous French actress, Sarah Bernhardt, has been again in Boston, but I did not see her. The fame of her extreme thinness has reached far and wide. A common man, driving by here in a cart, with a poor lank horse, gave him a cut with his whip crying, 'Get up! Sarah Bernhardt!'"[45]

Her thinness was, nonetheless, a cause célèbre. Jules Lemaître attributed Bernhardt's allure to her slight figure and her exoticism:

> It is especially in the case of actresses that physical appearance is of extreme importance. Now heaven has endowed Madame Sarah Bernhardt with exceptional gifts: it has made her strange, surprisingly slender and supple, and it has covered her thin face with the disturbing grace of a Bohemian, a gipsy, a Tartar . . . something which makes one think of Salome, of Salammbo, of the Queen of Sheba. . . . Even in modern parts she keeps this strangeness which is given her by her elegant thinness and her Oriental, Jewish type.[46]

More significant than his reference to her figure, however, is Lemaître's attribution of "strangeness" to her "Oriental, Jewish type," which allows her to play multiple

fig. 12 Georges Jules Victor
Clairin (French, 1843–
1919), *Sarah Bernhardt as
Théodora*, 1902. Poster,
78 3/4 x 30 7/8 in. (200 x
78 cm). Bibliothèque
Nationale de France,
Département
des Estampes, Paris

roles. In listing the "exotic" sorts Bernhardt evokes—Bohemian, Gypsy, Tartar, and various non-Western personages—Lemaître exemplifies the position taken by a number of Bernhardt's contemporaries.

Although Bernhardt was distinguished by her ability to play a range of characters, including male roles, critics often disparaged her for putting too much of herself into these characters rather than becoming the role she was playing. Chekhov reviewed her Moscow performances in 1881: "[Bernhardt] remakes her heroine into exactly the same sort of unusual woman she is herself. . . . You watch *Adrienne Lecouvreur* and you see not Adrienne Lecouvreur in her but the ultra-clever, ultra-sensational Sarah Bernhardt. . . . [She] goes in pursuit not of the natural but of the extraordinary. Her goal is to startle, to amaze, to dazzle. . . . Every step she takes is profoundly thought out, a stunt."[47] Similarly, George Bernard Shaw compared Bernhardt unfavorably with the naturalistic Eleonora Duse: "[Bernhardt] does not enter the leading character [but] substitutes herself for it. . . . [The] dress, the title of the play, the order of the words may vary, but the woman [onstage] is always the same."[48]

Bernhardt was also extensively compared with the earlier famed Jewish actress Rachel. Matthew Arnold, for one, preferred Rachel's intellect to Bernhardt's passion:

> One talks vaguely of genius, but I had never till now comprehended how much of Rachel's superiority was purely in intellectual power, how eminently this power counts in the actor's art as in all art. . . . Temperament and quick intelligence, passion, nervous mobility, grace, smile, voice, charm, poetry,— Mlle Sarah Bernhardt has them all. One watches her with pleasure, with admiration,—and yet not without a secret disquietude. Something is wanting, or, at least, not present in sufficient force; something which alone can secure and fix her administration of all the charming gifts which she has, can alone keep them fresh, keep them sincere, save them from perils by caprice, perils by mannerism. That something is high intellectual power. It was here that Rachel was so great; she began . . . almost where Mlle Sarah Bernhardt ends.[49]

The preeminent actress of her time, Bernhardt was also a reputable painter and sculptor who showed her work in the Paris Salons. Capable though Bernhardt was as an artist, her many talents earned her criticism both from those who believed that her painting and sculpting were mere publicity stunts and from those who sought to confine her to the single role of actress. The French novelist and poet Arsène Houssaye wryly observed: "She has her enemies and her critics, but the more of her statues you break, the more there are made for her. Moreover, she takes a hand in the matter herself."[50]

One theater critic, Pierre Véron, believing sculpture to be a masculine occupation, accused Bernhardt of becoming a man when she modeled clay. Indeed, she did wear a pants suit while sculpting (see Ockman essay, fig. 28), although, while playing with androgyny, it was distinctly feminine attire. In an article titled

fig. 13 Sarah Bernhardt
(French, 1844–1923),
Bust of Victorien Sardou,
1895–1900. Bronze,
28 3/8 x 21 1/4 x 15 3/4 in.
(72.1 x 54 x 40 cm).
Petit Palais, Musée des
Beaux-Arts de la Ville
de Paris

"Monsieur Sarah Bernhardt," Véron bantered: "Outside . . . her studio, Sarah Bernhardt is a woman, and a charming one. But as soon as she crosses the threshold of the sanctuary where she models clay, she is a man. . . . Only a man could share this disdain of flirtation, this energy of will, this resistance to fatigue."[51]

Reviewing the Paris Salon in May 1876 for the *New-York Tribune*, Henry James criticized the portraits of Bernhardt by others (see Ockman essay, fig. 9) but commented with admiration on what she had produced:

A work which has at the least its share of gazers is a huge representation, by M. [Georges] Clairin, of Mlle. Sarah Bernhardt, the bright particular star of the Comédie Française. Considering the very small space which this young lady takes up in nature—her thinness is quite phenomenal—she occupies a very large one at the Salon. . . . Clairin's portrait [see p. 30, fig. 9] is vast and superficially brilliant, but really, I think, not above mediocrity. There is a remarkable white satin wrapper, in which the actress, who is lolling on a sort of oriental divan, is twisted and entangled with something of her peculiar snake-like grace, and which shines from afar; and there are draperies and plants and rugs, and a great deerhound. The only thing wanting is Mlle.

fig. 14   Jean-Léon Gérôme
(French, 1824–1904),
Sarah Bernhardt, c. 1895.
Marble with pigment,
27 1/8 x 16 1/8 x 11 3/8 in.
(69 x 41 x 29 cm). Musée
d'Orsay, Paris, Bequest of
the artist, 1904 (RF 1393)

Bernhardt herself. She is wanting even more in her second portrait, by Mlle. Louise Abbéma, in which she is standing, in a black walking dress; and in this almost equally large work there are no accessories, good or bad, to make up for the deficiency. . . . Not to be utterly incomplete I must say that Mlle. Sarah Bernhardt, the actress, has a huge group of an old peasant woman holding in her lap, in a frenzied posture, the body of her drowned grandson [see p. 43, fig. 27]. The thing is extremely amateurish, but it is surprisingly good for a young lady whom the public knows to draw upon her artistic ingenuity for so many other purposes.[52]

Émile Zola, a friend of Bernhardt's whom she publicly supported in his defense of Captain Alfred Dreyfus, defended her aspiration to create visual art as well as act. As he wrote to a newspaper: "She is reproached for not having stuck straight to dramatic art . . . to have taken up sculpture, painting, heaven knows what else. How droll! Not content with finding her thin, or declaring her mad, they want to regulate her daily activities. One is freer in prison. To be accurate, she is not denied the right to sculpt. She is simply denied the right to exhibit her works. This is the height of farce. Let a law be passed immediately to present the cumulation of talent."[53]

Auguste Rodin, among others, simply didn't like her style of sculpting; he called it "old-fashioned tripe."[54] Bernhardt did make traditional portrait busts, but she also worked in current Art Nouveau fashion, as seen in sculptures that took such organic forms as algae (see Bergman-Carton essay, fig. 3).

Actress, artist, celebrity, and grande dame of Parisian society: Sarah Bernhardt's renown continues long after her death, due in large part to the outpouring of commentary from her contemporaries. When the legendary actress died in 1923, her funeral procession extended for miles along Paris's streets, constituting a spectacle appropriate for a creature both divine and infernal. Befitting her extraordinary persona, the words written about her life and death were as flowery and grandiose as was the funeral cortege. English painter and illustrator Graham Robertson, who painted Bernhardt in her home in 1889, wrote: "This passing of almost the last Great Romantic Figure of the past century seems to emphasize the death of Art and Beauty and to reveal the full dreariness of the ugly desert stretched around us."[55]

Entr'acte

BERNHARDT AND ADVERTISING

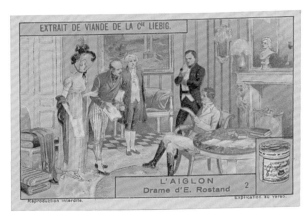

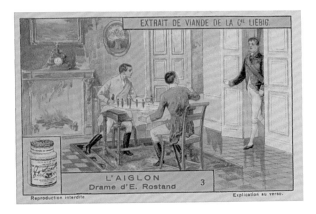

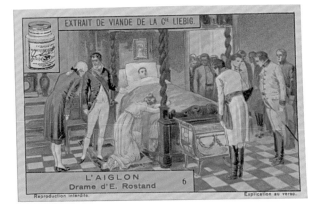

Postcard advertisement for "Le Fédora" dessert, 1883. 4 1/8 x 2 5/8 in. (10.5 x 6.7 cm). Bibliothèque Nationale de France, Département des Arts du Spectacle, Paris

opposite:

Advertisements for L'Extrait de la viande (Beef Bouillon) with Sarah Bernhardt as L'Aiglon, c. 1900. Six lithographed trading cards, each 2 3/4 x 4 in. (7 x 10.2 cm). Laurence Senelick Collection of Theatrical Imagery, West Medford, Massachusetts

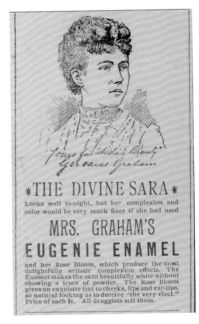

Postcard advertisement for Lefèvre-Utile biscuits with scene from *Théodora* and image from *La princesse lointaine*, c. 1904. 6 3/4 x 3 5/8 in. (17 x 9.2 cm). Bibliothèque Nationale de France, Département des Arts du Spectacle, Paris

Advertisement for Mrs. Graham's Eugenie Enamel in program for *Théodora*, 1891. 12 x 9 3/8 in. (30.5 x 23.9 cm). Harvard Theatre Collection, Houghton Library, Cambridge, Massachusetts

Sarah Bernhardt trading card for Red Cross Tea with image from *Théodora*, c. 1890. Lithograph on trading card, 5 1/2 x 7 in. (14 x 17.8 cm). Laurence Senelick Collection of Theatrical Imagery, West Medford, Massachusetts

Advertisement for Marmon car with Sarah Bernhardt, in Illinois Theatre program, 1918. 9 9/16 x 7 1/8 in. (24.1 x 18.1 cm). Harvard Theatre Collection, Houghton Library, Cambridge, Massachusetts

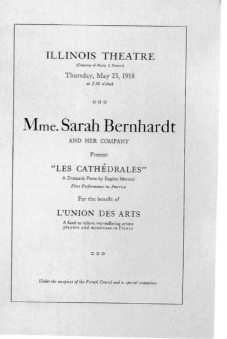

Carol Ockman and Kenneth E. Silver

BERNHARDT IN THE NEW WORLD

A Photographic Essay

I put my head out of my porthole and caught sight of some men, busy cutting us a passage down the river. The Hudson was frozen. . . . A pale pink sun was rising, dissipating the mist and gleaming on the ice as the workmen's efforts sent a thousand icy sparks flying into the air. I was entering the New World in the midst of an icy firework display.

—Sarah Bernhardt, My Double Life

Sarah Bernhardt considered her first view of America, on October 27, 1880, as auspicious, and she was right. Over nearly four decades, she made nine tours of the United States. Between this first tour and the last, which ended in 1918, Bernhardt spent almost eight years in America. She was both a colossal success and a controversial figure. Like so many others, including Charles Dickens, Jenny Lind, Oscar Wilde, and her distinguished predecessor Rachel, Bernhardt came to America to make her fortune. From New York City to Waco, Texas, to Berkeley, California, she filled theaters, opera houses, circus tents, convention halls, and an occasional skating rink, performing solely in French. She traveled from city to town, through cornfields and over mountain passes, on her own train, "Le Sarah Bernhardt," also known as "The Sarah Bernhardt Special." During her first tour, her luggage contained more than three hundred pairs of gloves, seventy-five pairs of shoes, and at least forty dresses.[1] On subsequent tours, she was said to have traveled with her entire art collection—and a coffin. The pages that follow give a sense of the variety of Bernhardt's experience in the United States as working professional, as tourist attraction and tourist, and as honorary national treasure.

fig. 2 Sarah Bernhardt with Harry and Bess Houdini, n.d. Gelatin silver print, 8 x 10 in. (20.3 x 25.4 cm). Billy Rose Theatre Collection, The New York Public Library for the Performing Arts

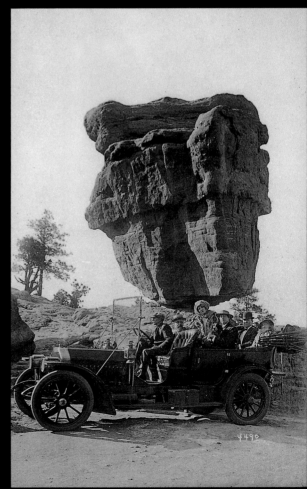

fig. 3 A. T. Russell (American, dates unknown), *Audience for Sarah Bernhardt inside Convention Hall in Kansas City, Missouri*, 1906. Collodion print, 8 1/4 x 10 3/16 in. (21 x 26 cm). Gift of Frederick R. Koch, 1983; Harvard Theatre Collection, Houghton Library, Cambridge, Massachusetts

fig. 4 Paul Goerke & Son, *Sarah Bernhardt and Troupe in Automobile, Garden of the Gods, Colorado*, 1905–6. Albumen print, 20 1/16 x 16 1/8 in. (50.9 x 41 cm). Gift of Frederick R. Koch, 1983; Harvard Theatre Collection, Houghton Library, Cambridge, Massachusetts

fig. 5 Sarah Bernhardt and troupe at Niagara Falls, 1891. Albumen print, 5 1/8 x 7 1/8 in. (13 x 18.1 cm). Gift of Frederick R. Koch, 1983; Harvard Theatre Collection, Houghton Library, Cambridge, Massachusetts

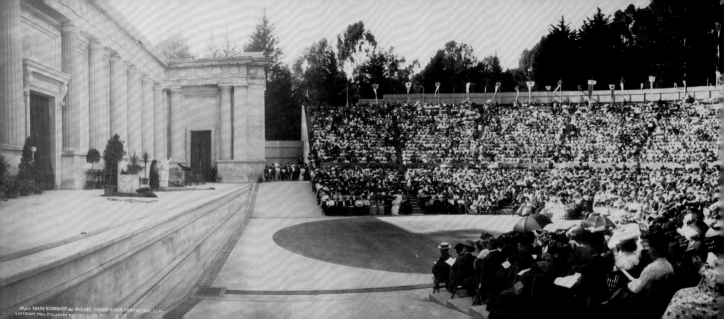

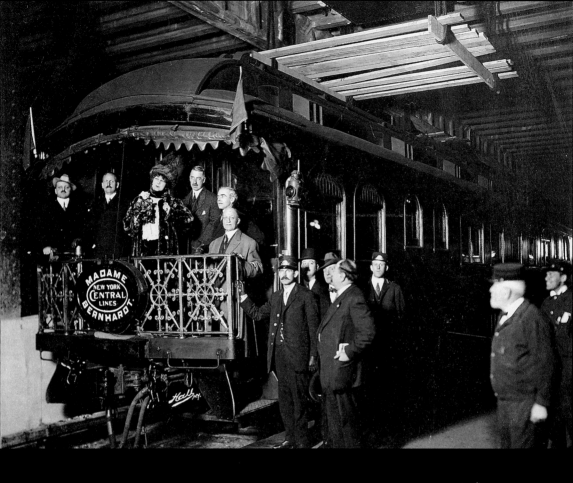

fig. 7 Hall, Sarah Bernhardt
on Caboose of Her Private
Pullman Car, "Le Sarah
Bernhardt," 1912. Gelatin
silver print, 10 1/4 x
13 1/4 in. (26 x 33.7 cm).
Museum of the City
of New York, Theater
Collection (28.67.47)

opposite:

fig. 8 Moffett Studio (American,
active early 20th century),
Sarah Bernhardt Standing
inside Her Train "Le Sarah
Bernhardt," 1912. Albumen
or platinotype, 9 x 6 in.
(22.9 x 15.2 cm). Gift
of Frederick R. Koch,
1983; Harvard Theatre
Collection, Houghton
Library, Cambridge,
Massachusetts

POST OFFICE TELEGRAPHS.

FOR INWARD FOREIGN AND COLONIAL TELEGRAMS.

C S/M or B S/M F

No. of Telegram.

L PARIS 97317 119 27 7 55 =

Time handed in.

Service Instructions.

Recd. from

At

By

Sent or Sent out at

To

By

Charges to pay.

SHUBERT CARLTON HOTEL LONDON = DURING MY PREVIOUS TOURS
IN AMERICA I ALWAYS RECEIVED AT LEAST ONE HUNDRED FIFTY
THOUSAND FRANCS ADVANCES I ONLY ASK FROM YOU SEVENTYFIVE
THOUSAND TWENTY FIVE THOUSAND AT SIGNATURE OF CONTRACT AT
THE LATEST ON JUNE FIRST AND FIFTY THOUSAND ONE MONTH BEFORE
DEPARTURE FROM PARIS BEING COMPELLED MYSELF TO GIVE
ADVANCES TO ARTISTS ACCOMPANYING ME THIS SUM OF SEVENTYFIVE
THOUSAND FRANCS WOULD BE PAID BACK TO YOU AT THE RATE OF
ONE THOUSAND FRANCS PER DAY DURING THE LAST SEVENTY FIVE
PERFORMANCES OF TOUR IF THIS IS ACCEPTED BY YOU WE
WOULD AGREE ON ALL PRINCIPAL POINTS AS TO THE SMALL DETAILS
WE SHALL DISCUSS SAME WHEN SIGNING CONTRACT COMPLIMENTS =
SARAH BERNHARDT =

obtained on application at the office from which it was delivered.

N.B.—This form must accompany any inquiry made.

£ s. d.

JAS. TRUSCOTT & SON, LTD., PRINTERS, LONDON.

fig. 11   Panoramic view of
Chicago tent with
portrait inset of Sarah
Bernhardt, c. 1906.
Gelatin silver print,
7.5 x 26 in. (19 x 66 cm).
Library of Congress,
Prints and Photographs
Division, Washington,
D.C.

fig. 12   Telegram to one of
the Shubert brothers
from Sarah Bernhardt,
March 27, 1905. 8 1/2 x
8 1/4 in. (21.6 x 21 cm).
The Shubert Archive,
New York

fig. 13 Cup with photographic reproduction of Sarah Bernhardt in *La dame aux camélias* (stamped "Rockefeller Center" on bottom), 1929 or after. Ceramic, height 3 in. (7.6 cm). Musée Carnavalet—Histoire de Paris (C 2361)

fig. 14 Sign for Sarah Bernhardt's train reading "The Sarah Bernhardt Special," 1906? Cardboard, 9 5/8 x 12 1/2 in. (24.6 x 31.9 cm). Bibliothèque Nationale de France, Département des Arts du Spectacle, Paris

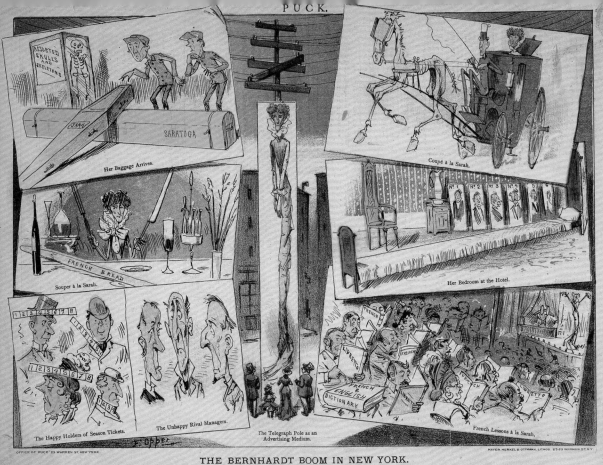

THE BERNHARDT BOOM IN NEW YORK.

BERNHARDT'S BOSTON BOOM--Sara's Bust-on Beans. SEE VERSES PAGE 8
SARA--"Mille Tonnères, what have I swallow--a earthquake--a tornado?"

fig. 15 "Bernhardt's Boston Boom—Sarah's Bust-on Beans," caricature, n.d. Museum of the City of New York, Theater Collection

fig. 16 "The Bernhardt Boom in New York," caricature of Sarah Bernhardt's American Tour, published in Puck, n.d. Museum of the City of New York, Theater Collection

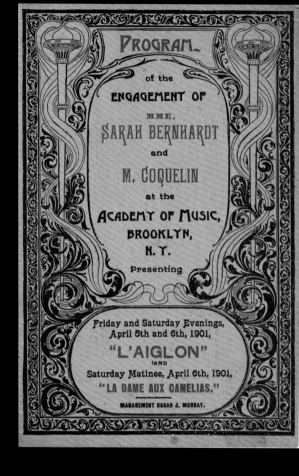

fig. 17 Printed play text in English from Sarah Bernhardt's Farewell Tour, "The Last Visit to America," 1916, published by Fred Rullman. 10 7/8 x 7 7/8 in. (25.7 x 20 cm). Harvard Theatre Collection, Houghton Library, Cambridge, Massachusetts

fig. 18 Program cover: Sarah Bernhardt and Constantin Coquelin in L'Aiglon and La dame aux camélias, Academy of Music, Brooklyn, New York, April 6, 1901. 8 1/4 x 5 1/2 in. (21 x 14 cm). Museum of the City of New York, Theater Collection, Gift of Elwin M. Eldredge (41.161.44)

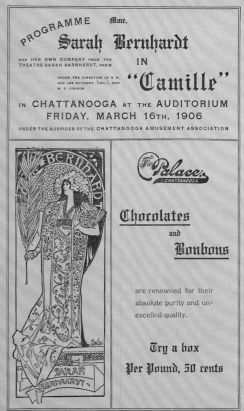

fig. 19 **Program for the Greenwall Theatre, New Orleans, March 1906. 8 x 5 1/2 in. (20.4 x 13.9 cm). Bibliothèque Nationale de France, Département des Arts du Spectacle, Paris**

fig. 20 **Program for Camille at the Auditorium, Chattanooga, Friday, March 16, 1906. 9 1/4 x 5 7/8 in. (23.5 x 15 cm). Bibliothèque Nationale de France, Département des Arts**

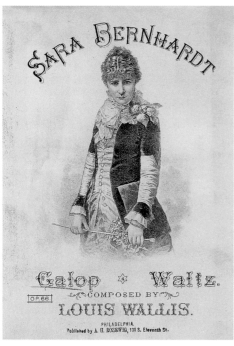

fig. 21 Sheet music for "Sara[h] Bernhardt Galop-Waltz," composed by Louis Wallis, published by A. H. Rosewig, 1880. 14 x 10 3/4 in. (35.6 x 27.3 cm). Museum of the City of New York, Garrison P. Sherwood Collection (40.281.1229)

fig. 22 Souvenir spoons of American cities and sites, n.d. Silver plate, each 4 in. (10.2 cm). Bibliothèque-Musèe de la Comédie Française, Paris

fig. 23 Henry Clogenson
(American, active
late 19th– early 20th
centuries), *Sarah
Bernhardt in Front of
Circus Tent, Dallas, Texas,
1906.* Gelatin silver print,
7 x 9 1/4 in. (17.9 x 23.5 cm).
Harvard Theatre
Collection, Houghton
Library, Cambridge,
Massachusetts,
Frederick R. Koch
Collection

fig. 24 Presentation of laurel
wreath to Sarah
Bernhardt at the Palace
Theatre, New York, June
1913. Gelatin silver print,
Harvard Theatre
Collection, Houghton
Library, Cambridge,
Massachusetts

fig. 25 Sarah Bernhardt's
arrival in New York with
Martin Beck, 1911–13.
Gelatin silver print.
Harvard Theatre
Collection, Houghton
Library, Cambridge,
Massachusetts

opposite:

fig. 26 Sarah Bernhardt's
arrival in New York with
Martin Beck, 1911–13.
Gelatin silver print.
Harvard Theatre
Collection, Houghton
Library, Cambridge,
Massachusetts

RUE D'ANJOU S⁺ H^RÉ 51.
(HÔTEL PRIVÉ)

Suzanne Schwarz Zuber

CHRONOLOGY OF SARAH BERNHARDT'S LIFE

fig. 1 Paul Nadar (French, 1856–1939), Sarah Bernhardt as Lady Macbeth, c. 1884. Albumen print cabinet card, 6 1/2 x 4 1/4 in. (16.5 x 10.8 cm). Bequest of Evert Jansen Wendell, 1918; Harvard Theatre Collection, Houghton Library, Cambridge, Massachusetts

The facts of Sarah Bernhardt's life are difficult to ascertain. Much of the standard information is derived from her memoirs, *Ma double vie* (*My Double Life*), first published in 1907, which is a mixture of fact and fiction. Subsequent biographies— such as those in French by Madame Pierre Berton, Ernest Pronier, Louis Verneuil, and her granddaughter Lysiane Bernhardt, and in English by Cornelia Otis Skinner and by Arthur Gold and Robert Fizdale—are based, at least for her early years, on Bernhardt's willfully compromised memoirs. The following text adheres to the most plausible facts of the actress's life.

1844–50
Sarah Bernhardt is born in Paris on September 25, 1844, according to her baptismal certificate, and given the name Sara-Marie-Henriette Bernhardt. She is the illegitimate daughter of Youle van Hard—a Dutch or German Jew who became a demimondaine (courtesan) on her arrival in Paris—and possibly Édouard Bernhardt, a law student from Le Havre. She is raised by a nanny in Brittany, and then in a Paris suburb, while her mother travels. After being seriously injured in a fall, the five-year-old Bernhardt goes to live with her mother on the rue Saint-Honoré in Paris.

1851–58

From age seven until age fourteen, Bernhardt receives a basic education at two boarding schools: a pension for girls run by a Madame Fressard, and the convent of Grandchamps in Versailles. Bernhardt has her first taste of the theater by participating in school performances. It is at Grandchamps that she catches a glimpse of the famous actress Rachel, who has come to visit one of the students.

Bernhardt is baptized a Catholic in 1856. In 1858 she is taken out of the convent school and receives lessons at home.

1859–60

The influential Duc de Morny, a friend and client of her mother's (and the illegitimate half brother of Emperor Napoleon III), secures an audition for Bernhardt at the Conservatoire. Run by the Comédie Française, it is the premier acting school in France. Initially, she is not interested in acting and vows to become a nun instead. But after seeing Jean Racine's *Britannicus* and Molière's *Amphytrion* at the Théâtre Français, she is convinced that her future lies in the theater. In 1860, she is accepted into the Conservatoire.

1862

Having been hired by the Comédie Française, Bernhardt debuts in Racine's *Iphigénie*. Around this time she adopts the motto "Quand même" ("No matter what").

1863–64

In 1863, Bernhardt resigns from the Comédie Française, refusing to accept the loss of a lead role she has been promised for a premiere. Through the contacts of her godfather, Régis Lavolé, she obtains a position at the Théâtre du Gymnase, where she performs in Eugène Labiche and Raymond Deslandes's *Un mari qui lance sa femme* (A Husband Who Launches His Wife). She finds the Gymnase repertory unsuitable and soon leaves.

After a period away from Paris, Bernhardt returns pregnant (probably by the Belgian prince Charles de Ligne). Her son, Maurice, is born on December 22, 1864, in the rue Duphot. During the next two years, Bernhardt performs at the Théâtre de la Porte Saint-Martin in the Coniard brothers' *La biche au bois* (The Doe in the Woods), an entertaining play of the *féerie* genre.

1866

With the help of the Conservatoire's director, Camille Doucet, Bernhardt earns a position at the Odéon, a theater on the Left Bank known for its contemporary repertory. Despite an insignificant debut, she later becomes popular with the student audience, most memorably in the revival of *Kean*, by Alexandre Dumas père, in 1868.

1869–71

In 1869, Bernhardt persuades the directors of the Odéon, Félix Duquesnel and Charles-Marie de Chilly, to stage *Le passant* (*The Passerby*), by the young François Coppée, and herself takes the role of the young Florentine troubadour Zanetto. The play premieres on January 14, and the company later gives a special performance at the Tuileries for Napoleon III and Empress Eugénie. Bernhardt goes on to act in the role 140 times.

In this period she is close with the French writer Count Robert de Montesquiou and the Jewish society figure Charles Haas. Years later, Bernhardt and Haas will serve as models for the central characters Berma and Charles Swann in Marcel Proust's *À la recherche du temps perdu* (*In Search of Lost Time*).

Bernhardt loses her apartment on the rue Auber in a fire, but is saved from ruin by the proceeds of a benefit gala held in her honor at the Odéon.

She performs the lead role in George Sand's *L'autre* (*The Other*) in 1870. Her acting wins the respect of the author.

On July 19, 1870, France declares war on Prussia. During the siege of Paris, from September through the following January, state-owned theaters are closed. Bernhardt, however, obtains special permission from the prefect of police and the Ministry of War to keep the Odéon open as an *ambulance*, or military infirmary. She procures supplies from high-ranking sources, including a chocolate magnate, Meunier, and Baron Alphonse de Rothschild. Besides directing the *ambulance*, Bernhardt accompanies a group of nuns and clerics to the battlefield of Chatillon to recover the dead and wounded. For her wartime efforts, she is later awarded a medal by the Société d'Encouragement au Bien.

When the Odéon is damaged in a bombardment, Bernhardt is forced to close the infirmary. She moves the more serious cases to a military hospital and shelters others in a rented apartment on the rue Taitbout. France surrenders on January 28, 1871. Bernhardt retrieves her mother, her son, and other members of her family from Germany, where they have taken refuge.

fig. 2 Reutlinger Studio (French, active 1850–1930), Sarah Bernhardt in "Hernani," c. 1877. Albumen print, 6 3/8 x 4 1/4 in. (16.2 x 10.8 cm). Harvard Theatre Collection, Houghton Library, Cambridge, Massachusetts

fig. 2 Etienne Carjat (French, 1828–1906), Sarah Bernhardt as Doña Maria de Neubourg in Victor Hugo's "Ruy Blas," c. 1872. Albumen print, 3 3/8 x 4 7/8 in. (8.5 x 12.5 cm). Bibliothèque Nationale de France, Département des Estampes, Paris

1872

Victor Hugo, who returned from two decades of political exile after the fall of the Second Empire in September 1870, is hailed as a national hero in France. The Odéon, which has resumed performances, celebrates his return by presenting his play *Ruy Blas*; it premieres on February 19, with Bernhardt as Doña Maria de Neubourg, Queen of Spain. Critics praise the actress for her regal beauty, excellent projection, and remarkable voice and for the variety of her gestures and expressions. Despite her success at the Odéon, she returns to the Comédie Française, which has offered her a lucrative position with a larger salary. For this breach of contract, she must pay a large penalty.

At the Comédie Française, Bernhardt, as Junie, costars with Jean Mounet-Sully, as Nero, in Racine's *Britannicus*. Subsequently they are cast together in numerous performances at the Comédie.

1873–74

After Bernhardt's sister Régine dies of tuberculosis, Bernhardt is diagnosed with anemia; she spends several months recuperating in Brittany in 1874.

Since the previous year, she has been taking sculpting lessons in a studio in Montmartre. Her first teachers are Jules Franceschi and Roland Mathieu-Meusnier (she later takes painting lessons from Alfred Stevens). On her return to Paris from Brittany, she participates for the first time in the Salon des Artistes, exhibiting several works.

On December 21, 1874, Bernhardt makes her premiere in the coveted role of Phaedra in Racine's play. With her new, sensual interpretation, she reshapes the classic tale of incest and guilt, making *Phèdre*—which for years was identified with her famous predecessor Rachel—her own.

1875

In January, Bernhardt is promoted to the status of *sociétaire*, official member of the Comédie Française. She performs the title role in Viscount Henri de Bornier's *La fille de Roland* (Roland's Daughter).

By this time, Bernhardt is achieving international status. Among those who review her performances is Peter Ilyich Tchaikovsky, who praises her in Racine's *Andromaque*.

With the inheritance left by a great-aunt, Bernhardt hires the prominent architect Félix Escalier to design and build a house at the corner of the rue de Fortuny and the avenue de Villiers. She studies sculpture with Gustave Doré and secures a commission from the architect Charles Garnier for a sculpture to adorn the façade of the casino he has designed at Monte Carlo. Bernhardt's sculpture *Le chant*, a winged figure carrying a lyre and representing music, appears alongside Doré's *La danse*.

fig. 4 Paul Nadar (French,
1856–1939), *Sarah
Bernhardt as Phèdre with
Handmaidens*, n.d.
Albumen print, 14 7/8 x
10 1/2 in. (37.9 x 26.7 cm).
Bibliothèque Nationale
de France, Département
des Estampes, Paris

1876

Youle van Hard dies.

At this year's Salon des Artistes, Bernhardt receives honorable mention for her sculpture *Après la tempête* (After the Storm). Also displayed are two portraits of the actress, one by Georges Clairin, the other by Louise Abbéma; the two artists are part of Bernhardt's intimate circle.

At the Comédie Française, Bernhardt performs the controversial role of Mrs. Clarkson, daughter of a mulatto slave and a Carolina planter, in *L'Étrangère* (The Foreigner) by Alexandre Dumas *fils*.

1877

On November 21, Bernhardt triumphs at the Comédie Française, as Doña Sol in a revival of Victor Hugo's *Hernani*.

1878

During the Universal Exposition, Bernhardt ascends from the Tuileries gardens in a tethered hot-air balloon, manned by Henri Giffard, inventor of the dirigible. She then arranges for a free flight in an untethered balloon, the specially prepared *Doña Sol*. Criticized by her employer for engaging in such unconventional behavior,

Bernhardt threatens to resign from the Comédie Française, but the minister of fine arts defuses the tension and she stays on. She later publishes an entertaining account of her ascent, *Dans les nuages: Impressions d'une chaise* (In the Clouds: Impressions of a Chair).

1879

Under the condition that she be promoted to the highest rank, *sociétaire à part entière*, Bernhardt agrees to travel with the Comédie Française in June for its summer season at the Gaiety Theatre in London. On her arrival, she is greeted by great crowds, among them the young Oscar Wilde. All of the Comédie's performances featuring Bernhardt are sold out. While in London, she shows a number of her paintings and sculptures at a gallery in Piccadilly.

Bernhardt's English success is met with resentment by the French press. On June 27, Le Figaro publishes a particularly caustic letter in which the critic Albert Wolff attacks the actress for, among other things, her aspirations as a commercial artist. As part of her retort in the next day's Figaro, Bernhardt publicly considers resigning from the Comédie Française.

1880

Bernhardt is cast against her will in Émile Augier's play L'aventurière (The Adventuress), which is set to open on April 17; the day after the opening, she announces her resignation, breaking a twenty-year contract with the Comédie

fig. 5 Gebbie and Co. after Paul Nadar (French, 1856–1939), *Sarah Bernhardt in "L'Étrangère,"* 1887. Photoengraving, 17 1/16 x 11 3/4 in. (43.2 x 29.9 cm). Bequest of Evert Jansen Wendell, 1918; Harvard Theatre Collection, Houghton Library, Cambridge, Massachusetts

Française. She presents her letter of resignation to *Le Figaro*, which publishes it on May 26. The Comédie Française sues the actress; a court subsequently rules in favor of the theater company, and Bernhardt is ordered to pay the considerable sum of 100,000 francs.

She accepts an offer from the theatrical agent William Edward Jarrett for a tour of the United States. On October 15, Bernhardt departs for her first tour of North America with a handpicked troupe; she is now her own director and manager. The group will travel to some fifty cities in the United States and Canada, giving a total of 150 performances.

Bernhardt's first appearance on the American stage, on November 8, is met with adulation when she performs in Eugène Scribe and Ernest Legouvé's *Adrienne Lecouvreur* at Booth's Theatre in New York City. She also performs the title role in Dumas fils's *La dame aux camélias* (*The Lady of the Camellias*), an addition to her repertory that will become the most performed role of her career. Bernhardt visits Thomas Alva Edison in New Jersey, and he records her voice on the recently invented phonograph.

1882

In Turin on February 25, Eleonora Duse first sees Bernhardt perform, as Marguerite Gautier in *La dame aux camélias*.

Bernhardt marries Jacques (Aristides) Damala, a former attaché at the Greek embassy in Paris, on April 4. Damala had joined her acting troupe after having met Bernhardt during one of her performances in Russia—one of the stops on her six-month European tour begun in the summer of 1881.

In autumn, Bernhardt leases the Théâtre de l'Ambigu and appoints as manager her seventeen-year-old son, Maurice. She premieres in Victorien Sardou's melodrama *Fédora* on December 12 at the Théâtre de Vaudeville in Paris.

1883

A former friend and actress in her company, Marie Colombier, publishes a vicious pseudobiography under the title *Les mémoires de Sarah Barnum*—an allusion to the American showman P. T. Barnum.

Bernhardt co-leases the Théâtre de la Porte Saint-Martin.

1884

Bernhardt's sister Jeanne dies, addicted to drugs.

In May, Bernhardt performs the role of Lady Macbeth in a new translation by Jean Richepin of Shakespeare's *Macbeth*.

On December 26, she premieres the title role in Sardou's *Théodora*, a historical melodrama set in sixth-century Constantinople. For the design of the costumes and jewelry, Bernhardt has traveled to Ravenna to view the Byzantine mosaics in the church of San Vitale that portray Empress Theodora and Emperor Justinian.

fig. 6 **Walter Barnett (Australian, 1862–1934), Sarah Bernhardt as Camille in "La dame aux camélias," 1891. Photographic print, 5 5/8 x 3 3/4 in. (14.3 x 9.4 cm). Victoria and Albert Museum, London (444-1952)**

1886

In the spring, Bernhardt departs for an extensive tour of the Americas.

1887

Back in Paris after the American tour and performances in Britain and Ireland, Bernhardt buys a house at 56 boulevard Péreire. She also acquires as a residence an old fort at Belle-Isle, in Brittany, where she has studios built for her friends Clairin and Abbéma.

Her son marries the Polish princess Maria (Marie-Thérèse) Jablonowska.

On November 24, Bernhardt first performs the lead role in La Tosca, a melodrama by Sardou, which will become more famous as Giacomo Puccini's opera Tosca in 1900.

1889

She tours Egypt and Turkey. In May, after her return to Paris, Bernhardt rents the Théâtre des Variétés and casts herself and Jacques Damala in La dame aux camélias. Damala, who is addicted to morphine, dies four months later.

Bernhardt's first granddaughter, Simone, is born.

fig. 8 Paul Nadar (French, 1856–1939), Sarah Bernhardt as Tosca with Dead Body of Scarpia, Act IV, 1888. Albumen print cabinet card, 6 1/2 x 4 3/4 in. (16.4 x 11 cm). Bibliothèque Nationale de France, Département des Arts du Spectacle, Paris

fig. 7 Alfred Stevens (Belgian, 1823–1906), Sarah Bernhardt, n.d. Oil on canvas, 25 11/16 x 18 1/4 in. (65.3 x 46.4 cm). Armand Hammer Museum of Art, Los Angeles, The Armand Hammer Collection, Gift of the Armand Hammer Foundation (AH.90.73)

fig. 9 Edmond Lachenal (French, 1855–1900), Faience plate with portrait of Sarah Bernhardt, 1891. Ceramic, diam. 9 in. (22.9 cm). Petit Palais, Musée des Beaux-Arts de la Ville de Paris (PPS 3348)

fig. 10 Napoleon Sarony (American, b. Canada, 1821–1896), Sarah Bernhardt as Cléopâtre with Handmaiden, 1891. Albumen print cabinet card, 6 5/8 x 4 5/16 in. (16.8 x 10.8 cm). Bequest of Evert Jansen Wendell, 1918; Harvard Theatre Collection, Houghton Library, Cambridge, Massachusetts

1890

Bernhardt premieres in Jules Barbier's *Jeanne d'Arc* on January 3 and in Sardou's *Cléopâtre* on October 23.

1891–93

In 1891, the actress embarks on the most extensive tour of her career, which includes Europe, Australia, Africa, the Americas, Russia, Turkey, and Tahiti. In Boston, she first performs the title role in Albert Darmont's drama *Léah* (in which the Jewish heroine is forsaken by her lover for a Christian and is persecuted by her community). Bernhardt prepares to stage Oscar Wilde's *Salomé*, which he has written with her in mind. The play is banned by the Lord Chamberlain's Office, on the grounds that biblical subjects shall not appear on the British stage. Wilde later asks Bernhardt to buy the rights to the play, but she does not.

In March 1893, Bernhardt sells her shares in the Théâtre de la Porte Saint-Martin and buys the Théâtre de la Renaissance. Marcel Proust is among the spectators at her matinee performances of *Phèdre*.

1894–95

On October 1, 1894, French army captain Alfred Dreyfus, a Jew, is arrested on questionable charges of high treason; in December, Dreyfus is tried and found guilty. The next month he is stripped of his rank, and in April 1895 he is incarcerated on Devil's Island.

On October 31, 1894, Bernhardt stars in Sardou's *Gismonda*, which she also directs and produces. The poster for the play, by the Czech artist Alphonse Mucha, is the first of seven the actress commissions from him.

In 1895, Bernhardt produces and stars in Edmond Rostand's *La princesse lointaine* (*The Faraway Princess*), which premieres on April 5.

Her second granddaughter, Lysiane, is born. Lysiane will later write a book about her grandmother.

1896

After another American tour and a stint in London, where her popularity continues, Bernhardt returns to Paris. She premieres the lead in *Lorenzaccio* by Alfred de Musset on December 3. The play, set in Renaissance Italy, is a hit, and Bernhardt is acclaimed in the title role.

On December 9, the actress is honored in Paris with "La Journée Sarah Bernhardt"—Sarah Bernhardt Day. The celebration, organized by a loyal group of friends, consists of a banquet, with tributes, at the Grand Hôtel, followed by Bernhardt's performance of excerpts from *Phèdre* and Alexandre Parodi's *Rome vaincue* (*Rome Vanquished*) at the Théâtre de la Renaissance.

1897

During Easter week, Bernhardt premieres in the title role of Rostand's *La samaritaine*. In the summer, she hosts her sometime rival Eleonora Duse at the Théâtre de la Renaissance.

1898

On January 13, Émile Zola publishes "J'accuse" in support of Dreyfus. The next day Bernhardt writes Zola a letter of encouragement, thanking him for his efforts on Dreyfus's behalf.

Bernhardt sells the Théâtre de la Renaissance. One of her last roles there is the lead in Catulle Mendès's *Médée*, which premieres on October 28.

1899

Bernhardt inaugurates her newly acquired theater on the place du Châtelet. The first production at the Théâtre Sarah Bernhardt is Sardou's *La Tosca*, which opens on January 14. From now on, this will be the only place where she performs in Paris.

During May and June, she tours Europe in her controversial and immensely popular role as Hamlet.

fig. 11   Aimé Dupont (French,
1842–1900), Sarah Bernhardt
in "L'Aiglon," c. 1900.
Albumen print cabinet
card, 6 9/16 x 4 5/16 in. (16.5
x 10.8 cm). Harvard Theatre
Collection, Houghton
Library, Cambridge,
Massachusetts

1900

On March 15, Bernhardt premieres in Rostand's *L'Aiglon* (*The Eaglet*), written expressly for her. She takes the tragic role of the seventeen-year-old Duke de Reichstadt, son of Napoleon Bonaparte.

The Universal Exposition opens in Paris on April 14.

Bernhardt stars in her first film, *Le duel d'Hamlet*, directed by Clément Maurice. Together with Constant Coquelin, the star of Rostand's *Cyrano de Bergerac*, she departs for her fifth American tour in November.

1903

Bernhardt's longtime friend Robert de Montesquiou holds a party in her honor, at which she and Marcel Proust meet.

The actress enjoys great success with the premiere of Sardou's *La sorcière* (*The Witch*) on December 15. She presents *matinées classiques*, where she performs Racine's *Andromaque* and other revered mainstays of French theater.

1905

In late April, Bernhardt performs the male role of Pelléas in Maurice Maeterlinck's *Pelléas et Mélisande*, alongside Mrs. Patrick Campbell.

Bernhardt embarks on her sixth American tour. Because of a conflict between

fig. 12 W. & D. Downey (British, active 1863–1910s), *Pelléas et Mélisande*, 1904. Albumen print cabinet card, 6 1/2 x 4 1/4 in. (16.6 x 10.8 cm). Bibliothèque Nationale de France, Département des Arts du Spectacle, Paris

the theatrical syndicate and the Shubert brothers, her producers, she performs in alternative spaces—including skating rinks and circus tents.

While onstage in Rio de Janeiro, she sustains a serious knee injury.

1906
In observation of Henrik Ibsen's death, Bernhardt gives a single performance of his play *The Lady from the Sea*.

1907
She publishes *Ma double vie* (*My Double Life*), an account of her life until 1881.

More than four decades after her entry into the Conservatoire, Bernhardt returns to teach.

1908
She stars in the film version of *La tosca* and undertakes an extensive tour of Europe as well as Turkey and Egypt.

1910–11
When her daughter-in-law dies, Bernhardt takes in her granddaughter Lysiane.

Bernhardt costars in the film version of *La dame aux camélias* (*Camille*) with Lou Tellegen (which premieres in 1912). In October 1910, she embarks on her seventh American tour.

fig. 13 Henry Clogenson (American, active late 19th–early 20th centuries), *Sarah Bernhardt in Her Carriage, Dallas*, 1906. Inscribed: "Moi et mon ménage arrivant à l'hotel. Suzanne est descendue!" (Me and my troupe arriving at the hotel. Suzanne has descended!). Gelatin silver print, 7 3/8 x 9 3/4 in. (18.6 x 24.7 cm). Bibliothèque Nationale de France, Département des Estampes, Paris

1912

Les amours de la reine Elisabeth, starring Bernhardt as Elizabeth I of England, is released in New York in July. Directed by Louis Mercanton and Henri Desfontaines, it is the greatest box-office success of her films.

1913

After returning from another extensive tour of the United States, which began in the previous year, Bernhardt produces and performs in Tristan Bernard's naturalist drama *Jeanne Doré,* a financial success, and films *Adrienne Lecouvreur,* directed by Mercanton and Desfontaines.

1914

In January, Bernhardt is made a Chevalier of the Legion of Honor.

In August, World War I begins.

1915

In February, Bernhardt's right leg is amputated in Bordeaux.

She performs in a number of patriotic plays, including *Du théâtre au champ d'honneur* (From the Theater to the Field of Honor) and Eugène Morand's *Les cathédrales,* and stars in the film version of *Jeanne Doré,* directed by Louis Mercanton.

1916–17

In late September 1916, Bernhardt departs on her ninth and final American tour. During her travels, she becomes seriously ill. On April 17, 1917, she has a kidney operation at Mount Sinai Hospital in New York. Undaunted, she resumes her tour in Atlantic City, New Jersey, with two performances on August 26.

1922

In Paris, she performs for the last time onstage in *Régine Arnaud,* written for her by her grandson-in-law, Louis Verneuil.

1923

Bernhardt begins filming Louis Mercanton and Leon Abrams's *La voyante* (The Fortune-teller) and rehearses for Sacha Guitry's play *Un sujet de roman* (A Subject for a Novel).

She dies at home in Paris on March 26.

Her funeral procession on March 29 travels from the church of Saint-François-de-Sales in the Seventeenth Arrondissement, past the Théâtre Sarah Bernhardt, to Père-Lachaise cemetery, where she is buried. According to *The New York Times* of March 30, the cemetery is "filled with what old residents of Paris termed the greatest crowd in its history. . . . The police estimated that there were at least 1,000,000 people between La Madeleine and the Théâtre Sarah Bernhardt."

fig. 14   Sarah Bernhardt and Raymond Bernard in *Jeanne Doré* (Universal Pictures, 1915), directed by Louis Mercanton. Cinémathèque Française, Bois d'Arcy, France

Exhibition Checklist

Paintings

1. Marie-Désiré Bourgoin (French, 1839–1912)
Sarah Bernhardt's Studio, 1879
Watercolor and gouache over graphite on paper, 26 11/16 x 20 7/8 in. (67.8 x 53.1 cm)
The Metropolitan Museum of Art, New York, Gift of Helen O. Brice, 1942 (42.64.10)
Page 46, fig. 31

2. Georges Jules Victor Clairin (French, 1843–1919)
Portrait of Sarah Bernhardt, 1876
Oil on canvas, 98 1/2 x 78 3/4 in. (250 x 200 cm)
Musée du Petit Palais, Paris (PPP 0744)
Page 30, fig. 9

3. Georges Jules Victor Clairin (French, 1843–1919)
Sarah Bernhardt as Doña Maria de Neubourg in Victor Hugo's "Ruy Blas," 1879
Oil on canvas, 21 5/8 x 12 5/8 in. (55 x 32 cm)
Collections de la Comédie Française, Paris

(1236)
Page 32, fig. 11

4. André Gill (French, 1840–1885)
Sarah Bernhardt as Chimera, caricature, c. 1880
Oil on panel, 24 x 16 1/2 in. (61 x 42 cm)
Mutuelle Nationale des Artistes, Couilly-Pont-aux-Dames, France
Page 81, fig. 7

5. Dudley Hardy (British, 1867–1922)
Sarah Bernhardt, 1889
Oil on panel, 9 1/2 x 6 1/2 in. (24 x 16.5 cm)
Sterling and Francine Clark Art Institute, Williamstown, Massachusetts (1955.760)
Page 15, fig. 16

6. René Lelong (French, 1860–1912)
Sarah Bernhardt Conversing with Mr. Gladstone at Her London Exhibition, c. 1879
Oil on canvas laid down on board, 19 3/6 x

14 in. (49.2 x 35.6 cm)
Dahesh Museum of Art, New York (2002.25)

7. Walford Graham Robertson (British, 1866–1948)
The Actress Sarah Bernhardt in Her Salon, 1889
Oil on panel, 17 1/4 x 12 in. (44.3 x 30.5 cm)
Private collection, Paris
Page 101, fig. 4

8. Walter Spindler (French, 1878–1940)
Sarah Bernhardt Invoking Diotima (Homage to Sarah Bernhardt), 1908
Watercolor and crayon on paper, 7 1/8 x 9 1/2 in. (18.1 x 24.1 cm)
Collection of Robert A. Zehil, Monte Carlo, Monaco
Page 98, fig. 1

9. Alfred Stevens (Belgian, 1823–1906)
Sarah Bernhardt, n.d.

Oil on canvas, 25 11/16 x 18 1/4 in.
(65.3 x 46.4 cm)
Armand Hammer Museum of Art, Los
Angeles, The Armand Hammer Collection,
Gift of the Armand Hammer Foundation
(AH.90.73)
Page 174, fig. 7

Sculpture

10. Louise Abbéma (French, 1858–1927)
Plaque of Sarah Bernhardt, 1875
Bronze, diam. 4 1/8 in. (10.5 cm)
Billy Rose Theatre Collection, The New York
Public Library for the Performing Arts
Page 48, fig. 33

11. Sarah Bernhardt (French, 1844–1923)
Algae, 1900
Bronze, 4 x 19 1/4 in. (10 x 49 cm)
Mutuelle Nationale des Artistes, Couilly-Pont-
aux-Dames, France
Page 100, fig. 3

12. Sarah Bernhardt (French, 1844–1923)
Bust of Victorien Sardou, 1895–1900
Bronze, 28 3/8 x 21 1/4 x 15 3/4 in.
(72.1 x 54 x 40 cm)
Petit Palais, Musée des Beaux-Arts de la Ville
de Paris
Page 141, fig. 13

13. Sarah Bernhardt (French, 1844–1923)
Fantastic Inkwell (Self-Portrait as a Sphinx), 1880
Bronze, 12 1/2 x 7 1/2 x 9 in.
(31.8 x 19.1 x 22.9 cm)
Museum of Fine Arts, Boston, Helen and
Alice Colburn Fund (1973.551)
Page 50, fig. 35

14. Sarah Bernhardt (French, 1844–1923)
*La fille de Roland (Self-Portrait as Roland's
Daughter),* 1876
Terra-cotta, 7 3/4 x 6 1/2 x 5 1/4 in.
(19.7 x 16.5 x 13.3 cm)
The Jewish Museum, New York; Purchase: Gift
of Mr. and Mrs. Steven D. Bloom, by exchange,
and Maurice I. Parasier Foundation Fund,
1998-111
Page 78, fig. 4

15. Sarah Bernhardt (French, 1844–1923)
Portrait Bust of Louise Abbéma, 1878
Marble, 16 1/2 x 10 5/8 x 8 5/8 in.
(42 x 27 x 22 cm)

Musée d'Orsay, Paris (RF 3756)
Page 53, fig. 38

16. Sarah Bernhardt (French, 1844–1923)
Portrait of Louise Abbéma, 1875 (?), or *Self-Portrait,*
1878 (?)
Bronze, 8 7/16 x 7 1/8 x 1 1/2 in.
(21.1 x 18.1 x 3.8 cm)
Museum of Fine Arts, Boston, Otis Norcross
Fund and Gift of Robert A. Radloff and Ann
Beha (1989.196)
Page 49, fig. 34

17. Sarah Bernhardt (French, 1844–1923)
Self-Portrait Bust, n.d.
Ceramic, 9 1/2 x 6 1/4 x 4 in.
(3 3/4 x 2 1/2 x 1 5/8 cm)
Victor and Gretha Arwas Collection, London

18. Jean-Léon Gérôme (French, 1824–1904)
Sarah Bernhardt, c. 1895
Marble with pigment, 27 1/8 x 16 1/8 x 11 3/8 in.
(69 x 41 x 29 cm)
Musée d'Orsay, Paris, Bequest of the artist,
1904 (RF 1393)
Page 142, fig. 14

19. René Lalique (French, 1860–1945)
Plaquette of Sarah Bernhardt, c. 1890–1900
Silvered-gilt struck bronze, height 1 1/2 in.
(3.8 cm)
Victoria and Albert Museum, London
(A 28-1924)

20. René Lalique (French, 1860–1945)
Portrait Medal of Sarah Bernhardt, 1896
Silver, diam. 4 1/8 in. (10.5 cm)
The Jewish Museum, New York; Purchase:
Miriam and Milton Handler Endowment
Fund, 1998-112
Page 112, fig. 16

21. L. Raphael (French, 1885–?)
L'Aiglon Statuette, c. 1900
Bronze, 8 x 2 1/4 x 2 1/2 in. (20.2 x 5.8 x 6.2 cm)
Garrick Club, London

22. L. Raphael (French, 1885–?)
L'Aiglon Statuette, c. 1900
Bronze, 7 1/4 x 1 3/4 x 1 3/4 in.
(18.4 x 4.5 x 4.5 cm)
Museum of the City of New York, Theater
Collection, Gift of Mrs. Frederick Rullman
(28.67.75)

23. L. Raphael (French, 1885–?)
L'Aiglon Statuette, c. 1900
Bronze, 7 1/4 x 1 3/4 x 2 in. (18.4 x 4.5 x 5.1 cm)
Laurence Senelick Collection of Theatrical
Imagery, West Medford, Massachusetts
Page 122, fig. 25

Photographs

24. Walter Barnett (Australian, 1862–1934)
*Sarah Bernhardt as Camille in "La dame aux
camélias,"* 1891
Photographic print, 5 5/8 x 3 3/4 in.
(14.3 x 9.4 cm)
Victoria and Albert Museum, London (444-1952)
Page 173, fig. 6

25. Henri de la Blanchère (French, 1821–1880)
Rachel as Phèdre (Act II, Scene 5), 1846,
printed 1859
Albumen print, 7 1/2 x 5 1/2 in. (19 x 14 cm)
Collections de la Comédie Française, Paris
Page 5, fig. 6

26. Paul Boyer (French, active late 19th century)
Sarah Bernhardt in "L'Aiglon," 1900
Albumen print, 6 1/2 x 4 1/4 in. (16.5 x 10.8 cm)
Gift of Copenhagen Theatre Museum, 1978;
Harvard Theatre Collection, Houghton
Library, Cambridge, Massachusetts

27. Paul Boyer (French, active late 19th century)
Sarah Bernhardt in "L'Aiglon," 1900
Albumen print, 6 1/2 x 4 1/4 in. (16.5 x 10.8 cm)
Gift of Frederick R. Koch, 1983; Harvard
Theatre Collection, Houghton Library,
Cambridge, Massachusetts

28. Etienne Carjat (French, 1828–1906)
*Sarah Bernhardt as Doña Maria de Neubourg
in Victor Hugo's "Ruy Blas,"* c. 1872
Albumen print, 4 7/8 x 3 3/8 in. (12.5 x 8.5 cm)
Bibliothèque Nationale de France,
Département des Estampes, Paris
Page 169, fig. 3

29. Chalot & Co., Paris (French, active
1879–1884)
Jacques Damala, n.d.
Gelatin silver print cabinet card, 6 1/2 x 4 1/4 in.
(16.5 x 10.8 cm)
Performing Arts Collection, Harry Ransom
Humanities Research Center, The University
of Texas at Austin
Page 29, fig. 8

30. Henry Clogenson (American, active late 19th–early 20th centuries)
Sarah Bernhardt in Carriage, Dallas (with inscription), 1906
Gelatin silver print, 7 3/8 x 9 3/4 in
(18.6 x 24.7 cm)
Bibliothèque Nationale de France, Département des Estampes, Paris
Page 178, fig. 13

31. Henry Clogenson (American, active late 19th–early 20th centuries)
Sarah Bernhardt in Front of Circus Tent, Dallas, Texas (inscribed to Louise Abbéma), 1906
Gelatin silver print, 9 7/8 x 11 3/4 in.
(25 x 30 cm)
Bibliothèque Nationale de France, Département des Estampes, Paris
Page 67, fig. 53

32. André Adolphe-Eugène Disdéri (French, 1819–1889)
Sarah Bernhardt in Eight Poses; Seven Standing, One Sitting, 1866
Albumen contact sheet, 7 7/8 x 9 1/2 in. (20 x 24 cm)
Musée d'Orsay, Paris (Inv. PHO 1995-25-42)

33. W. & D. Downey (British, active 1863–1910s)
Pelléas et Mélisande, 1904
Albumen print cabinet card, 6 1/2 x 4 1/4 in.
(16.6 x 10.8 cm)
Bibliothèque Nationale de France, Département des Arts du Spectacle, Paris
Page 178, fig. 12

34. W. & D. Downey (British, active 1863–1910s)
Sarah Bernhardt as Adrienne Lecouvreur, c. 1880
Albumen print cabinet card, 6 5/8 x 4 5/16 in.
(16.8 x 10.8 cm)
Bequest of Evert Jansen Wendell, 1918; Harvard Theatre Collection, Houghton Library, Cambridge, Massachusetts
Page 34, fig. 15

35. W. & D. Downey (British, active 1863–1910s)
Sarah Bernhardt as Izéyl, 1903
Albumen print cabinet card, 6 9/16 x 4 5/16 in.
(16.5 x 10.8 cm)
Gift of the Copenhagen Theatre Museum, 1978; Harvard Theatre Collection, Houghton Library, Cambridge, Massachusetts
Page 34, fig. 14

36. W. & D. Downey (British, active 1863–1910s)
Sarah Bernhardt as Théodora, c. 1884
Albumen print cabinet card, 6 9/16 x 4 1/4 in.
(16.5 x 10.8 cm)
Bequest of Evert Jansen Wendell, 1918; Harvard Theatre Collection, Houghton Library, Cambridge, Massachusetts
Page 108, fig. 11

37. W. & D. Downey (British, active 1863–1910s)
Sarah Bernhardt in "Le passant," 1869
Albumen print cabinet card, 6 1/2 x 4 3/8 in.
(16.5 x 11 cm)
Bibliothèque Nationale de France, Département des Arts du Spectacle, Paris
Page 41, fig. 25

38. W. & D. Downey (British, active 1863–1910s)
Sarah Bernhardt in Personal Wardrobe, 1902
Albumen print cabinet card, 6 1/2 x 4 1/4 in.
(16.6 x 10.8 cm)
Bibliothèque Nationale de France, Département des Arts du Spectacle, Paris
Page 107, fig. 9

39. Aimé Dupont (French, 1842–1900)
Sarah Bernhardt in "L'Aiglon," c. 1900
Albumen print cabinet card, 6 9/16 x 4 5/16 in.
(16.5 x 10.8 cm)
Harvard Theatre Collection, Houghton Library, Cambridge, Massachusetts
Page 177, fig. 11

40. Aimé Dupont (French, 1842–1900)
Sarah Bernhardt in "L'Aiglon", c. 1900
Albumen print cabinet card, 6 9/16 x 4 1/4 in.
(16.6 x 10.8 cm)
Harvard Theatre Collection, Houghton Library, Cambridge, Massachusetts

41. Aimé Dupont (French, 1842–1900)
Sarah Bernhardt in "L'Aiglon" (standing, looking up), c. 1900
Albumen print cabinet card, 6 9/16 x 4 5/16 in.
(16.6 x 10.8 cm)
Harvard Theatre Collection, Houghton Library, Cambridge, Massachusetts

42. Falk Studio (New York; Benjamin J. Falk, American, 1853–1925)
La dame aux camélias, c. 1891
Cabinet card, 6 1/2 x 4 1/4 in. (16.5 x 10.9 cm)
Bibliothèque Nationale de France, Département des Arts du Spectacle, Paris
Page 31, fig. 10

43. Gebbie and Co. after Paul Nadar (French, 1856–1939)
Sarah Bernhardt in "L'Étrangère," 1887
Photoengraving, 17 1/16 x 11 3/4 in.
(43.2 x 29.9 cm)
Bequest of Evert Jansen Wendell, 1918; Harvard Theatre Collection, Houghton Library, Cambridge, Massachusetts
Page 172, fig. 5

44. Paul Goerke & Son
Sarah Bernhardt and Troupe in Automobile, Garden of the Gods, Colorado, 1905–6
Albumen print, 20 1/16 x 16 1/8 in.
(50.9 x 41 cm)
Gift of Frederick R. Koch, 1983; Harvard Theatre Collection, Houghton Library, Cambridge, Massachusetts
Page 150, fig. 4

45. Hall
Sarah Bernhardt on Caboose of Her Private Pullman Car, "Le Sarah Bernhardt," 1912
Gelatin silver print, 10 1/4 x 13 1/4 in.
(26 x 33.7 cm)
Museum of the City of New York, Theater Collection (28.67.47)
Page 154, fig. 7

46. Lafayette (British, 1853–1923)
Sarah Bernhardt as Hamlet, c. 1899
Gelatin silver print, 14 1/4 x 11 in.
(36.2 x 27.9 cm)
Gift of Frederick R. Koch, 1992; Harvard Theatre Collection, Houghton Library, Cambridge, Massachusetts
Page 42, fig. 26

47. Charles Latham (British, 1888–1970?)
G. Paul Smith as Sarah Bernhardt, inscribed "Sincerely, G. Paul Smith," c. 1890
Cabinet card, 6 1/2 x 4 1/4 in. (16.5 x 10.8 cm)
Laurence Senelick Collection of Theatrical Imagery, West Medford, Massachusetts

48. Melandri (French, active c. 1860s–80s)
Sarah Bernhardt Posing in Her Coffin, c. 1880
Albumen print cabinet card, 6 1/2 x 4 1/4 in.
(16.5 x 10.7 cm)
Bibliothèque Nationale de France, Département des Estampes, Paris
Page 52, fig. 37

49. Melandri (French, active c. 1860s–80s)
Sarah Bernhardt Sculpting, c. 1875

Albumen print cabinet card, 6 1/2 x 4 1/2 in.
(16.5 x 11.4 cm)
Bequest of Evert Jansen Wendell, 1918;
Harvard Theatre Collection, Houghton
Library, Cambridge, Massachusetts
Page 44, fig. 28

50. Melandri (French, active c. 1860s–80s)
Sarah Bernhardt with Her Son Maurice, n.d.
Albumen print, 6 1/2 x 4 1/4 in. (16.5 x 10.8 cm)
Bequest of Evert Jansen Wendell, 1918;
Harvard Theatre Collection, Houghton
Library, Cambridge, Massachusetts

51. Moffett Studio (American, active early
20th century)
*Sarah Bernhardt Standing inside Her Train
"Le Sarah Bernhardt,"* 1912
Albumen or platinotype, 9 x 6 in.
(22.9 x 15.2 cm)
Gift of Frederick R. Koch, 1983; Harvard
Theatre Collection, Houghton Library,
Cambridge, Massachusetts
Page 154, fig. 8

52. Félix Nadar (French, 1820–1910)
Sarah Bernhardt, c. 1860
Albumen print, 8 5/8 x 6 3/8 in. (21.8 x 16.3 cm)
Bibliothèque Nationale de France,
Département des Estampes, Paris
Page 26, fig. 3

53. Félix Nadar (French, 1820–1910)
Sarah Bernhardt, c. 1860
Albumen print, 8 1/2 x 6 3/8 (21.6 x 16.3 cm)
Bibliothèque Nationale de France,
Département des Estampes, Paris
Page 27, fig. 5

54. Félix Nadar (French, 1820–1910)
Sarah Bernhardt, c. 1860
Albumen print, 8 7/8 x 6 7/8 in. (22.5 x 17.5 cm)
Bibliothèque Nationale de France,
Département des Estampes, Paris
Page 27, fig. 4

55. Félix Nadar (French, 1820–1910)
Sarah Bernhardt in "Hernani," c. 1877
Albumen print, 5 3/8 x 3 3/4 in. (13.7 x 9.5 cm)
Musée d'Orsay, Paris (Inv. PHO 2001 11 19)

56. Paul Nadar (French, 1856–1939)
Sarah Bernhardt as Gismonda, c. 1894
Albumen print on cardboard, 6 7/16 x 4 5/16 in
(16.4 x 10.9 cm)

The Jewish Museum, New York; Purchase: Fine
Arts Acquisitions Committee, 1998-64.3

57. Paul Nadar (French, 1856–1939)
Sarah Bernhardt as Jeanne d'Arc, 1890
Albumen print cabinet card, 6 9/16 x 4 5/16 in.
(16.5 x 10.8 cm)
Harvard Theatre Collection, Houghton
Library, Cambridge, Massachusetts
Page 76, fig. 2

58. Paul Nadar (French, 1856–1939)
Sarah Bernhardt as Lady Macbeth, c. 1884
Albumen print cabinet card, 6 1/2 x 4 1/4 in.
(16.5 x 10.8 cm)
Bequest of Evert Jansen Wendell, 1918;
Harvard Theatre Collection, Houghton
Library, Cambridge, Massachusetts
Page 166, fig. 1

59. Paul Nadar (French, 1856–1939)
Sarah Bernhardt as Phèdre with Handmaidens,
n.d.
Albumen print, 14 7/8 x 10 1/2 in.
(37.9 x 26.7 cm)
Bibliothèque Nationale de France,
Département des Estampes, Paris
Page 171, fig. 4

60. Paul Nadar (French, 1856–1939)
Sarah Bernhardt as Théodora, c. 1884
Albumen print on card, 13 1/4 x 7 11/16 in.
(33.7 x 19.4 cm)
Harvard Theatre Collection, Houghton
Library, Cambridge, Massachusetts
Page 33, fig. 12

61. Paul Nadar (French, 1856–1939)
Sarah Bernhardt as Théodora with Fortune Teller,
c. 1884
Albumen prints mounted on board, 21 7/8 x
28 5/8 in. (55.5 x 72.8 cm)
Bibliothèque Nationale de France,
Département des Estampes, Paris
Page 6, fig. 7a

62. Paul Nadar (French, 1856–1939)
*Sarah Bernhardt as Tosca with Dead Body of
Scarpia, Act IV,* 1888
Albumen print cabinet card, 6 1/2 x 4 3/4 in.
(16.4 x 11 cm)
Bibliothèque Nationale de France,
Département des Arts du Spectacle, Paris
Page 174, fig. 8

63. Paul Nadar (French, 1856–1939)
Sarah Bernhardt in "Pierrot Assassin," c. 1883
Albumen print, 13 3/4 x 9 7/8 in. (35 x 25.2 cm)
Bibliothèque Nationale de France,
Département des Estampes, Paris

64. Otto (French, active c. 1892–1917)
Sarah Bernhardt in Personal Wardrobe (Bat Hat),
1880
Albumen print cabinet card, 6 1/2 x 4 3/16 in.
(16.4 x 10.7 cm)
Harvard Theatre Collection, Houghton
Library, Cambridge, Massachusetts
Page 116, fig. 21

65. Otto (French, active c. 1892–1917)
Sarah Bernhardt in Personal Wardrobe, 1893
Albumen print cabinet card, 6 1/2 x 4 1/4 in.
(16.6 x 10.8 cm)
Bibliothèque Nationale de France,
Département des Arts du Spectacle, Paris
Page 107, fig. 10

66. Reutlinger Studio (French, active
1850–1930)
La princesse lointaine, c. 1895
Albumen print cabinet card, 6 1/2 x 4 1/4 in.
(16.5 x 10.8 cm)
Harvard Theatre Collection, Houghton
Library, Cambridge, Massachusetts
Page 59, fig. 43

67. Reutlinger Studio (French, active 1850–1930)
Sarah Bernhardt in "Hernani," c. 1877
Albumen print, 6 3/8 x 4 1/4 in. (16.2 x 10.8 cm)
Harvard Theatre Collection, Houghton
Library, Cambridge, Massachusetts
Page 169, fig. 2

68. Reutlinger Studio (French, active
1850–1930)
Sarah Bernhardt in Personal Wardrobe, n.d.
Photographic print, 4 3/4 x 6 1/2 in.
(12 x 16.5 cm)
Bibliothèque Nationale de France,
Département des Estampes, Paris
Page 106, fig. 8

69. Rochlitz Studio
Sarah Bernhardt as Phèdre, after 1915
Tinted gelatin silver print, 11 1/8 x 7 1/4 in.
(28.3 x 18 .4 cm)
Harvard Theatre Collection, Houghton
Library, Cambridge, Massachusetts
Page 130, fig. 5

70. A. T. Russell (American, dates unknown)
Audience for Sarah Bernhardt inside Convention Hall in Kansas City, Missouri, 1906
Collodion print, 8 1/4 x 10 3/16 in. (21 x 26 cm)
Gift of Frederick R. Koch, 1983; Harvard Theatre Collection, Houghton Library, Cambridge, Massachusetts
Page 150, fig. 3

71. Napoleon Sarony (American, b. Canada, 1821–1896)
Death Scene from "La dame aux camélias," 1880
Albumen print cabinet card, 6 9/16 x 4 1/4 in. (16.5 x 10.8 cm)
Bequest of Evert Jansen Wendell, 1918; Harvard Theatre Collection, Houghton Library, Cambridge, Massachusetts
Page 55, fig. 39

72. Napoleon Sarony Studio
Maude Adams as L'Aiglon, c. 1901
Gelatin silver print, 5 1/4 x 3 3/4 in. (13.3 x 9.5 cm)
Museum of the City of New York, Theater Collection
Page 71, fig. 57

73. Napoleon Sarony (American, b. Canada, 1821–1896)
Sarah Bernhardt as Camille, 1880
Albumen or collodion print, 6 1/2 x 4 1/4 in. (16.5 x 10.8 cm)
Bequest of Evert Jansen Wendell, 1918; Harvard Theatre Collection, Houghton Library, Cambridge, Massachusetts

74. Napoleon Sarony (American, b. Canada, 1821–1896)
Sarah Bernhardt as Cléopâtre, 1891
Albumen print cabinet card, 4 5/16 x 6 5/8 in. (10.8 x 16.8 cm)
Bequest of Evert Jansen Wendell, 1918; Harvard Theatre Collection, Houghton Library, Cambridge, Massachusetts
Page 35, fig. 16

75. Napoleon Sarony (American, b. Canada, 1821–1896)
Sarah Bernhardt as Cléopâtre with Handmaiden, 1891
Albumen print cabinet card, 6 5/8 x 4 5/16 in. (16.8 x 10.8 cm)
Bequest of Evert Jansen Wendell, 1918; Harvard Theatre Collection, Houghton

Library, Cambridge, Massachusetts
Page 175, fig. 10

76. Napoleon Sarony (American, b. Canada, 1821–1896)
Sarah Bernhardt as Cléopâtre with Handmaiden, 1891
Albumen print, 6 9/16 x 4 1/4 in. (16.6 x 10.8 cm)
Bequest of Evert Jansen Wendell, 1918; Harvard Theatre Collection, Houghton Library, Cambridge, Massachusetts

77. Napoleon Sarony (American, b. Canada, 1821–1896)
Sarah Bernhardt as Léah, 1892
Collodion printing-out paper on card, 6 9/16 x 4 1/4 in. (16.5 x 10.8 cm)
Bequest of Robert P. Bowler, 1919; Harvard Theatre Collection, Houghton Library, Cambridge, Massachusetts
Page 80, fig. 6

78. Napoleon Sarony (American, b. Canada, 1821–1896)
Sarah Bernhardt in "Hernani," c. 1877
Albumen print, 6 1/2 x 4 1/4 in. (16.5 x 10.8 cm)
Bequest of Evert Jansen Wendell, 1918; Harvard Theatre Collection, Houghton Library, Cambridge, Massachusetts

79. Napoleon Sarony (American, b.Canada, 1821–1896)
Sarah Bernhardt in "Frou Frou," 1880
Albumen print on card, 6 11/16 x 4 5/8 in. (16.8 x 11.8 cm)
Harvard Theatre Collection, Houghton Library, Cambridge, Massachusetts
Page 40, fig. 23

80. *Death scene from Adrienne Lecouvreur,* n.d.
Gelatin silver print, 11 x 14 in. (27.9 x 35.6 cm)
Museum of the City of New York, Theater Collection, Gift of Mrs. Robert Burns Mantle (48.210.1933)

81. *Eva Le Gallienne as L'Aiglon (with Ethel Barrymore),* 1934
Gelatin silver print, 8 x 10 in. (20.3 x 25.4 cm)
Museum of the City of New York, Theater Collection, Gift of Mr. and Mrs. Spencer Merriam Berger (50.178.679)
Page 70, fig. 56

82. *Interior of Sarah Bernhardt's home on the boulevard Péreire,* 1887 or after
Gelatin silver print, 5 1/4 x 7 1/4 in. (13.3 x 18.4 cm)
Museum of the City of New York, Theater Collection

83. *Louise Abbéma,* n.d.
Photographic print, 6 7/8 x 4 7/8 in. (17.5 x 12.5 cm)
Bibliothèque Nationale de France, Département des Estampes, Paris
Page 47, fig. 32

84. *Louise Abbéma as pasha and Sarah Bernhardt as odalisque,* n.d.
Cabinet card, 6 1/2 x 4 3/4 in. (16.4 x 12.1 cm)
Bibliothèque Nationale de France, Département des Arts du Spectacle, Paris
Page 51, fig. 36

85. *Louise Abbéma in Sarah Bernhardt's home on the boulevard Péreire,* 1887 or after
Photographic print
Musée Carnavalet—Histoire de Paris (PH 8685)

86. *Panoramic view of Chicago tent with portrait inset of Sarah Bernhardt,* c. 1906
Gelatin silver print, 7.5 x 26 in. (19 x 66 cm)
Library of Congress, Prints and Photographs Division, Washington, D.C.
Page 157, fig. 11

87. *Sarah Bernhardt,* c. 1865–70
Ferrotype, 3 x 2 in. (7.6 x 5.1 cm)
Musée Carnavalet—Histoire de Paris (PH 9023)
Page 126, fig. 2

88. *Sarah Bernhardt and Edmond Rostand Playing cards,* n.d.
Photographic print, 4 5/8 x 6 3/4 in. (11.8 x 17 cm)
Bibliothèque Nationale de France, Département des Estampes, Paris

89. *Sarah Bernhardt and friends on rug,* c. 1880
Photographic print on card, 6 1/2 x 4 1/4 in. (16.5 x 10.8 cm)
Laurence Senelick Collection of Theatrical Imagery, West Medford, Massachusetts
Page 2, fig. 2

90. *Sarah Bernhardt and troupe at Niagara Falls,* 1891
Albumen print, 5 1/8 x 7 1/8 in. (13 x 18.1 cm)

Gift of Frederick R. Koch, 1983; Harvard
Theatre Collection, Houghton Library,
Cambridge, Massachusetts
Page 151, fig. 5

91. Sarah Bernhardt entering carriage in front
of the Palace Theatre, New York, Wreath
Ceremony, 1913
Gelatin silver print, 11 x 14 in. (27.9 x 35.6 cm)
Performing Arts Collection, Harry Ransom
Humanities Research Center, The University
of Texas at Austin
Page 156, fig. 9

92. Sarah Bernhardt in Phèdre, Act III, Hearst
Greek Theatre, May 17, 1906
Gelatin silver print, 9.5 x 38 in. (24 x 96.5 cm)
Library of Congress, Prints and Photographs
Division, Washington, D.C.
Pages 152–53, fig. 6

93. Sarah Bernhardt wearing dark glasses,
filming La voyante (The Fortune-teller), 1923
Gelatin silver print, 6 3/4 x 9 1/8 in.
(17.1 x 23.1 cm)
Bibliothèque Nationale de France,
Département des Arts du Spectacle, Paris
Page 69, fig. 55

94. Sarah Bernhardt with friends at Belle-Isle,
1895 or after
Gelatin silver print, 5 1/4 x 7 1/4 in.
(13.3 x 18.4 cm)
Museum of the City of New York, Theater
Collection, Gift of Mrs. Joseph Verner Reed
(75.120.39)
Page 29, fig. 7

95. Sarah Bernhardt with Harry and Bess
Houdini, n.d.
Gelatin silver print, 8 x 10 in. (20.3 x 25.4 cm)
Billy Rose Theatre Collection, The New York
Public Library for the Performing Arts
Page 150, fig. 2

Posters

96. Édouard Bernard (French, 1879–1950)
Advertisement for Quinquina Michaud,
c. 1900
Poster, 23 7/8 x 32 1/4 in. (60.6 x 81.9 cm)
Musée de la Publicité, Paris (13440)

97. Jules Chéret (French, 1836–1932)
Advertisement for La Diaphane, Poudre de riz
Sarah Bernhardt, 1890

Poster, 47 1/4 x 31 1/2 in. (120 x 80 cm)
Bibliothèque Nationale de France,
Département des Estampes, Paris
Page 64, fig. 50

98. Georges Jules Victor Clairin (French,
1843–1919)
Sarah Bernhardt as Théodora, 1902
Poster, 78 3/4 x 30 7/8 in. (200 x 78 cm)
Bibliothèque Nationale de France,
Département des Estampes, Paris
Page 139, fig. 12

99. Emmanuel Coulange-Lautrec (French,
1824–1898)
L'Aiglon, quinquina apéritif P. Serve, 1900
Poster, 59 x 49 1/4 in. (150 x 125 cm)
Bibliothèque Forney, Paris (BF No 198523)
Page 92, fig. 14

100. Eugène Grasset (French, 1841–1917)
Sarah Bernhardt as Jeanne d'Arc (second version),
1894
Poster, 47 1/4 x 31 1/2 in. (120 x 80 cm)
Bibliothèque Nationale de France,
Département des Estampes, Paris
Page 74, fig. 1

101. Robert Kastor (French, active late
19th–early 20th centuries)
Au Cinématographe: La dame aux camélias,
1911–12
Poster for the film directed by André
Calmettes and Henri Pouctal, starring Sarah
Bernhardt (Cinémathèque Française, 1912)
63 x 47 1/4 in. (160 x 120 cm)
Collection of Mr. and Mrs. Jack Rennert,
New York
Page 17, fig. 18

102. Alphonse Mucha (Czech, 1860–1939)
La dame aux camélias, 1896
Color lithograph, 81 1/2 x 30 in. (207 x 76.2 cm)
Collection of Mr. and Mrs. Joel Schur,
Greenwich, Connecticut
Page 62, fig. 46

103. Alphonse Mucha (Czech, 1860–1939)
Farewell American Tour Sarah Bernhardt 1905–6,
1905
Color lithograph, 80 x 30 in. (203 x 76 cm)
Laura Gold, Park South Gallery at Carnegie
Hall, New York
Page 148, fig. 1

104. Alphonse Mucha (Czech, 1860–1939)
Gismonda, 1894
Color lithograph, 84 x 29 1/8 in. (213.4 x 74 cm)
Collection of Mr. and Mrs. Jack Rennert,
New York
Page 57, fig. 41

105. Alphonse Mucha (Czech, 1860–1939)
Lorenzaccio, 1896
Color lithograph, 80 1/2 x 29 7/8 in.
(204 x 76 cm)
Private collection, Maryland
Page 62, fig. 47

106. Alphonse Mucha (Czech, 1860–1939)
Médée, 1898
Color lithograph, 81 x 30 in. (206 x 76.2 cm)
Laura Gold, Park South Gallery at Carnegie
Hall, New York
Page 102, fig. 5

107. Alphonse Mucha (Czech, 1860–1939)
La samaritaine, 1897
Color lithograph, 68 1/8 x 23 in. (173 x 58.4 cm)
Collection of Mr. Albert Malumed and Ms.
Jacqueline Morris, New York
Page 3, fig. 3

108. Alphonse Mucha (Czech, 1860–1939)
Sarah Bernhardt, 1896
Color lithograph, 26 1/4 x 19 in. (66.7 x 48.3 cm)
Collection of Norma Canelas and William D.
Roth, Winter Haven, Florida, and New York
Page 60, fig. 44

109. Alphonse Mucha (Czech, 1860–1939)
La Tosca, 1899
Color lithograph, 41 x 15 in. (104 x 38 cm)
Posters Please, Inc., New York
Page 63, fig. 48

110. Alphonse Mucha (Czech, 1860–1939)
Tragique histoire d'Hamlet, 1899
Color lithograph, 81 1/2 x 30 1/4 in.
(207 x 76.8 cm)
Collection of Mr. and Mrs. Ivan Lendl,
New York
Page 63, fig. 49

111. William Nicholson (British, 1872–1949)
Poster for the Grand Théâtre de Génève, 1897
Wood-block print, 10 5/8 x 10 in. (27 x 25.5 cm)
Bibliothèque Nationale de France,
Département des Arts du Spectacle, Paris
Page 132, fig. 7

112. "The Only Leon" as Sarah Bernhardt, n.d.
Poster, 18 x 10 in. (45.7 x 25.4 cm)
Harvard Theatre Collection, Houghton
Library, Cambridge, Massachusetts
Page 66, fig. 52

Postcards

113. Hand-tinted postcard of Sarah Bernhardt
as L'Aiglon, c. 1900
3 3/8 x 5 3/8 in. (8.7 x 13.7 cm)
Bibliothèque Nationale de France,
Département des Arts du Spectacle, Paris
Page 89, fig. 12

114. Postcard advertisement for Lefèvre-Utile
biscuits with scene from *Théodora* and image
from *La princesse lointaine*, c. 1904
6 3/4 x 3 5/8 in. (17 x 9.2 cm)
Bibliothèque Nationale de France,
Département des Arts du Spectacle, Paris
Page 146

115. Postcard advertisement for "Le Fédora"
dessert, c. 1883
4 1/8 x 2 5/8 in. (10.5 x 6.7 cm)
Bibliothèque Nationale de France,
Département des Arts du Spectacle, Paris
Page 145

116. Postcard of château, Belle-Isle-en-Mer, n.d.
3 1/2 x 5 1/2 in. (8.9 x 14 cm)
Museum of the City of New York, Theater
Collection

117. Postcard of Fort Sarah Bernhardt, Belle-
Isle-en-Mer, n.d.
3 5/16 x 5 6/16 in. (8.3 x 14 cm)
Museum of the City of New York, Theater
Collection

118. Sarah Bernhardt with her mother and her
sister Régine, 1860s
Postcard, 5 1/2 x 3 1/2 in. (13.9 x 9 cm)
Bibliothèque Nationale de France,
Département des Arts du Spectacle, Paris
Page 28, fig. 6

119. Puzzle made of postcards of Sarah
Bernhardt in a variety of roles forming portrait
of Bernhardt as L'Aiglon, after 1906
17 1/2 x 10 7/8 in. (44.5 x 27.7 cm)
Bibliothèque Nationale de France,
Département des Arts du Spectacle, Paris
Page 1, fig. 1

Other Works on Paper

120. Sarah Bernhardt (French, 1844–1923),
engraved by Gaucherel
La jeune fille et la mort (Death and the Maiden),
1880
Engraving after a drawing, 11 x 9 in.
(4 3/8 x 3 1/2 cm)
Victor and Gretha Arwas Collection, London

121. Paul Berthon (French, 1872–1909)
*Sarah Bernhardt as Mélisande in "La princesse
lointaine,"* 1901
Color lithograph on paper, 25 3/4 x 19 3/4 in.
(65.3 x 50.2 cm)
Victoria and Albert Museum, London
(E 133-1981)
Page 104, fig. 7

122. Émile Bertin (French, 1878–1957)
Maquette for *La sorcière*, Act IV, c. 1903
Watercolor on paper, approx. 10 x 12 in.
(25.4 x 30.5 cm)
Bibliothèque Nationale de France,
Département des Arts du Spectacle, Paris
Page 136, fig. 10

123. Cabriol (Georges Lorin, French)
Sarah Bernhardt, caricature printed as cover
page of *Les hydropathes*, April 5, 1879
11 x 9 in. (27.9 x 22.9 cm)
Herbert D. and Ruth Schimmel Rare Book
Purchase Fund, Jane Voorhees Zimmerli
Museum, Rutgers, The State University of
New Jersey, New Brunswick
Page 44, fig. 29

124. Leonetto Cappiello (Italian, 1875–1942)
Cover of *Le théâtre*, 1903
Color lithograph, 14 1/4 x 10 1/2 in.
(36.2 x 26.7 cm)
Posters Please, Inc., New York
Page 131, fig. 6

125. Henri Demare (French, 1846–1888)
Sarah Bernhardt with Louise Abbéma, caricature
published in *Le grelot*, February 18, 1883
19 1/8 x 15 1/2 in. (48.5 x 39.5 cm)
Bibliothèque Nationale de France,
Département des Arts du Spectacle, Paris
Page 110, fig. 13

126. André Gill (French, 1840–1885)
Sarah Bernhardt as a Sphinx, caricature,
published in *La lune rousse*, October 6, 1878
25 x 18 1/8 in. (63.5 x 46 cm)

Bibliothèque Nationale de France,
Département des Arts du Spectacle, Paris
Page 45, fig. 30

127. Alfred Le Petit (French, 1841–1909)
Cover of *Les contemporains*, caricature, n.d.
11 3/4 x 15 3/4 in. (29.9 x 40 cm)
Bibliothèque Nationale de France,
Département des Arts du Spectacle, Paris
Page 37, fig. 20

128. Alfred Le Petit (French, 1841–1909)
"La poule aux oeufs d'or" ("The 'Tart' That Laid
the Golden Eggs"), caricature of Sarah
Bernhardt with Victorien Sardou published in
Le grelot, December 31, 1882
12 3/4 x 11 1/8 in. (32.3 x 28.3 cm)
Collection of Philippe Lechat, Paris
Page 37, fig. 19

129. Alfred Le Petit (French, 1841–1909)
Une rude lutteuse, caricature of Sarah Bernhardt
as a skinny boxer with Jean Richepin,
published in *Le grelot*, January 6, 1884
12 1/2 x 10 7/8 in. (31.8 x 27.7 cm)
Bibliothèque Nationale de France,
Département des Arts du Spectacle, Paris
Page 138, fig. 11

130. Manuel Luque (Spanish, 1854–1881)
Sarah Bernhardt Sweeping Money, caricature,
published in *Le grelot*, January 1884
19 5/8 x 12 3/8 in. (50 x 31.4 cm)
Bibliothèque Nationale de France,
Département des Arts du Spectacle, Paris

131. Marcelin (Émile Planat) (French, 1830–1887)
"The Great Tragedienne Begins Her 190th
Season," caricature of Rachel published in
Le journal pour rire, November 20, 1852
17 3/8 x 12 5/8 in. (44 x 32 cm)
Bibliothèque Nationale de France,
Département des Estampes, Paris
Page 38, fig. 22

132. Alphonse Mucha (Czech, 1860–1939)
Studies for *La dame aux camélias* (cover designs
and interior of special program), 1896
Pencil and watercolor on paper, 11 x 18 1/8 in.
(28 x 46 cm)
Mucha Trust, London
Page 61, fig. 45

133. Alphonse Mucha (Czech, 1860–1939)
Study for *L'Aiglon*, 1900

Pencil on paper, 10 5/8 x 7 7/8 in. (27 x 20 cm)
Mucha Trust, London

134. Alphonse Mucha (Czech, 1860–1939)
Study for *Hamlet* costume, 1899
Pencil on paper, 9 x 7 5/8 in. (22.9 x 19.4 cm)
Mucha Trust, London

135. Alphonse Mucha (Czech, 1860–1939)
Study for *Hamlet* costume, 1899
Pencil and watercolor on paper, 9 x 7 5/8 in.
(22.9 x 19.4 cm)
Mucha Trust, London

136. Alphonse Mucha (Czech, 1860–1939)
Study for *Lorenzaccio* poster: arms and legs of
Sarah Bernhardt, 1896
Pencil on paper, 18 1/2 x 12 1/4 in. (47 x 31.1 cm)
Mucha Trust, London

137. Alphonse Mucha (Czech, 1860–1939)
Study for *Médée* poster, 1898
Pencil on paper, 17 3/4 x 13 in. (45.1 x 33 cm)
Mucha Trust, London

138. Orens (Orens Denizard) (French, 1879–?)
Hamlet with Skull, caricature, 1905
5 3/4 in. x 3 3/4 in. (14.5 x 9.4 cm)
Bibliothèque Nationale de France,
Département des Arts du Spectacle, Paris

139. Reutlinger Studio (French, active
1850–1930)
Sarah Bernhardt Advertising Chocolat Sadla,
c. 1890
Photogravure trading card, 2 1/2 x 4 in.
(6.4 x 10.2 cm)
Laurence Senelick Collection of Theatrical
Imagery, West Medford, Massachusetts

140. Edmond Rostand (French, 1868–1918)
Letter from Edmond Rostand to Sarah
Bernhardt with sketches for *L'Aiglon*, late 1899
Bibliothèque Nationale de France,
Département des Arts du Spectacle, Paris
Page 90, fig. 13

141. Henri-Marie-Raymond de Toulouse-
Lautrec (French, 1864–1901)
*At the Théâtre de la Renaissance: Sarah Bernhardt
in "Phèdre,"* 1893
Lithograph on Japan paper, 18 1/8 x 12 3/16 in.
(46 x 31 cm)
The Metropolitan Museum of Art, New York,
Bequest of Scofield Thayer, 1982 (1984.1203.157)
Page 128, fig. 4

142. Andy Warhol (American, 1928–1987)
*Sarah Bernhardt from Ten Portraits of Jews of the
Twentieth Century*, 1980
Silkscreen print, 40 x 32 in. (101.6 x 81.3 cm)
The Jewish Museum, New York; Promised gift
of Lorraine and Martin Beitler, P.1.2001
Page 14, fig. 15

143. Advertisement for cigarettes with reproduction of Reutlinger photograph of Sarah
Bernhardt as Roxane in *Cyrano de Bergerac*,
c. 1890
1 1/2 x 1 1/4 in. (3.8 x 3.2 cm)
Laurence Senelick Collection of Theatrical
Imagery, West Medford, Massachusetts

144. Advertisement for cigarettes with
reproduction of Reutlinger photograph of
Sarah Bernhardt as Tosca, c. 1890
1 1/2 x 2 1/2 in. (3.8 x 6.4 cm)
Laurence Senelick Collection of Theatrical
Imagery, West Medford, Massachusetts

145. Advertisement for Milk Weed Cream
(Detroit), n.d.
11 x 8 3/4 in. (27.9 x 8.3 cm)
Performing Arts Collection, Harry Ransom
Humanities Research Center, The University
of Texas at Austin

146. Advertisement for Marmon car with Sarah
Bernhardt, in Illinois Theatre program, 1918
9 9/16 x 7 1/8 in. (24.1 x 18.1 cm)
Harvard Theatre Collection, Houghton
Library, Cambridge, Massachusetts
Page 147

147. Advertisement for Mrs. Graham's Eugenie
Enamel in program for *Théodora*, 1891
12 x 9 3/8 in. (30.5 x 23.9 cm)
Harvard Theatre Collection, Houghton
Library, Cambridge, Massachusetts
Page 146

148. Advertisement for real estate in the Bronx:
"319 Lots on the Morris Park Race Track to Be
Sold," in Program for Palace Theater, May 5, 1913
9 x 12 in. (22.9 x 30.5 cm)
Museum of the City of New York, Theater
Collection, Gift of Gaston J. Cramer (39.319.16)

149. Advertisement for Studebaker Brothers
Mfg. Co. in Program for Broadway Theater,
Sarah Bernhardt and Constantin Coquelin in
L'Aiglon, February 6, 1901

13 1/2 x 8 7/8, in. (34.3 x 22.7 cm)
Museum of the City of New York, Theater
Collection, Gift of Miss Fanny F. Campbell
(34.363.4)

150. Advertisements for *L'Extrait de la viande*
(*Beef Bouillon*) with Sarah Bernhardt as
L'Aiglon, c. 1900
Six lithographed trading cards, each 2 3/4 x
4 in. (7 x 10.2 cm)
Laurence Senelick Collection of Theatrical
Imagery, West Medford, Massachusetts
Page 144

151. Caricature of Sarah Bernhardt dying
and killing, published in *La vie parisienne*,
December 5, 1896
13 x 18 1/2 in. (33 x 47 cm)
Bibliothèque Nationale de France,
Département des Arts du Spectacle, Paris
Page 56, fig. 40

152. Cover of *Femina*, Sarah Bernhardt at
San Quentin Prison: "Je joue devant les
condamnés à mort" (I perform for those
condemned to die), 1913
13 1/8 x 9 7/8 in. (33.3 x 25 cm)
Bibliothèque Nationale de France,
Département des Arts du Spectacle, Paris
Page 156, fig. 10

153. Map of Sarah Bernhardt tour route
("All Roads Lead to Texas"), 1905–6
14.5 x 9 in. (36.8 x 22.9 cm)
Museum of the City of New York, Theater
Collection, Gift of Mrs. Walter Lowe Fairchild
(40.18.170)
Page 65, fig. 51

154. Marquis d'Angelsy as L'Aiglon, in
The Sketch, January 1, 1902
8 x 10 in. (20.3 x 25.4 cm)
British Library, London

155. Program with product endorsement for
Sozodont Antiseptic, November 12, 1900
The Shubert Archive, New York

156. Sarah Bernhardt as amputee on the front
in her sedan chair, published in *Literary Digest*,
c. 1916–17
The General Research Division, The New York
Public Library, Astor, Lenox and Tilden
Foundation
See equivalent on page 96, fig. 17

157. "Sarah Bernhardt—New York's Latest High Pressure Craze," caricature of Bernhardt's Farewell American Tour, 1905–6
12 x 8 in. (30.5 x 20.3 cm)
Billy Rose Theatre Collection, The New York Public Library for the Performing Arts
Page 135, fig. 9

158. Sarah Bernhardt trading card for *Red Cross Tea* with image from *Théodora*, c. 1890
Lithograph on trading card, 5 1/2 x 7 in. (14 x 17.8 cm)
Laurence Senelick Collection of Theatrical Imagery, West Medford, Massachusetts
Page 147

159. "Some Suggestions à la Bernhardt to Supplant the Old Diamond Dodge," caricature of Sarah Bernhardt's American Tour, n.d.
Lithograph
Private collection, New York

160. William Henry Rice in *Sarah Heartburn*, 1881
7 x 5 in. (17.8 x 12.7 cm)
Harvard Theatre Collection, Houghton Library, Cambridge, Massachusetts

Wardrobe and Accessories

161. Georges Jules Victor Clairin (French, 1843–1919)
Fan with portrait of Sarah Bernhardt and names of Bernhardt productions, 1881
Watercolor with tortoiseshell frame, 12 1/4 x 24 3/8 in. (31 x 62 cm)
Musée Galliera, Musée de la Mode de la Ville de Paris (GAL 1989.254.1)
Page 127, fig. 3

162. Réne Lalique (French, 1860–1945)
Brooch dedicated to Sarah Bernhardt and given to the Comédie Française by André Malraux, 1896
5 1/8 x 5 3/4 in. (13 x 14.5 cm)
Collections de la Comédie Française, Paris
Page 100, fig. 2

163. René Lalique (French, 1860–1945)
Ornament with birds, c. 1900
Gold, enamel, diamonds
Private collection, Paris

164. Théophile Thomas (French, 1846–1916)
Cape for *Théodora*, c. 1884

Fabric embroidered with silk thread, glass beads
Bibliothèque Nationale de France, Département des Arts du Spectacle, Paris
Page 21

165. Théophile Thomas (French, 1846–1916)
Capelet for *Théodora*, 1884 and 1902
Fabric with gilt thread, gilt buttons, colored stones, pearls, 15 3/8 x 31 1/2 in. (39 x 80 cm)
Bibliothèque Nationale de France, Département des Arts du Spectacle, Paris
Page 21

166. Théophile Thomas (French, 1846–1916)
Jeanne d'Arc cuirass with bag, 1890
White leather with multicolored embroidery, metal, 34 1/4 x 22 7/8 in. (87 x 58 cm); 9 1/4 x 8 5/8 in. (23.5 x 22 cm)
Bibliothèque Nationale de France, Département des Arts du Spectacle, Paris
Page 77, fig. 3

167. Théophile Thomas (French, 1846–1916)
Tunic costume for Euphratas in *Théodora*, 1884 and 1902
Fabric with gilt thread, pearls, semiprecious stones, 56 3/4 x 15 in. (144 x 38 cm)
Bibliothèque Nationale de France, Département des Arts du Spectacle, Paris
Page 10, fig. 10

168. Vallet (French, 1856–before 1934)
Kid gloves, c. 1910
Leather with multicolored and gold thread, 14 x 6 in. (35 x 15 cm)
Musée Galliera, Musée de la Mode de la Ville de Paris (GAL 1983.26.1 AB)
Page 18

169. *L'Aiglon* buttons (four), 1900 or after
Brass, each diam. 1 in. (2.5 cm)
Collection of Amy Bedik, New York

170. Arm bracelet for *Cléopâtre*, 1890 or after
Diam. 7 in. (17.8 cm)
Museum of the City of New York, Theater Collection, Museum purchase (74.170.2a)

171. Belt with buckle inscribed "Sarah Bernhardt," n.d.
Metal ornament on velvet, approx. 30 in. (76.2 cm)
Musée Carnavalet—Histoire de Paris (OM 3403)
Page 9, fig. 9

172. Bird ornaments for *Cléopâtre* (two), c. 1890
Metal, pearls, semiprecious stones (amethyst, lapis, turquoise), 5 1/8 x 9 1/2 in. (13 x 24 cm); 3 1/2 x 5 1/2 in. (9 x 14 cm)
Bibliothèque Nationale de France, Département des Arts du Spectacle, Paris

173. Bracelets for *Cléopâtre* (five), c. 1890
Gilded metal, glass beads, gold
Bibliothèque Nationale de France, Département des Arts du Spectacle, Paris

174. Bracelets studded with semiprecious stones for *Cléopâtre* (two), 1890
Metal and gems, each approx. 4 3/4 in. x 3 1/2 in. diam. (12 x 9 cm)
Mutuelle Nationale des Artistes, Couilly-Pont-aux-Dames, France

175. Corset worn in *Hernani*, 1877
Metal with rhinestones, pearls, gold thread, 12 1/2 x 24 3/4 in. (31 x 63 cm)
Bibliothèque Nationale de France, Département des Arts du Spectacle, Paris

176. Crown for *Ruy Blas*, c. 1872
Metal, rhinestones, artificial pearls, diam. 12 in. (30.5 cm)
Collections de la Comédie Française, Paris (0.7)

177. Cuff links depicting Sarah Bernhardt as Franz, Duke of Reichstadt, in *L'Aiglon*, 1900 or after
Gold, each 1/2 in. (1.25 cm)
Museum of the City of New York, Theater Collection, Museum purchase (74.170.4ab)
Page 93, fig. 15

178. Dagger and sheath for *Lorenzaccio* and *Hamlet*, 1896
2 x 15 in. (5 x 38 cm)
Mutuelle Nationale des Artistes, Couilly-Pont-aux-Dames, France

179. Diadem for *La princesse lointaine*, c. 1895
Metal and pearls, 6 1/4 x 12 5/8 x 10 1/4 in. (16 x 32 x 26 cm)
Bibliothèque Nationale de France, Musée et Bibliothèque de l'Opéra, Paris
Page 58, fig. 42

180. Double-eagle crown for *Théodora*, 1902
Velour and metal inset with opals, amethysts, and turquoise, 5 7/8 x 13 3/8 x 7 1/2 in. (15 x 34 x 19 cm)

Mutuelle Nationale des Artistes, Couilly-Pont-aux-Dames, France
Page 11, fig. 11

181. Ermine capelet with high collar,
c. 1898–1900
33 1/2 x 26 3/4 in. (85 x 68 cm)
Musée Galliera, Musée de la Mode de la Ville de Paris (GAL 1985.1.108)
Page 39, fig. 23

182. Feathered fan, c. 1905
Feathers, silver pailettes, mother-of-pearl,
9 7/8 x 14 1/4 in. (25 x 36 cm)
Musée Galliera, Musée de la Mode de la Ville de Paris (GAL 2003.17.2)
Page 19

183. Handkerchief embroidered with "Sarah," accompanied by letter dated 1955 from Julie Harris to Susan Strasberg
11 1/4 x 11 1/4 in. (28 x 28 cm)
Cherry Jones, New York
Page xiv

184. Pectoral and belt for Cléopâtre, 1890
Metal, pearls, beads, sequins, gold thread
Bibliothèque Nationale de France, Département des Arts du Spectacle, Paris
Page 12, fig. 12

185. Purse for Gismonda, 1896
Fabric with gilt thread, pearls, amethysts,
10 5/8 x 17 3/8 in. (27 x 45 cm)
Mutuelle Nationale des Artistes, Couilly-Pont-aux-Dames, France
Page 20

186. Shawl from Phèdre, c. 1898
Embroidered silk
Bibliothèque Nationale de France, Département des Arts du Spectacle, Paris

187. Topaz ring given by daughter of Mathilde Herron, Bijou Fernandez, n.d.
Topaz in gold mount
The Hampden-Booth Theatre Library, New York

188. Purses (three), for unidentified roles of Sarah Bernhardt's, n.d.
Velvet, 1 3/4 x 6 7/8 in. (4.5 x 17.5 cm); 1 3/4 x 5 1/8 in. (4.5 x 13 cm); 6 1/4 x 6 1/4 in. (16 x 16 cm)
Bibliothèque Nationale de France, Département des Arts du Spectacle, Paris
Page 20

Decorative Arts

189. Sarah Bernhardt (French, 1844–1923)
Letter opener with fantastic animal motifs, 1900
Wood, 2 x 15 3/8 in. (5 x 39 cm)
Mutuelle Nationale des Artistes, Couilly-Pont-aux-Dames, France

190. Paul François Berthoud (French, 1870–1939)
Jardinière of Sarah Bernhardt, 1905
Bronze, 15 x 20 x 10 in. (38.1 x 50.8 x 25.4 cm)
Collection of Raphael Benjamin Sinai, London
Page 112, fig. 15

191. Christofle and Henin
Three serving utensils with Sarah Bernhardt's motto, "Quand même," n.d.
Silver, each 11 in. (27.9 cm)
Collection of Robert A. Zehil, Monte Carlo, Monaco
Page 113, fig. 17

192. Kayserzinn Company
Plate with Sarah Bernhardt's motto, "Quand même," 1911
Pewter, diam. 13 in. (33 cm)
Collection Beatrix Ost and Ludwig Kuttner, New York
Page 113, fig. 18

193. Edmond Lachenal (French, 1855–1900)
Faience plate with portrait of Sarah Bernhardt, 1891
Ceramic, diam. 9 in. (22.9 cm)
Petit Palais, Musée des Beaux-Arts de la Ville de Paris (PPS 3348)
Page 175, fig. 9

194. Édouard Lièvre (French, 1829–1886)
Sarah Bernhardt's standing mirror with her motto, "Quand même," n.d.
Wood with mounted brass and silver "Quand même" shield, gilt bronze mounts, inlaid enamel panels, mirrored glass, 9 x 4 x 2 ft. (274.5 x 122 x 61 cm)
Ariodante, Paris
Page 8, fig. 8

195. Candelabra with Sarah Bernhardt's motto, "Quand même," n.d.
Height of each approx. 6 in. (15.2 cm)
Private collection, Paris

196. Cup with photographic reproduction of Sarah Bernhardt in La dame aux camélias

(stamped "Rockefeller Center" on bottom), 1929 or after
Ceramic, height 3 in. (7.6 cm)
Musée Carnavalet—Histoire de Paris (C 2361)
Page 158, fig. 13

197. Pots for Sarah Bernhardt's tea service (three), n.d.
Silver
Collection of Alain Campignon, Paris

198. Retractable pencil inscribed "For Sarah Bernhardt, January 9, '92," presented to William Seymour by May Davenport Seymour
Gold and silver
The Hampden-Booth Theatre Library, New York

199. Souvenir spoons of American cities and sites (eighteen), n.d.
Silver plate, each 4 in. (10.2 cm)
Bibliothèque-Musée de la Comédie Française, Paris
Page 162, fig. 22

200. Stationery with Sarah Bernhardt's motto, "Quand même" (note dated 1903)
Mutuelle Nationale des Artistes, Couilly-Pont-aux-Dames, France
Page 25, fig. 2

Films Featuring Sarah Bernhardt

201. Les amours de la reine Elisabeth (Queen Elizabeth) (Famous Players, 1912), directed by Henri Desfontaines and Louis Mercanton, starring Sarah Bernhardt

202. La dame aux camélias (Camille) (Cinémathèque Française, 1912), directed by André Calmettes and Henri Pouctal, starring Sarah Bernhardt
Cinémathèque Française, Bois d'Arcy, France

203. Le duel d'Hamlet (Duel scene from Hamlet) (George Klein Optical Company, 1900), directed by Louis Mercanton, produced by Clement Maurice, starring Sarah Bernhardt
Cinémathèque Française, Bois d'Arcy, France

204. Funeral procession for Sarah Bernhardt, 1923
Gaumont–Pathé Archives, Saint-Ouen, France

205. Jeanne Doré (Universal Pictures, 1916), directed by Louis Mercanton, starring Sarah Bernhardt

Cinémathèque Française, Bois d'Arcy, France
Page 179, fig. 14

206. Mères françaises (Mothers of France) (1917), directed by René Hervil and Louis Mercanton, starring Sarah Bernhardt
Cinémathèque Française, Bois d'Arcy, France

207. Sarah Bernhardt à Belle-Isle (Sarah Bernhardt at Home) (1912), directed by Louis Mercanton, featuring Sarah Bernhardt
Cinémathèque Française, Bois d'Arcy, France

Films Evoking Sarah Bernhardt

208. All About Eve (Twentieth Century Fox, 1950), directed by Joseph Mankiewicz, starring Bette Davis
Footage from All About Eve courtesy of Twentieth Century Fox. All rights reserved.

209. Babes on Broadway (MGM, 1941), directed by Busby Berkeley, starring Judy Garland
Academy of Motion Picture Arts and Sciences, Beverly Hills, California
Page 72, fig. 58

210. The Barkleys of Broadway (MGM, 1949), directed by Charles Walters, starring Fred Astaire and Ginger Rogers
Page 73, fig. 59

211. Moulin Rouge! (Twentieth Century Fox, 2001), directed by Baz Luhrmann, starring Nicole Kidman and Ewan McGregor
Footage from Moulin Rouge! courtesy of Twentieth Century Fox. All rights reserved.

212. Nancy Goes to Rio (MGM, 1950), directed by Robert Z. Leonard, starring Jane Powell and Ann Sothern

213. Portrait of Jennie (Selznick, 1948), directed by William Dieterle, starring Jennifer Jones and Joseph Cotten

214. The Seven Year Itch (Twentieth Century Fox, 1955), directed by Billy Wilder, starring Marilyn Monroe and Tom Ewell
The Seven Year Itch © 1955 Twentieth Century Fox. All rights reserved. TM 2005 Marilyn Monroe LLC by CMG Worldwide, Inc./www.MarilynMonroe.com
Page 22, fig. 1

215. Star! (Twentieth Century Fox, 1968), directed by Robert Wise, starring Julie Andrews

Footage from Star! courtesy of Twentieth Century Fox. All rights reserved.

216. Topsy Turvy (Goldwyn Films, 1999), directed by Mike Leigh, starring Jim Broadbent and Allan Corduner

217. Twentieth Century (Columbia, 1934), directed by Howard Hawks, starring John Barrymore and Carole Lombard

218. Without You I'm Nothing (MCEG Productions, 1990), directed by John Boskovich, starring Sandra Bernhard

219. Breakfast for Two (RKO, 1937), directed by Alfred Santell, starring Barbara Stanwyck and Herbert Marshall

Books, Booklets, Authorized Editions, Programs

220. Sarah Bernhardt (French, 1844–1923)
L'art du théâtre (Art of the Theater), 1923
Book, 7 1/2 x 5 x 1/2 in. (19.1 x 12.7 x 1.25 cm)
Laurence Senelick Collection of Theatrical Imagery, West Medford, Massachusetts

221. Sarah Bernhardt (French, 1844–1923)
Dans les nuages: Impressions d'une chaise (In the Clouds: Impressions of a Chair), 1878
With illustrations by Georges Clairin
Book, 12 x 9 in. (30.5 x 22.9 cm)
The Metropolitan Museum of Art, New York, The Elisha Whittlesey Collection, The Elisha Whittlesey Fund, 1963 (63.602)
Page 117, fig. 22

222. Marie Colombier (French, 1844–1910)
The Memoirs of Sarah Barnum, 1884
Book, 7 5/8 x 5 x 1/2 in. (19.2 x 12.7 x 1.3 cm)
Laurence Senelick Collection of Theatrical Imagery, West Medford, Massachusetts
Page 38, fig. 21

223. Paulo Guglielm
Three programs for performances at the Théâtre Sarah Bernhardt (Dame aux camélias, Adrienne Lecouvreur, Jeanne Doré), Paris, 1903
11 x 4.5 in. (28 x 11.5 cm); 8 1/2 x 6 1/2 in. (20.5 x 16.5 cm); 9 1/2 x 6 1/4 in. (24 x 16 cm)
Bibliothèque Nationale de France, Musée et Bibliothèque de l'Opéra, Paris

224. Edmond Rostand (French, 1868–1918)
La princesse lointaine (The Faraway Princess)

(book given by Edmond Rostand to Sarah Bernhardt), 1911
Moroccan leather binding with metal filigree and semiprecious stones
Private collection, New York
Page 115, fig. 19

225. Printed play text in English: The Bernhardt Edition: Jeanne d'Arc, 1890
Published by Fred Rullman
10 1/8 x 6 7/8 (25.7 x 17.5 cm)
Harvard Theatre Collection, Houghton Library, Cambridge, Massachusetts

226. Printed play text in English: The Bernhardt Edition: La Tosca
Published by Fred Rullman
10 1/4 x 6 7/8 in. (26 x 17.5 cm)
Harvard Theatre Collection, Houghton Library, Cambridge, Massachusetts
Page 67, fig. 54

227. Printed play text in English: La Sorcière (synopsis)
Published by J. Miles & Co.
8 1/4 x 5 7/16 in. (21 x 14 cm)
Harvard Theatre Collection, Houghton Library, Cambridge, Massachusetts

228. Printed play text in English from Sarah Bernhardt's Farewell Tour, "The Last Visit to America, 1905–6": Camille
Published by Fred Rullman
10 1/8 x 7 3/4 in. (25.7 x 19.7 cm)
Harvard Theatre Collection, Houghton Library, Cambridge, Massachusetts

229. Printed play text in English from Sarah Bernhardt's Farewell Tour, "The Last Visit to America, 1910–11": Phaedra
Published by Fred Rullman
10 1/8 x 7 7/8 in. (25.7 x 20 cm)
Harvard Theatre Collection, Houghton Library, Cambridge, Massachusetts (HTC 32.132)

230. Printed play text in English from Sarah Bernhardt's Farewell Tour, "The Last Visit to America," 1916
Published by Fred Rullman
10 1/8 x 7 7/8 in. (25.7 x 20 cm)
Harvard Theatre Collection, Houghton Library, Cambridge, Massachusetts
Page 160, fig. 17

231. *The Home of Sarah Bernhardt in Paris,*
after 1890
Booklet, 7 1/2 x 5 1/2 in. (19 x 14 cm)
Mutuelle Nationale des Artistes, Couilly-Pont-
aux-Dames, France
Page 119, fig. 23

232. Program cover: Sarah Bernhardt and
Constantin Coquelin in *L'Aiglon* and *La dame
aux camélias,* Academy of Music, Brooklyn,
New York, April 6, 1901
8 1/4 x 5 1/2 in. (21 x 14 cm)
Museum of the City of New York, Theater
Collection, Gift of Elwin M. Eldredge
(41.161.44)
Page 160, fig. 18

233. Program for *Camille* at the Auditorium,
Chattanooga, Friday, March 16, 1906
9 1/4 x 5 7/8 in. (23.5 x 15 cm)
Bibliothèque Nationale de France,
Département des Arts du Spectacle, Paris
Page 161, fig. 20

234. Program for the Greenwall Theatre,
New Orleans, March 1906
8 x 5 1/2 in. (20.4 x 13.9 cm)
Bibliothèque Nationale de France,
Département des Arts du Spectacle, Paris
Page 161, fig. 19

235. *Too Thin or Skeleton Sarah,* n.d.
Booklet published by Evans and Kelly
Harvard Theatre Collection, Houghton
Library, Cambridge, Massachusetts

Miscellany

236. Human skull given and inscribed by
Victor Hugo to Sarah Bernhardt, n.d.
7 x 6 in. (17.8 x 15.2 cm)
Victoria and Albert Museum, London (S117-1981)
Page 13, fig. 13

237. Plate with caricature of Sarah Bernhardt as
"Vegetable Salsify" and poem by Alfred Le
Petit, n.d.
Ceramic, diam. 7 in. (17.8 cm)
Musée Carnavalet—Histoire de Paris (C 1517)
Page 36, fig. 17

238. Rosary given to Sarah Bernhardt by Pope
Leo XIII at Castel Gandolfo, n.d.
Silver and wood beads, silver cross with
feathers; beads: 26 1/2 in. (67.3 cm), pendant:
4 x 3 1/4 in. (10.2 x 8.3 cm)

Laurence Senelick Collection of Theatrical
Imagery, West Medford, Massachusetts
Page 82, fig. 8

239. Sarah Bernhardt's note to Émile Zola in
support of Alfred Dreyfus, January 14, 1898
Bibliothèque Nationale de France,
Département des Manuscrits, Paris
Page 85, fig. 10

240. Sheet music for "Sara[h] Bernhardt
Galop-Waltz," composed by Louis Wallis,
published by A. H. Rosewig, 1880
14 x 10 3/4 in. (35.6 x 27.3 cm)
Museum of the City of New York, Garrison
P. Sherwood Collection (40.281.1229)
Page 162, fig. 21

241. Sign for Sarah Bernhardt's train reading
"The Sarah Bernhardt Special," 1906
Cardboard, 9 5/8 x 12 1/2 in. (24.6 x 31.9 cm)
Bibliothèque Nationale de France,
Département des Arts du Spectacle, Paris
Page 158, fig. 14

242. Sound recording of Sarah Bernhardt's
performance of *L'Aiglon,* 1910
Bibliothèque Nationale de France, Audiovisuel,
Paris

243. Telegram to one of the Shubert brothers
from Sarah Bernhardt, March 27, 1905
8 1/2 x 8 1/4 in. (21.6 x 21 cm)
The Shubert Archive, New York
Page 157, fig. 12

244. Ticket stubs for *Hécube,* Brooklyn
Academy of Music, December 30, 1916
Each 1 3/4 x 2 in. (4.5 x 5.1 cm)
Performing Arts Collection, Harry Ransom
Humanities Research Center, The University
of Texas at Austin

Notes

Introduction

1. See Robyn Asleson et al., *A Passion for Performance: Sarah Siddons and Her Portraitists* (Los Angeles: J. Paul Getty Museum, 1999).

2. For portraits of Rachel, including Jean-Léon Gérôme's *La Tragédie* (1859; Collections de la Comédie Française), see *Rachel: Une vie pour le théâtre, 1821–1858* (Paris: Musée d'Art et d'Histoire du Judaïsme, 2004). For portraits of nineteenth-century French actresses contemporary with Bernhardt, including Mademoiselle Mars and Mademoiselle George, see *La Comédie-Française, 1680–1980* (Paris: Bibliothèque Nationale, 1980), especially 111, 113.

3. "Squelette, qu'as tu fait de l'âme? / Lampe, qu'as tu fait de la flamme? / Cage déserte, qu'as tu fait? / De ton bel oiseau qui chantait? / Volcan, qu'as tu fait de la lave? / Qu'as tu fait de ton maître, esclave?" (English translation ours.)

Was She Magnificent?

Author's note: I thank Kenneth E. Silver for peerless assistance in editing this essay. I gratefully acknowledge the support of Williams College, my home institution, and the Mary Ingraham Bunting Institute (the Radcliffe Research Institute at Harvard University), where I had a fellowship in 1997–98 to develop my work on Bernhardt. This essay builds on my previous publications on the actress: "Sarah Bernhardt: Death and the Icon," in Christopher Balme, Robert Erenstein, and Cesare Molinari, eds., *European Theatre Iconography: Proceedings of the European Science Foundation Network* (Rome: Bulzoni, 2002), 331–39; "Women, Icons and Power," in Aruna D'Souza, ed., *Self and History: A Festschrift in Honor of Linda Nochlin* (New York: Thames and Hudson, 2001), 103–15; and "When Is a Jewish Star Just a Star? Interpreting Images of Sarah Bernhardt," in Linda Nochlin and Tamar Garb, eds., *The Jew in the Text: Modernity and the Construction of Identity* (New York: Thames and Hudson, 1995), 121–39. My unpublished papers also inform this essay: "Sarah Bernhardt on Stage and in the Studio," presented in *Demanding Attention: Women and Artistic Training in the Nineteenth Century*, a symposium (cosponsored by the Institute of Fine Arts, New York University, and the Association of Historians of Nineteenth-Century Art) held in conjunction with the exhibition *Overcoming All Obstacles: The Women of the Académie Julian*, Dahesh Museum, New York, April 29, 2000; "Casting the Diva: Bernhardt, Mucha, Nadar, and Edison," presented in conjunction with the exhibition *Alphonse Mucha: The Spirit of Art Nouveau*, Worcester Art Museum, Worcester, Mass., November 2, 1999, and Philbrook Museum of Art, Tulsa, April 24, 1999; "Sarah Bernhardt Live!" delivered at University

College London, January 1999, and the Humanities Center, Harvard University, May 5, 1998; "Dying Nightly: Sarah Bernhardt Plays the Orient," presented in *The Oriental Mirage: Orientalism in Context*, a symposium (cosponsored by the Art Gallery of New South Wales, the Centre for Cross-Cultural Research, and the Australian National University) in conjunction with the exhibition *Orientalism: Delacroix to Klee*, Art Gallery of New South Wales, Sydney, February 14, 1998; and "Death and the Icon: Sarah Bernhardt's Nine Tours in America," presented at the Bunting Institute, January 14, 1998. Unless otherwise noted, translations in this essay are mine.

Epigraph: Jean Cocteau, *Professional Secrets*, trans. Richard Howard (New York: Farrar, Straus and Giroux, 1970), 35.

1. If his parents let him, Tom Ewell, born in 1909—and thirty-eight-year-old Richard Sherman, were he real—could have seen Bernhardt.

2. Writing within a year of Bernhardt's death, one author asserted that "the name Sarah Bernhardt . . . had been printed so often in newspapers and magazines and on bills, programmes, and the like, that the letters would bridge the Atlantic." Cited in "The Book of the Week by T.P.—The Tragedy of a Beautiful Woman," *T.P. and Cassell's Weekly*, January 19, 1942, 447.

3. Citations are from Sarah Bernhardt, *My Double Life: The Memoirs of Sarah Bernhardt*, trans. Victoria Tietze Larson (Albany: State University of New York Press, 1999), 215, 8, 194. Among other versions are, in French, *Ma double vie: Mémoires de Sarah Bernhardt*, ed. Claudine Hermann (Paris: Éditions des Femmes, 1980), and in English, Sarah Bernhardt, *Memories of My Life: Being My Personal, Professional, and Social Recollections as Woman and Artist* (New York: D. Appleton, 1907).

4. Bernhardt, *My Double Life*, 57. According to one friend, the artist Graham Robertson, it was "hard to find the real Sarah because of her talent and power as an actress." W. Graham Robertson, *Life Was Worth Living* (New York: Harper and Brothers, 1931), 107. Similarly, the

critic Max Beerbohm observed: "It is clear that even in her most terrific moments one half of her soul was in the position of spectator, applauding vigorously." Beerbohm, *Around Theatres* (New York: Greenwood, 1930), 486.

5. For an excellent discussion, see Tracy C. Davis, *Actresses as Working Women: Their Social Identity in Victorian Culture* (New York: Routledge, 1991), esp. 69ff.

6. There is much debate about Sarah Bernhardt's origins. It is said that her birth certificate was destroyed by fire in 1871, during the Commune. A copy of her baptismal certificate from the parish of Saint-Louis in Versailles identifies her as "Sara, Marie, Henriette, born in Paris, twelfth arrondissement, September 25, 1844, daughter of M. Edouard Bernhardt, resident of Le Havre, no. 2, rue des Arcades, and of Mme Judith von Hard, resident of Paris, 265 rue Saint-Honoré." The longer French text, from an unidentified newspaper clipping in the Bibliothèque de la Comédie Française, Paris, reads:

> L'an 1856, le 21 mai, a été baptisée par nous soussigné chapelain de la communauté de Grandchamp, dûment autorisé par Monsigneur l'évêque de Versailles, Sara, Marie, Henriette, née à Paris, douzième arrondissement, le 25 septembre 1844, fille de M. Edouard Bernhardt demeurant actuellement au Havre, rue des Arcades, n. 2, et de Mme Judith von Hard, demeurant à Paris, rue Saint-Honoré, 265.
>
> Le parrain, a été M. Régis Lavolé, rue de la Chaussée-d'Antin, 65, à Paris, réprésenté par M. Nicolas Murcier, rue Saint-Honoré, 24 à Versailles et la marraine, Mme. Anna van Hard, Veuve Bruck tante de l'enfant.
> S.-M.-H. Bernhardt.
> Vve Bruck.-Murcier
> Gourd, chanoine honoraire, chapelain de Grandchamp.

In secondary sources, Sarah Bernhardt's name is usually recorded as Henriette-Rosine or Rosine Bernard. Her mother's maiden name is given as either van Hard or van Hardt, but more often as Bernard or Bernhardt. Her father's identity is more mysterious: Édouard Bernard, a law student who became a successful notary (the majority opinion according to Cornelia Otis Skinner, *Madame Sarah* [New

York: Dell, 1966], 24); Édouard Ker-Bernhardt—her uncle whom certain descendants of Sarah Bernhardt are convinced was her father—who took the Breton form of his name and emigrated to Chile (Arthur Gold and Robert Fizdale, *The Divine Sarah: A Life of Sarah Bernhardt* [New York: Alfred A. Knopf, 1991], 11); or a rich naval cadet named Morel (Georges Bernier, *Sarah Bernhardt and Her Times* [New York: Wildenstein, 1984], 66). On the actress's origins, see also Ernest Pronier, *Une vie au théâtre* (Geneva: Alexandre Jullien, n.d.), 26; Louis Verneuil (husband of Bernhardt's granddaughter Lysiane), *La vie merveilleuse de Sarah Bernhardt* (Montreal: Éditions Variétés, 1942), 26–43; Basil Woon (from material supplied by Madame Pierre Berton), *The Real Sarah Bernhardt, Whom Her Audiences Never Knew* (New York: Boni and Liveright, 1924), 32–47; and, more recently, Mary Louise Roberts, *Disruptive Acts: The New Woman in Fin-de-Siècle France* (Chicago: University of Chicago Press, 2002), 208–10.

7. Bernhardt's relationships with Clairin and Abbéma date to the 1870s. When the actress purchased her home at Belle-Isle-en-Mer, in Brittany, in 1886, she had studios built for them there. Clairin died at Belle-Isle in 1919. Abbéma outlived Bernhardt and led her funeral procession, together with the actress's son and other family members. Abbéma's large oil of Bernhardt and herself on the lake in the Bois de Boulogne (repr. in Noëlle Guibert, ed., *Portrait(s) de Sarah Bernhardt* [Paris: Bibliothèque Nationale de France, 2000], 104) was painted "par Louise Abbéma, le jour anniversaire de leur liaison amoureuse" ("by Louise Abbéma, on the anniversary of their amorous liaison"), according to a letter, accompanying the bequest of the picture to the Comédie Française in 1990, from Madame Christian Ayoub-Sinano to Noëlle Guibert (then curator of the Bibliothèque-Musée de la Comédie Française), March 18, 1990.

8. Émile Zola, "Deux expositions d'art au mois de mai: Salon de 1876 et 2e Exposition Impressioniste," *Le messager de l'Europe*, June 1876. For additional critical responses to this picture, see Ockman, "Sarah Bernhardt on Stage and in the Studio."

9. Hahn continued: "When she sits, it's in a spiral; her dress sweeps around her, embraces her in the tender movement of the spiral, and the train falls on the ground in the design of a spiral whose form her head and chest adopt above, in the opposite direction." Reynaldo Hahn, *La grande Sarah: Souvenirs* (Paris: Hachette, 1930), 48.

10. Joseph-Isidore Samson, cited in Gerda Taranow, *Sarah Bernhardt: The Art within the Legend* (Princeton, N.J.: Princeton University Press, 1972), 5. Bernhardt perfected a formula invented by her collaborator Victorien Sardou: any action onstage would unfold in three consecutive phases, from glance to gesture to word. I am indebted to Taranow's excellent discussions of Bernhardt as actress.

11. Tom Taylor, cited ibid., 111, 113; Anatole France, cited in Robert Horville, "The Stage Techniques of Sarah Bernhardt," in Eric Salmon, ed., *Bernhardt and the Theatre of Her Time* (Westport, Conn.: Greenwood, 1984), 51; reporter, undated clipping, *The New York Times*, Box 2, Sarah Bernhardt star clippings, Harvard Theatre Collection.

12. Marguerite Coe, "Sarah and Coq: Contrasts in Acting Styles," in Salmon, *Bernhardt and the Theatre of Her Time*, 71.

13. Jokes about Bernhardt's thinness are legion: "Her mother often traveled, and the child was so thin, so thin! . . . that she gave birth without anyone noticing." "If an importune visitor tried to get in, she hid in an umbrella stand." "When a friend arrived and Bernhardt was on her way out, she pulled off the bell cord and substituted herself for it." "Her hair is always very tangled. . . . When she goes to comb it, she can't, because at each stroke, her entire body passes through the teeth of the comb." "Mlle Sarah Bernhardt sculpts in her spare time; one of her disappointments is that she can't make a self-portrait medallion in relief. Her spirit is very sharp, her elbows too." Touchatout [Léon-Charles Bienvenu], *Le Trombinoscope*, October 1881.

14. Bernhardt, *My Double Life*, 55.

15. The full quatrain reads: "Quelqu'un venu de sa province / Tout épaté, se dit comment / Le salsifis, qu'on voit si mince / Contient-il un si grand talent?"

16. "Sarah, comme les hirondelles, / Avec mai, vient à tire-d'elles. / La divine, malgré les ans, / Enchâine jeunesse et printemps." *Les contemporains*, n.d. An article by Félicien Champsaur accompanies the caricature; in detailing Bernhardt's oddities, he recounts a story he supposedly heard her tell colleagues at the theater. She intended to kill her little black dog for "no reason," Champsaur claims, adding by way of explanation that the impulse came from "her Jewish and nomadic blood."

17. Rachel's thinness was frequently a target of caricaturists as well. Unlike Bernhardt, however, she was likened to a classical column, and her ramrod stance is evident in many paintings, caricatures, and photographs. On Rachel, see *Rachel: Une vie pour le théâtre, 1821–1858* (Paris: Musée d'Art et d'Histoire du Judaïsme, 2004); Rachel M. Brownstein, *Tragic Muse: Rachel of the Comédie Française* (New York: Alfred A. Knopf, 1993); Sylvie Chevalley, *Rachel* (Alençon: Calmann-Lévy, 1989).

18. The hexagram, as employed by Willette, Cabriol, Gill, and others, is hardly neutral. But taken on its own, what we know as the Jewish star didn't have to be Jewish. A host of nineteenth-century popular entertainers, the famous chanteuse Thérésa among them, were shown with a six-pointed star as often as they were with a five-pointed one; a star could be just a star. It wasn't until the founding of Zionism that the six-pointed star unequivocally came to stand for Jewishness. On caricatures of Bernhardt and the valence of the Jewish star, see Ockman, "When Is a Jewish Star Just a Star?" On Bernhardt's Jewishness, see also Janis Bergman-Carton, "Negotiating the Categories: Sarah Bernhardt and the Possibilities of Jewishness," *Art Journal* 55, no. 2 (Summer 1996), 55–64; Ann Pellegrini, *Performance Anxieties: Staging Psychoanalysis, Staging Race* (New York: Routledge, 1997), 39–47; Sander L. Gilman, "Salome, Syphilis, Sarah Bernhardt, and the Modern Jewess," in Nochlin and Garb, *The Jew in the Text*, 97–120; Roberts, *Disruptive Acts*, 165–219; and Susan A. Glenn, *Female Spectacle: The Theatrical Roots of Modern Feminism* (Cambridge, Mass.: Harvard University Press, 2000), 31–34. For Bernhardt as Jewish actress, see Harley Erdman, *Staging the Jew: The Performance of an American Ethnicity, 1860–1920* (New Brunswick, N.J.: Rutgers University Press, 1997), 48–50.

19. On the nineteenth-century *belle juive*, see Carol Ockman, "Two Large Eyebrows à l'orientale: The Baronne de Rothschild," in *Ingres's Eroticized Bodies: Retracing the Serpentine Line* (New Haven and London: Yale University Press, 1995), 66–83; and Erdman, *Staging the Jew*, 40–60.

20. Definitions are from *Merriam-Webster's Collegiate Dictionary*, 11th ed. (Springfield, Mass.: Merriam-Webster, 2003), 504.

21. On Cushman's male roles, see Lisa Merrill, *When Romeo Was a Woman: Charlotte Cushman and Her Circle of Female Spectators* (Ann Arbor: University of Michigan Press, 1999), esp. 110–37.

22. On Bernhardt's breeches roles, see Gerda Taranow, *The Bernhardt Hamlet: Culture and Context* (Bern: Peter Lang, 1998); Laurence Senelick, *The Changing Room: Sex, Drag and Theatre* (London: Routledge, 2000), esp. 275–80; Martha Vicinus, "Turn-of-the-Century Male Impersonation: Rewriting the Roman Plot," in Andrew H. Miller and James Eli Adams, eds., *Sexualities in Victorian Britain* (Bloomington: Indiana University Press, 1996), 187–213, and "The Adolescent Boy: Fin-de-Siècle Femme Fatale?" *Journal of the History of Sexuality* 5 (July 1994), 90–114; and Jill Edmonds, "Prince Hamlet," in Vivien Gardner and Susan Rutherford, eds., *The New Woman and Her Sisters: Feminism and Theatre, 1850–1914* (Ann Arbor: University of Michigan Press, 1992), 62ff.

23. The first version of *The Lady of the Camellias* in the United States was *Camille; or, The Fate of a Coquette* (1856). William D. Howarth, "The Lady of the Camelias [sic] (*La dame aux camélias*)," in Mark Hawkins-Dady, ed., *International Dictionary of Theatre* (Chicago: St. James, 1992), vol. 1 (Plays), 406–8.

24. Sarah Bernhardt, "Men's Rôles as Played by Women," *Harper's Bazaar*, December 15, 2000, 2114–15, Box 1, Sarah Bernhardt star clippings, Harvard Theatre Collection.

25. At least one reviewer lamented: "I feel that those who now see her for the first time would have formed a juster idea of her powers had she appeared in one of her great feminine roles." *Reynolds Newspaper* (London), September 25, 1910.

26. Box 1, Sarah Bernhardt press clippings, Harvard Theatre Collection.

27. The name "Hydropathes," coined by Émile Goudeau, refers to a group of writers committed to Truth, Art, and Beauty, including Goudeau himself, Jean Richepin, André Gill, and Jean Moréas, who began to meet around 1878. Bernhardt was the first woman to be included in the group's journal. See Jules Lévy, *Les Hydropathes* (Paris: André Delpeuch, 1928).

28. On the critical response to the portrait by Abbéma, see Ockman, "Sarah Bernhardt on Stage and in the Studio."

29. Although the Museum of Fine Arts, Boston, which owns a cast of the plaque by Bernhardt, identifies it as a self-portrait and dates it 1878, the Service de Documentation at the Musée d'Orsay identifies the work as a portrait of Louise Abbéma and dates it 1875. The plaque is inscribed "À Mon Amie Louise Abbéma, Sarah Bernhardt," followed by the date, which I am inclined to read as 1875. Miranda Mason's paper "Is There Room in Queer for Me? Reading Sarah Bernhardt's Bust of Louise Abbéma (1878) with Scholarly Lesbian Desire" (presented in the session "Queer Visual Culture, 1870–1914" [chair: Whitney Davis], at the conference InterseXions, sponsored by the Center for Lesbian and Gay Studies at the City University of New York, the Queer Caucus for Art, the Ph.D. Program in Art History at the CUNY Graduate Center, The Leslie–Lohman Gay Art Foundation, and Steven J. Goldstein, M.D., November 13, 2004) first suggested to me that the plaque depicts Abbéma. In addition to the arguments in the text above, there is the fact that the large bow with straight collar in this plaque is virtually identical to the one in Melandri's half-length photograph of Abbéma. While much more common in images of Bernhardt, including the plaque of her by Abbéma, Bernhardt's *Fantastic Inkwell (Self-Portrait as a Sphinx)*, and the many representations of her in studio costume, the bow is always accompanied by a frilly collar in images of Bernhardt.

For an interpretation confirming the artistic dialogue between Bernhardt and Abbéma, see Griselda Pollock's forthcoming essay, "Louise Abbéma's *Lunch* and Alfred Stevens's *Studio*: Theatricality, Feminine Subjectivity, and Space around Sarah Bernhardt, 1877–1888," in Janice Helland and Deborah Cherry, eds., *Studio, Space, and Sociality: New Narratives of Nineteenth-Century Women Artists* (Aldershot: Ashgate, 2006). At the University of Leeds, Miranda Mason is working on a Ph.D. thesis, "Re-Presenting Sarah Bernhardt: From Surface to Substance" (supervisors: Fred Orton and Griselda Pollock), in which the artistic and personal relationship between Bernhardt and Abbéma plays a principal role. On the specific challenges facing women artists at this time, see Tamar Garb, *Sisters of the Brush: Women's Artistic Culture in Late Nineteenth-Century Paris* (New Haven and London: Yale University Press, 1994); and Gabriel P. Weisberg and Jane R. Becker, eds., *Overcoming All Obstacles: The Women of the Académie Julian* (New Brunswick, N.J.: Rutgers University Press, and New York: Dahesh Museum, 1999).

30. This deliberately homoerotic inversion of Orientalist paradigms might be extended to the work of Georges Clairin and Henri Regnault. Regnault's provocative artistic production, as well as his close friendship and amorous liaison with Clairin, was cut short by his death in the Franco-Prussian War. For an important discussion of their relationship, see Hollis Clayson, *Paris in Despair: Art and Everyday Life under Siege (1870–71)* (Chicago: University of Chicago Press, 2002), 236ff.

31. Cited in Georges Lecocq, *Louise Abbéma* (first installment in the series *Peintres et sculpteurs*) (Paris: Librairie des Bibliophiles, 1879), 7–8.

32. See, for example, Gold and Fizdale, *The Divine Sarah*, fig. 27. Along with those by Cornelia Otis Skinner and Reynaldo Hahn, this is one of the best biographies of Bernhardt.

33. On the cult of invalidism, see the classic discussion by Bram Dijkstra, *Idols of Perversity: Fantasies of Feminine Evil in Fin-de-Siècle Culture* (New York: Oxford University Press, 1986), 25ff.

34. Bernhardt, *My Double Life*, 184.

35. Ibid., 309.

36. Max Beerbohm expresses a similar idea: "The tragedian cured the invalid. Doubtless, if she had not been by nature a tragedian, and if all her outbursts of emotion had come straight from her human heart, she could not have survived." Beerbohm, *Around Theatres*, 486. I disagree with the theater historian Leigh Woods, who argues that Bernhardt's appearances in vaudeville can be reduced to a reactionary stance inscribing "a narrow morality for women and the mortal penalty for such deviations from morality." Leigh Woods, "Two-a-Day Redemptions and Truncated Camille: The Vaudeville Repertoire of Sarah Bernhardt," *New Quarterly Review*, February 10, 1994, 22. See also Leigh Woods, "Sarah Bernhardt and the Refining of American Vaudeville," *Theatre Research International* 18, no. 1 (Spring 1993), 16–24.

37. See Skinner, *Madame Sarah*, 221–22, 252–53, 264; and http://www.andreas-praefcke.de/carthalia/france/f_paris_ville.htm.

38. Unidentified clipping, Box 2, Sarah Bernhardt star clippings, plays G–O, Harvard Theatre Collection.

39. Cited in "New York Magazine Program" (New York: New York Theatre Program Corp.), December 6, 1933.

40. For Mucha, see Jack Rennert and Alain Weill, *Alphonse Mucha: The Complete Posters and Panels* (Boston: G. K. Hall, 1984); and Victor Arwas, Jana Brabcová-Orlíková, and Anna Dvořák, *Alphonse Mucha—The Spirit of Art Nouveau* (Alexandria, Va.: Art Services International, in association with Yale University Press, 1998).

41. My discussion of the poster is indebted to Marcus Verhagen, "The Poster in Fin-de-Siècle Paris: 'That Mobile and Degenerate Art,'" in Leo Charney and Vanessa R. Schwartz, eds., *Cinema and the Invention of Modern Life* (Berkeley: University of California Press, 1995), 103–29. On the identification of woman and mass culture, see Rachel Bowlby, *Just Looking: Consumer Culture in Dreiser, Gissing and Zola* (New York: Methuen, 1985); Andreas Huyssen,

After the Great Divide: Modernism, Mass Culture, Postmodernism (London: Macmillan, 1988), chap. 3; and Mary Louise Roberts, "Review Essay: Gender, Consumption and Commodity Culture," American Historical Review 3 (June 1998), 817–44.

42. On Bernhardt in Canada, see Ramon Hathorn, Our Lady of the Snows: Sarah Bernhardt in Canada (New York: Peter Lang, 1996). On Bernhardt in Australia, see Corille Fraser, Come to Dazzle: Sarah Bernhardt's Australian Tour (Sydney: Currency, in association with the National Library of Australia, 1998). On the itinerary and repertory of Bernhardt's world tour, see Skinner, Madame Sarah, 281–83. The actress's luggage included forty-five crates of costumes; seventy-five trunks for her personal wardrobe, which included 250 pairs of shoes; a special trunk for perfumes, cosmetics, and makeup; and a chest containing a table and bed linens, including the five pillows on which she slept. Pronier, Une vie au théâtre (335–48), provides, albeit somewhat incompletely, the Bernhardt repertory for the tours as well as the Paris venues. The 1917–18 season was billed as the "Last Visit to America."

43. T. S. Eliot (1951), cited in Richard Anthony Baker, Marie Lloyd: Queen of the Music-halls (London: R. Hale, 1990), 28. When Lloyd was impersonating Bernhardt in 1902, Bernhardt was in London appearing at the Garrick Theatre, where the two met through Willie Clarkson, London's leading costumer and wigmaker. Of this meeting, Bernhardt remarked: "Now, the two great actresses are in the same theatre—but not upon the same stage. You, my dear, are the greatest living comedienne and I, Sarah Bernhardt, the greatest living tragedienne." Lloyd's Sunday News, cited ibid., 91. Lloyd is pictured as Bernhardt in the role of Izeyl; she performed Marguerite (from Faust), Sappho, and Prehistoric Woman on the same program. "The Revue at the Tivoli Music Hall," The Tatler, July 2, 1902, 28. The Parisian music-hall stars Jane May and Yvette Guilbert also had a go at Bernhardt: May imitated her as Hamlet (Ernest Short, Fifty Years of Vaudeville [London: Eyre and Spottiswoode, 1978], 159), while Guilbert satirized Bernhardt's thinness in the song "Le petit serpent de Sarah" (music

and lyrics by Léon Xanrof, Chansons parisiennes, no. 25 [Paris: G. Ondet, 1891], cited in Yvette Guilbert: Diseuse fin de siècle, exh. cat. [Paris: Bibliothèque Nationale de France, 1994]; see also Yvette Guilbert, La chanson de ma vie, mes mémoires [Paris: Grasset, 1927]).

44. Bernhardt would undoubtedly have known as well male impersonators—women who impersonated men—because they came to prominence in popular entertainment at the same time that she first played a breeches role in the late 1860s. Male impersonators like Vesta Tilley also showcased their legs, as Bernhardt did prominently in Le passant and in L'Aiglon thirty years later. For other Bernhardt impersonators, and transvestism in general, see Senelick, The Changing Room. See also Annemarie Bean, James V. Hatch, and Brooks McNamara, eds., Inside the Minstrel Mask: Readings in Nineteenth-Century Blackface Minstrelsy (Hanover, N.H.: Wesleyan University Press, 1996); and Laurence Senelick, "The Evolution of the Male Impersonator on the Nineteenth-Century Popular Stage," Essays in Theater 1, no. 1 (1982), 30–44.

45. "Martin Beck Offers Madame Sarah Bernhardt in Vaudeville," theater program, 1912, n.p., The New York Public Library for the Performing Arts.

46. Even on her first American tour, the criticism evoked by Bernhardt's sensual style of acting, and the content of a play like La dame aux camélias were held to be at odds with legitimate theater. See Patricia Marks, Sarah Bernhardt's First American Theatrical Tour, 1880–1881 (Jefferson, N.C.: McFarland, 2003).

47. Michael Denning goes so far as to say that "mass culture has won; there is nothing else." Denning, "The End of Mass Culture," in James Naremore and Patrick Brantlinger, eds., Modernity and Mass Culture (Bloomington: Indiana University Press, 1991), 257.

48. Unidentified clippings, Box 2, Sarah Bernhardt star clippings, Harvard Theatre Collection.

49. Cocteau has a glowing assessment of Bernhardt in the film La dame aux camélias: "At sixty, she acts the part of Marguerite Gautier. One is reminded of a famous Chinese

actor who said, at the same age, 'I'm beginning to play ingénues.' What actress will play the great amoureuses better than Sarah in this film? None. And when it is over, we find ourselves back in the modern life, like the diver who returns to the surface after having come face to face with a giant pink devilfish in tropic seas." Cocteau, Professional Secrets, 35–36.

50. These facts are substantiated by such reliable biographers as Skinner, in Madame Sarah, 317ff, and by Lysiane Bernhardt, the actress's granddaughter, in Sarah Bernhardt: Ma grand'mère (Paris: Éditions du Pavois, 1945), 337–42.

51. The Boston Herald, November 12, 1916.

52. Robert Grace, Boston Sunday Herald, June 13, 1915. Grace reversed the legs.

53. For testimonies to her indomitability during her last days, see David W. Menefee, Sarah Bernhardt in the Theatre of Films and Sound Recordings (Jefferson, N.C.: McFarland, 2003), 146–50.

54. Unidentified clipping, 1907, Box 2, Sarah Bernhardt star clippings, Harvard Theatre Collection. "Sarah Eats Shrimps," clipping from unidentified New York newspaper, 1912, Box 1, ibid.

55. Susan Sontag, "Notes on Camp" (1964), in Sontag, Against Interpretation and Other Essays (New York: Doubleday, 1966), 275–92. Quotations from this essay are from pages 285, 279, 277, and 287. On camp, see Pamela Robertson, Guilty Pleasures: Feminist Camp from Mae West to Madonna (Durham, N.C.: Duke University Press, 1996); Lesley Ferris, ed., Crossing the Stage: Controversies on Cross-Dressing (London: Routledge, 1993); David Bergman, ed., Camp Grounds: Style and Homosexuality (Amherst: University of Massachusetts Press, 1993); Moe Meyer, ed., The Politics and Poetics of Camp (London: Routledge, 1994); and Fabio Cleto, ed., Camp: Queer Aesthetics and the Performing Subject, a Reader (Ann Arbor: University of Michigan Press, 1999).

56. All but ten of Sontag's fifty-eight "jottings" on camp apply to Bernhardt at a much earlier stage of her career: among them, camp's intense love of artifice and exaggeration,

predilection for travesty and impersonation, emphasis on the force of personality, relation between parody and self-parody, and seriousness that cannot be taken altogether seriously because it is "too much." For a more extensive critique of Sontag, see my unpublished paper "Sarah Bernhardt Live" (see note 1, above), and an unpublished paper by Ann Pellegrini, "Notes on Jewish Camp" (c. 1997), courtesy the author.

57. Taranow, *Sarah Bernhardt*, provides the best discussion of voice, 3–82; for Hugo and *la voix d'or*, see 25. For Bernhardt audiography, from the unplayable tinfoil recording made in Edison's laboratory from 1880 to 1918, see ibid., 262–70. For filmography from 1900 to 1923, see ibid., 270–73.

58. On Brice, see Barbara W. Grossman, *Funny Woman: The Life and Times of Fanny Brice* (Bloomington: Indiana University Press, 1991).

59. See Richard Ellmann, *Oscar Wilde* (New York: Vintage, 1988), 371ff.

60. The major operas still in repertory are *Tosca* and *La traviata*; in her off-Broadway video *Without You I'm Nothing*, the comic Sandra Bernhard has herself repeatedly introduced as Sarah Bernhardt; Everett Quinton of the Ridiculous Theatrical Company starred as the Bernhardt-like Mimi London in the production *Call Me Sarah Bernhardt* (1996).

61. *Twentieth Century*: References to Bernhardt abound in this film about a Broadway Svengali figure, Oscar "O. J." Jaffe (John Barrymore), and his newest star, Lily Garland, aka Mildred Plotka (Carole Lombard), who manage their relationship though constant attempts to outdo each other overacting. In the opening scene, the stand-in director, Max Jacobs (Charles Lane) exclaims of Jaffe's newest protégée: "She's hopeless! And the worst of it is that Jaf is gonna blame me that a lingerie model hasn't turned out to be a Bernhardt." But after her first success, precisely as planned, Jaffe orders that a gold star be nailed to Garland's dressing room door, with the hushed pronouncement: "It once hung on Bernhardt's door. . . . I almost wish it weren't there. Why, it's the golden mark that henceforth sets you apart from anyone in the world, beyond the

reach of any one man to have and to hold." Boozy Owen O'Malley (Roscoe Karns) later greets Garland: "How's the baby Bernhardt?" and Jaffe, desperate to win her back after she's become a Hollywood star, instructs his confidants: "I just played a scene. Sardou might have written it," and "Tell her I'm dying. We're going to do this like the last act of *Camille*."

Portrait of Jennie: The painter Eben Adams (Joseph Cotten) meets Jennie Appleton (Jennifer Jones), a young woman whose parents, she says, are acrobats at Hammerstein's; but he knows the theater has been torn down years ago. Adams comes to discover that her story is true; over lunch, his Irish taxi-driver buddy (David Wayne) begins to read a newspaper in which Jennie has wrapped a scarf and exclaims, "Well, what do you know? Sarah Bernhardt's coming to America for a farewell tour!" "Sarah Bernhardt? Have you gone crazy?" replies Adams. But his friend continues: "Sarah Bernhardt, distinguished French tragedienne [which he mispronounces], arrives next month. Say, this paper's dated 1910." When Adams learns that Jennie's parents died when their high wire broke during a performance, he muses: "They knew they had something. But who do I think I am? Why should I believe that of all the thousands of struggling artists I'm the one who has something worth saying?"

Nancy Goes to Rio: After the author of the new play, in which Frances Elliot (Ann Sothern) is to act the lead, finds her too old for the role—"The part of Emily was intended for an eighteen-year-old"—he meets her daughter Nancy (Jane Powell). The impassioned speech she gives about young actors wins her the part: "They don't need big elaborate theaters and stars. . . . Maybe it's in a church or in a clubhouse or in a barn, but they're satisfied, and do you know why? Because it's the theater and it's theirs. They're not just people putting on plays in barns. They're the future of the theater, tomorrow's Oliviers and Bernhardts."

Star!: In this extravagant biopic, Gertrude Lawrence (Julie Andrews) begins her career in her father's song-and-dance act at a music hall. Infuriated by the tomato-throwing audience, Lawrence takes the show into her own hands. As they leave the stage, her father (Bruce

Forsyth) roundly scolds her: "You've only been in the profession two shakes of a donkey's tail! Who do you think you are—Sarah Bernhardt?"

Moulin Rouge!: The music-hall star Satine (Nicole Kidman) faints and falls from a trapeze. After coughing blood, the prelude to her death from consumption, she recovers and prepares for her rendezvous with the Duke: "With a patron like him you can be the next Sarah Bernhardt," her dresser remarks. As the camera cuts to a photograph of Bernhardt next to her dressing table, Satine replies: "Do you really think I could be like the great Sarah? . . . I'm going to be a real actress, Marie. A great actress."

Sarah Bernhardt and the Theatrics of French Nationalism

Author's note: Unless otherwise noted, translations in this essay are mine.

1. "The Symbolic Figure of Sarah Bernhardt at Three Score Years and Ten," clipping from unidentified magazine, January 1917, Harry Ransom Humanities Research Center, University of Texas at Austin. The anonymous author quotes a writer in the *Evening Mail*. I thank Carol Ockman for having shown me how I might contribute to the study of Sarah Bernhardt, a subject to which she herself has contributed so much, and for her sensitive editing of my text.

2. Henri Lavedan, "Courrier de Paris: Sarah," *L'illustration*, March 7, 1914, 170.

3. "Le 25 octobre 1844 / Ici naquit / Sarah Bernhardt / Gloire de notre Théâtre / Cette plaque a été apposée le 25 octobre 1944 par les soins de la Radiodiffusion Française, qui a porté ce jour-là le nom de Sarah Bernhardt à travers le monde, où Sarah Bernhardt porta si haut le nom de la France."

4. The first three possibilities are mentioned in Cornelia Otis Skinner, *Madame Sarah* (Cambridge, Mass.: Houghton Mifflin, 1967), 1; for the last, which is stated on Bernhardt's birth certificate, see essay by Carol Ockman in this volume, especially note 6, and Louis Verneuil, *The Fabulous Life of Sarah Bernhard*, trans. Ernest Boyd (New York and London: Harper and Brothers, 1942), 35.

5. Sarah Bernhardt, *My Double Life: The Memoirs of Sarah Bernhardt*, trans. Victoria Tietze Larson (Albany: State University of New York Press, 1999), 59.

6. Ibid.

7. Grasset made an earlier version of the poster, but Bernhardt apparently was upset by her coiffure, which she said resembled the "hair of a spaniel," and by her undergarment showing through beneath her cuirass. See William A. Emboden, *Sarah Bernhardt: Artist and Icon* (Irvine, Calif.: Severin Wunderman Museum, 1992), 82–83. The Bibliothèque Nationale de France, Paris, possesses both versions of the poster.

8. "Elle porte sur elle ce reflet de vitrail que les apparitions de saints ont laissé sur la belle illuminée de Domrémy." Cited in Noëlle Guibert, ed., *Portrait(s) de Sarah Bernhardt* (Paris: Bibliothèque Nationale de France, 2000), 44; English translation from Arthur Gold and Robert Fizdale, *The Divine Sarah: A Life of Sarah Bernhardt* (New York: Alfred A. Knopf, 1991), 244.

9. Cited in Stuart Jeffries, "Desperately Seeking Sarah," *The Guardian*, October 25, 2000; see http://www.guardian.co.uk/arts/story/0,3604,387 520,00.html. Bernhardt would play the great French heroine in another production, Émile Moreau's *Le procès de Jeanne d'Arc* (*The Trial of Joan of Arc*).

10. "On nous fit la lecture de la nouvelle pièce de Bornier, *La Fille de Roland*. Le rôle de Berthe me fut confié, et nous commençâmes de suite les répétitions de cette belle pièce, aux vers un peu plats, mais enveloppée d'un grand souffle patriotique." Sarah Bernhardt, *Ma double vie: Mémoires de Sarah Bernhardt* (Paris: Charpentier et Fasquelle, 1907), 351.

11. "La pièce eut un gros succès. . . . C'était peu de temps après la terrible guerre de 1870. La pièce contenait de fréquentes allusions. Et, grâce au chauvinisme du public, elle eut une carrière plus belle que ne le méritait l'oeuvre en elle-même." Ibid., 353.

12. Bernhardt, *My Double Life*, 101.

13. See Bernhardt's letter to the journalist Jean-Baptiste-Benoît Jouvin, of Le Figaro, translated in Skinner, *Madame Sarah*, 99.

14. "Emperor Napoléon III whom I very much liked." Bernhardt, *My Double Life*, 192.

15. Gold and Fizdale, *The Divine Sarah*, 13.

16. Bernhardt, *My Double Life*, 101.

17. Ibid., 113.

18. Ibid., 99–100.

19. Ibid., 251.

20. Cited in Susan A. Glenn, *Female Spectacle: The Theatrical Roots of Modern Feminism* (Cambridge, Mass.: Harvard University Press, 2000), 31. A number of important studies in the past decade place Bernhardt in the context of nineteenth-century anti-Semitism, including Carol Ockman, "When Is a Jewish Star Just a Star? Interpreting Images of Sarah Bernhardt," and Sander L. Gilman, "Salome, Syphilis, Sarah Bernhardt, and the Modern Jewess," both in Linda Nochlin and Tamar Garb, eds., *The Jew in the Text: Modernity and the Construction of Identity* (New York: Thames and Hudson, 1995), 121–39 and 97–120; and Janis Bergman-Carton, "Negotiating the Categories: Sarah Bernhardt and the Possibilities of Jewishness," *Art Journal* 55, no. 2 (Summer 1996), 55–63.

21. Interview in Le Figaro (October 1890), cited in Robert Horville, "The Stage Techniques of Sarah Bernhardt," in Eric Salmon, ed. *Bernhardt and the Theatre of Her Time* (Westport, Conn.: Greenwood, 1984), 49.

22. Cited in Jules Huret, *Sarah Bernhardt*, trans. G. A. Raper (London: Chapman and Hall, 1899), 37–38; see also Glenn, *Female Spectacle*, 31.

23. "Je casai ma grand'mère dans une maison de retraite. . . . Ma grand'mère était israélite et exécutait strictement et fidèlement les lois de sa religion." Bernhardt, *Ma double vie*, 197. Bernhardt, probably intentionally, complicates the matter of her ancestry and that of her grandmother (190): "Ma mère n'aimait pas cette femme, qui avait epousé mon grand-père alors qu'il avait déjà six grands enfants. . . . Cette seconde femme n'avait jamais eu d'enfants." Was this her grandmother or her step-grandmother? Does she mean that "this woman" had no children until she gave birth to Sarah's mother? Surely Bernhardt was being intentionally unclear on these and related points.

24. Marcel Proust to Robert de Montesquiou, [May 1896], *Marcel Proust: Selected Letters in English, 1880–1903*, ed. Philip Kolb, trans. Ralph Manheim (New York: Doubleday, 1983), vol. 1, 121.

25. Verneuil, *The Fabulous Life of Sarah Bernhardt*, 34. Verneuil was briefly married to Bernhardt's granddaughter.

26. Bernhardt, *My Double Life*, 13.

27. Marcel Proust, *Swann's Way*, vol. 1 of *In Search of Lost Time*, trans. C. K. Scott Moncrieff and Terence Kilmartin, rev. D. J. Enright (London: Chatto and Windus, 1992), 68.

28. In *La prisonnière* (*The Captive*), the narrator says: "Then she would find her tongue and say: 'My ——' or 'My darling ——' followed by my Christian name, which, if we give the narrator the same name as the author of this book, would be 'My Marcel,' or 'My darling Marcel.'" *The Captive*, vol. 3 of *Remembrance of Things Past* (*À la recherche du temps perdu*), trans. C. K. Scott Moncrieff, Terence Kilmartin, and Andreas Mayor (New York: Vintage, 1982), 69.

29. Reynaldo Hahn, *La grande Sarah: Souvenirs* (Paris: Hachette, 1930).

30. On Montesquiou, see Philippe Jullian, *Prince of Aesthetes: Count Robert de Montesquiou, 1855–1921*, trans. John Haylock and Francis King (New York: Viking, 1968); and Philippe Thiébaut and Jean-Michel Nectoux, *Robert de Montesquiou* (Paris: Réunion des Musées Nationaux, 1999).

31. Proust boasts of having magically turned the tables on Haas in *The Captive*, so that Haas's posterity is indebted to a young man he hardly took seriously: "And yet, my dear Charles ——, whom I used to know when I was still so young and you were nearing your grave, it is because he whom you must have regarded as a young idiot has made you the hero of one of his novels that people are beginning to speak of you again and that your name will perhaps live." Proust, *The Captive*, 199. It seems clear that Haas was the most important model for Swann, although, like all fictional characters, he is a product of the

imagination. Among the other real-life precedents for Swann, the rich and cultivated financier Charles Ephrussi is usually also mentioned, although Jean-Yves Tadié discounts this possibility, saying that he was neither handsome nor a dandy. See Tadié, *Marcel Proust*, trans. Euan Cameron (New York: Viking, 1996), 324.

The literature on Proust and Jewishness is considerable. See, for example, Albert Sonnenfeld, "Marcel Proust: Antisemite?" in Mary Ann Caws and Eugéne Nicole, eds., *Reading Proust Now* (New York: Peter Lang, 1990), 223–54; and Jonathan Freedman, "Coming out of the Jewish Closet with Marcel Proust," in Daniel Boyarin, ed., *Queer Theory and the Jewish Question* (New York: Columbia University Press, 2003), 334–64.

32. Proust, *Swann's Way* (*Du côté de chez Swann*), trans. C. K. Scott Moncrieff and Terence Kilmartin (New York: Random House, 1981), 80.

33. Proust, *Within a Budding Grove* (*À l'ombre des jeunes filles en fleurs*), trans. C. K. Scott Moncrieff and Terence Kilmartin (New York: Random House, 1981), 603.

34. Proust, *Swann's Way*, 219.

35. See Tadié, *Marcel Proust*, 300.

36. Translation from Gold and Fizdale, *The Divine Sarah*, 277; for the original French, which is preserved in the Department of Manuscripts at the Bibliothèque Nationale de France, Paris, see Guibert, *Portrait(s) de Sarah Bernhardt*, 96. Bernhardt also wrote to Dreyfus at the time of his final exoneration, on June 6, 1908: see Michael Burns, *France and the Dreyfus Affair: A Documentary History* (Boston: Bedford/St. Martin's, 1999), 180.

37. Michael Burns, *Dreyfus: A Family Affair, 1789–1945* (New York: HarperCollins, 1991), 150.

38. Ibid., 516 n. 29. Verneuil, in *The Fabulous Life of Sarah Bernhardt* (207), says that Bernhardt was among the "few privileged persons who had been present at the degradation of Captain Dreyfus."

39. Verneuil, *The Fabulous Life of Sarah Bernhardt*, 221.

40. Ibid., 222–23.

41. "No doubt Gilberte did not always go so far as when she insinuated that she was perhaps the natural daughter of some great personage; but as a rule she concealed her origins." Proust, *The Fugitive* (*Albertine disparue*), trans. C. K. Scott Moncrieff, Terence Kilmartin, and Andreas Mayor (New York: Vintage, 1982), 598.

42. Ibid., 674.

43. Lysiane Bernhardt, cited in Ruth Brandon, *Being Divine: A Biography of Sarah Bernhardt* (London: Mandarin, 1992), 356.

44. Gold and Fizdale, *Divine Sarah*, 275.

45. Maurice Baring, *Sarah Bernhardt* (New York: D. Appleton-Century, 1940), 138–39.

46. "Grand Dieu! Ce n'est pas une cause / Que j'attaque ou que je défends . . . / Et ceci n'est pas autre chose / Que l'histoire d'un pauvre enfant." These lines, which Rostand placed at the front of his published version of *L'Aiglon*, were added at the suggestion of the socialist leader Jean Jaurès, to avoid the play's political recuperation by the French right, according to Patrick Besnier, ed., Edmond Rostand, *L'Aiglon* (Paris: Gallimard, 1986), 414.

47. It is unclear to what extent Poiret contributed to the costume design for the Duke of Reichstadt in *L'Aiglon*. Palmer White says that he designed the famous white uniform but that a rude remark he made during a rehearsal led Bernhardt to demand that Poiret's employer, Jacques Doucet, fire him, which White says he did; see White, *Poiret le magnifique* (Paris: Payot, 1986), 47. Yvonne Deslandres says he was "charged with creating the costumes for Sarah Bernhardt in *L'Aiglon*" but was dismissed because of an arrogant remark; see Deslandres with Dorothée Lalanne, *Poiret: Paul Poiret, 1879–1944* (New York: Rizzoli, 1986), 36.

48. Edmond Rostand, *L'Aiglon*, trans. Louis N. Parker (New York: Harper and Brothers, 1900), act 3, 136.

49. Besnier, Edmond Rostand, *L'Aiglon*, 12.

50. Rostand, *L'Aiglon*, act 2, 113.

51. Ibid., act 2, 117.

52. Bernhardt always respected the repetition principle of fame, that is, that the more often something is repeated, the more ingrained it becomes in the mind of the public. It was reported in 1912 that having collected the money coin by coin each night at the Théâtre Sarah Bernhardt, she was donating twenty thousand francs to French military aviation to finance an airplane, which she wanted christened with "the beautiful name of Aiglon": "Mme Sarah Bernhardt vient de remettre pour l'aviation militaire une somme de 20,000 francs qu'elle a recueillie pièce par pièce en tendant la main chaque soir à ses spectateurs. L'oiseau qu'elle donne ainsi à la France portera, sur son désir, le beau nom d'Aiglon." "Une grande artiste patriote," *Dimanche illustré*, April 21, 1912, 11.

53. See Elisabeth Roudinesco, *Théroigne de Méricourt: A Melancholic Woman during the French Revolution*, trans. Martin Thom (London: Verso, 1991), 225–27.

54. Georges Lenotre was the pseudonym of Théodore Gosselin.

55. Bernhardt, *My Double Life*, 230–321.

56. Proust, *Time Regained* (*Le temps retrouvé*), trans. C. K. Scott Moncrieff, Terence Kilmartin, and Andreas Mayor (New York: Vintage, 1982), 854–55.

57. Ibid., 917.

58. Skinner, *Madame Sarah*, 320.

59. For Bernhardt's films, see David W. Menefee, *Sarah Bernhardt in the Theatre of Films and Sound Recordings* (Jefferson, N.C.: McFarland, 2003); and Victoria Duckett, "Sarah Bernhardt et le cinéma muet," in Guibert, *Portrait(s) de Sarah Bernhardt*, 182–96.

60. "We opened at the Palace in 1919 in a one act playlet called 'The Field of Honor,' written under the anonymous cloak of a nom de plume by Madame Bernhardt herself." Suzanne Caubaye, "The Golden Leg of Sarah Bernhardt," in program for *Sweet Charity* (New York: Palace Theater, 1966), 5.

61. "Bernhardt Has Spirit of France / Noted Actress Receives Ovation at Vendôme / Her Greatness Undimmed / Audience Aroused to Unbounded Enthusiasm by War Playlet,"

Nashville *Tennessean*, February 9, 1917. Julia Rather, at the State of Tennessee Archives, Nashville, communicated this anonymous article to Danielle Chamaillard, in the Department of the Arts du Spectacle of the Bibliothèque Nationale de France, Paris, who passed it on to me.

"A Vision of a Stained Glass Sarah"

Author's note: Unless noted otherwise, translations in this essay are mine. I am indebted to Carol Ockman and Kenneth E. Silver for informing me about their discovery of important decorative objects that are illustrated and discussed in this essay.

Epigraph: Helen Ten Broeck, "Bernhardt's Vision of Victory," *Theater*, September 1917, 150.

1. See Arthur Gold and Robert Fizdale, *The Divine Sarah: A Life of Sarah Bernhardt* (New York: Alfred A. Knopf, 1991), chap. 4.

2. See "Sarah Bernhardt par Gustave Kahn, Saint-Pol-Roux, Robert de Montesquiou . . . ," *La plume*, nos. 274 and 276 (September and October 1900).

3. The collaborations between Bernhardt and Mucha, particularly on theater posters, are among the most enduring expressions of the Art Nouveau aesthetic. They assimilate her trademark silhouette, the spiraling line she cultivated in clothing design, and the deportment of her body—what the writer Jean Lorrain called "a veritable arabesque." Her early establishment and imprint of that silhouette anticipate the design motif recurrent in Mucha's work and closely associated with Art Nouveau, the sinuous S-shaped curve.

4. Bernhardt left the Comédie Française, for the second time but on her own initiative, in 1880.

5. See Mary Louise Roberts, *Disruptive Acts: The New Woman in Fin-de-Siècle France* (Chicago: University of Chicago Press, 2002), 22.

6. See Debora L. Silverman, *Art Nouveau in Fin-de-Siècle France: Politics, Psychology, and Style* (Berkeley: University of California Press, 1989), 52–74.

7. Ibid., 1–42.

8. For discussions of the growing symbiosis in the nineteenth century among advanced art, commerce, and the mass press, and the myth of misunderstood genius it generated, see Martha Ward, "From Art Criticism to Art News: Journalistic Reviewing in Late-Nineteenth-Century Paris," and Dario Gamboni, "The Relative Autonomy of Art Criticism," both in Michael R. Orwicz, ed., *Art Criticism and Its Institutions in Nineteenth-Century France* (Manchester: Manchester University Press, 1994), 162–81 and 182–94; Nicolas Green, *The Spectacle of Nature: Landscape and Bourgeois Culture in Nineteenth-Century France* (Manchester: Manchester University Press, 1993); and Robert Jenson, *Marketing Modernism in Fin-de-Siècle Europe* (Princeton, N.J.: Princeton University Press, 1994). See also Malcolm Gee, "The Avant-Garde, Order and the Art Market, 1916–23," *Art History* 2, no. 1 (March 1979), 95–106.

9. The late-nineteenth-century impulse to encourage collaborations between the so-called fine arts and applied arts was international, strongly influenced by the theories of John Ruskin and William Morris's Arts and Crafts Movement. Despite the initial success, vitality, and diversity of the various artists, state administrators, critics, dealers, and museum personnel engaged in projects in the 1890s—a community that included Julius Meier-Graefe, Henry Van de Velde, Siegfried Bing, and Edmond and Jules de Goncourt—these movements increasingly abandoned the decorative arts in favor of modernist painting and sculpture, capitulating to xenophobic critiques that these arts were subject to dangerous foreign infiltration. See Jenson, *Marketing Modernism in Fin-de-Siècle Europe*; and Nancy Troy, *Modernism and the Decorative Arts in France: Art Nouveau to Le Corbusier* (New Haven and London: Yale University Press, 1991).

10. France's craft initiative was stimulated by the mid-century displays of British superiority in organizing the Universal Expositions. It began with the formation, in the 1860s, of the Central Union of Fine Arts Applied to Industry, whose purpose was to challenge the hierarchical valuing of the fine arts over the decorative arts as institutionalized after the Revolution. The craft initiative emphasized the restoration of rococo grace and unity of the arts. See Silverman, *Art Nouveau in Fin-de-Siècle France*, 138–39, 189–95.

11. As cited in Gold and Fizdale, *The Divine Sarah*, 67.

12. As cited in Ruth Brandon, *Being Divine: A Biography of Sarah Bernhardt* (London: Secker and Warburg, 1991), 175.

13. Rosalind Williams, *Dream Worlds: Mass Consumption in Late Nineteenth-Century France* (Berkeley: University of California Press, 1982), 64–72.

14. Cited in Roberts, *Disruptive Acts*, 226.

15. As cited in Brandon, *Being Divine*, 346.

16. See Sarah Bernhardt, *In the Clouds*, trans. Mariana Fitzpatrick, repr. in *The Memoirs of Sarah Bernhardt*, ed. and trans. Sandy Lesberg (New York: Peebles, 1977).

17. Ibid., 211.

18. Ibid., 252.

19. The bat motif may have been used to promote Bernhardt's revival of Octave Feuillet's *Le Sphynx* in 1880; in the play, which she had done at the Comédie seven years earlier, she had been cast in the role of Berthe de Savigny, secondary to the female lead, Le Sphynx, Blanche de Chelles, played by her rival Sophie Croizette. Though Bernhardt turned this minor role into a major triumph in 1873, she was eager to lay claim to what she believed was her rightful place as female lead. In 1880, when she launched her first tour as an independent agent in the United States and Canada, she included *Le Sphynx* among the eight plays in her company's repertory. This time she took the role of Blanche de Chelles, of whom it is said in the play's opening act: "Every woman is an enigma, and she, more than any other, has the right to take the sphinx as a symbol." Bernhardt seems to have done just that, in the bronze *Self-Portrait as a Sphinx*, which she produced that year and distributed among her friends in copies.

The motif of the bat was important in the decor of her good friend Robert de Montesquiou, in his apartment on the quai d'Orsay; bats provided the theme—indeed, the title—of his book of poetry Les chauves-souris (1892). The theme derived some of its popularity from the Vienna premiere in 1874 of Johann Strauss, Jr.'s Die Fledermaus, an opera based partly on the French vaudeville play Le reveillon, by Henri Meilhac and Ludovic Halévy. See Louis Verneuil, The Fabulous Life of Sarah Bernhardt, trans. Ernest Boyd (New York and London: Harper and Brothers, 1942), 94–97.

20. Charles Frederick Worth, the Englishman who redefined haute couture, was, like Bernhardt, a brilliant entrepreneur. The success of his Paris-based fashion house owed as much to the popularity of the theater as theater did to the popularity of fashion. Paris was the nineteenth-century capital of the fashion industry, and actresses were key signposts for new fashions; their costumes were discussed at length in the press. Bernhardt participated actively in the symbiotic relationship between the fashion and theater industries. Couturiers such as Worth came to exercise so much influence in the theater that Eugène Scribe, Victorien Sardou, and other dramatists deferred to him on the question of what his actress clients would wear in their plays.

Bernhardt's dissemination of her image in the Worth design kept her second career as sculptor in play. The atelier ensemble may also connect Bernhardt with another icon of art and theater, the commedia dell'arte's Pierrot, a role she herself performed in 1883 (see Chronology). The white pants and overshirt, and the oversize neck ruffle, recall the best loved of the commedia's stock characters. As a theatrical performer associated with a troupe renowned for its subversive challenges to official culture, Pierrot would have been a logical alter ego for Bernhardt—as he was and has continued to be for a succession of modern visual artists. Moreover, he suggested a historical convention that, like Bernhardt, conflated visual artist and actor with work of art.

21. The details of the narrator's life recall the stories of Bernhardt's dangerously fragile health as a young woman, her mother's indifference, and her "rescue" by various surrogates.

22. Bernhardt, The Memoirs of Sarah Bernhardt, 7–29.

23. Lysiane Bernhardt, Sarah Bernhardt, My Grandmother, trans. Vyvyan Holland (London: Hurst and Blackett, 1949), 47.

24. Alberty [pseud.], "Sarah Bernhardt: La veille d'une première," Le Figaro, October 9, 1894, 23.

25. Bernhardt, Sarah Bernhardt, My Grandmother, 71.

26. Roberts, Disruptive Acts, 226.

27. See Williams, Dream Worlds, 64–72.

28. In France, the second, more familiar phase of "Art Nouveau" dates to the 1890s and marks a retreat from the public spaces of the first phase as a response, in part, to the failures of the Third Republic's laissez-faire capitalism. It signals the economic and aesthetic reorientation of the French craft initiative from its original emphasis on industrial technology to the luxury trades.

29. See Paul Greenhalgh, ed., Art Nouveau: 1890–1914 (New York: Harry N. Abrams, 2000).

30. Matthew White, Jr., "The Queen of the French Stage," Munsey's, December 1895, 321, 324. See also Janis Bergman-Carton, "Negotiating the Categories: Sarah Bernhardt and the Possibilities of Jewishness," Art Journal 55, no. 2 (Summer 1996), 55–65; and Carol Ockman, "When Is a Jewish Star Just a Star? Interpreting Images of Sarah Bernhardt," in Linda Nochlin and Tamar Garb, eds., The Jew in the Text: Modernity and the Construction of Identity (London: Thames and Hudson, 1995), 121–39.

31. See Roberts, Disruptive Acts, 224–25.

32. As cited in Kenneth Silver, "The Other Fin-de-Siècle," Art in America 75, no. 12 (December 1987), 110.

33. Ibid., 104–11. For a broader discussion of the nationalistic, and specifically anti-Semitic, environment in which fin-de-siècle decorative arts movements were diminished, and the historiographical consequences, see Jenson, Marketing Modernism in Fin-de-Siècle Europe, chap. 8.

34. Roberts, Disruptive Acts, 207.

35. For a discussion of the cult of interior decoration as a form of self-expression, and late-nineteenth-century imagery in which the body is visually and symbolically integrated in a domestic space, see Susan Sidlauskas, Body, Place, and Self in Nineteenth-Century Painting (Cambridge: Cambridge University Press, 2000), 13–19.

36. Lisa Tiersten, "The Chic Interior and the Feminine Modern: Home Decorating as High Art in Turn-of-the-Century Paris," in Christopher Reed, ed., Not at Home: The Suppression of Domesticity in Modern Art and Architecture (London: Thames and Hudson, 1996), 18–20.

37. The 1870s and 1880s saw the beginnings of reform in women's education; the reestablishment of the right to divorce, a right suppressed since 1816; and the liberalization of laws that made possible the explosion of a mass-circulation press that counted many more female voices.

38. Roberts, Disruptive Acts, 167–68.

39. See, for instance, Victor Prouvé's portrait of the glassmaker Émile Gallé (1892; Musée de l'École de Nancy, France).

40. As cited in Laurence Senelick, "Chekhov's Response to Bernhardt," in Eric Salmon, ed., Bernhardt and the Theatre of Her Time (Westport, Conn.: Greenwood, 1984), 168. The comparison between a woman and a decorative art object, such as the statuette, was common in late-nineteenth-century literature and the literature of home decoration. The metaphor was employed in characterizations of the female statuette, by Joris-Karl Huysmans and other decadent writers, as a kind of sexual surrogate, an object to caress and rub against, which, unlike a living woman, could neither resist nor express its own desires. In the discourse of home decoration and decorative arts reform, women frequently were characterized as aesthetic consumers whose selection and arrangement of decorative objects for the home was an extension of their self-adornment rather than a creative act. See Jules Claretie, "La Femme," L'art de la mode 1, no. 4 (November 1880), 91.

41. Roberts, Disruptive Acts, 221–28; Gold and Fizdale, The Divine Sarah, 288.

42. The popularity of Mary Magdalene in

French art and literature throughout the nineteenth century is usually attributed to the saint's embodiment of the carnal and the sacred. That popularity is suggested by the cult of copies of Antonio Canova's sculpture of the *Penitent Magdalene* (c. 1794–96), frequently mentioned as the inspiration for private rituals in the 1800s. The writer Delphine de Girardin describes a party held during the Carnival season of 1844 whose climax was a ceremonial trip through the darkened galleries of a private home to a small room in which a copy of Canova's work had been kept secluded in preparation for this moment of "rebirth." Delphine de Girardin, "Lettres parisiennes (26 février 1844)," in *Oeuvres complètes de madame Émile de Girardin, née Delphine Gay* (Paris: H. Plon, 1860–61), vol. 5, 224.

43. Acting was considered a disreputable profession; Jean-Jacques Rousseau's *Lettre à d'Alembert sur les spectacles* (Letter to d'Alembert on the Theater; 1758) only reinforced that view. Because she depended on the arts of deceit and duplicity, Rousseau argued, the actress, already skilled in artifice as a woman, was doubly dangerous.

44. As cited in Gold and Fizdale, *The Divine Sarah*, 266–67.

The Divine Sarah and the Infernal Sally

Author's note: Where possible, original publishing information is provided for passages quoted here from secondary sources.

Epigraph: Cited in Arthur Gold and Robert Fizdale, *The Divine Sarah: A Life of Sarah Bernhardt* (New York: Alfred A. Knopf, 1991), 198.

1. Oscar Wilde, review in *The Times* (London), March 2, 1893; reprinted in *Complete Works of Oscar Wilde*, vol. 10: *Miscellanies*, ed. Robert Ross (Boston: Wyman-Fogg, 1905–9), 170; cited in Gerda Taranow, *Sarah Bernhardt: The Art within the Legend* (Princeton, N.J.: Princeton University Press, 1972), 201.

2. Henry James, "The Comédie Française in London," *The Nation*, July 31, 1879; reprinted in Henry James, *The Scenic Art: Notes on Acting and the Drama, 1872–1901*, ed. Allan Wade (New Brunswick, N.J.: Rutgers University Press, 1948), 128–29.

3. James, *The Scenic Art*, 129.

4. Cited in Basil Woon (from material supplied by Madame Pierre Berton), *The Real Sarah Bernhardt, Whom Her Audiences Never Knew* (New York: Boni and Liveright, 1924), 173; cited in Gamaliel Bradford, *Daughters of Eve* (Boston: Houghton Mifflin, 1930; repr., Port Washington, N.Y.: Kennikat, 1969), 254.

5. Cited in Maurice Baring, *Sarah Bernhardt* (New York: D. Appleton-Century, 1934), 30.

6. See Carol Armstrong, *Odd Man Out: Readings of the Work and Reputation of Edgar Degas* (Chicago: University of Chicago Press, 1991), 54, 257 n. 47.

7. See Robert L. Herbert, *Impressionism: Art, Leisure, and Parisian Society* (New Haven and London: Yale University Press, 1988), 103–14.

8. Cited in Gold and Fizdale, *The Divine Sarah*, 3.

9. Cited in Sheridan Morley, *The Quotable Oscar Wilde* (Philadelphia: Running Press, 2000).

10. Cited in Gold and Fizdale, *The Divine Sarah*, 3–4.

11. Henri Fouquier, *Le Figaro*, January 28, 1894; cited in Heather McPherson, *The Modern Portrait in Nineteenth-Century France* (Cambridge: Cambridge University Press, 2000), 77.

12. Théodore de Banville, *La lanterne magique* (Paris: G. Charpentier, 1883), 313; cited in McPherson, *The Modern Portrait in Nineteenth-Century France*, 79.

13. Francisque Sarcey, *Quarante ans de théâtre (Feuilletons dramatiques)* (Paris: Bibliothèque des Annales Politiques et Littéraires, 1900–1902), vol. 3, 230; cited in Baring, *Sarah Bernhardt*, 99.

14. Fanny Fair, *New York Telegram*, December 1905, 6; cited in Susan A. Glenn, *Female Spectacle: The Theatrical Roots of Modern Feminism* (Cambridge, Mass.: Harvard University Press, 2000), 37–38.

15. Lytton Strachey, "Sarah Bernhardt," *Century Magazine* 106 (July 1923), 470.

16. Jules Lemaître, *Les contemporains: Études et portraits littéraires* (Paris: H. Lecène et H. Oudin, 1886–87), vol. 2, 209; cited in Baring, *Sarah Bernhardt*, 125–26.

17. Alice B. Toklas, *What Is Remembered* (New York: Holt, Rinehart and Winston, 1963), 23; cited in Ruth Brandon, *Being Divine: A Biography of Sarah Bernhardt* (London: Secker and Warburg, 1991), 345.

18. Sigmund Freud to Martha Bernays, November 8, 1885; cited in Gold and Fizdale, *The Divine Sarah*, 4.

19. Freud to Bernays, November 8, 1885; this additional portion of the letter is cited in Ann Pellegrini, *Performance Anxieties: Staging Psychoanalysis, Staging Race* (New York: Routledge, 1997), 39–40.

20. *Chicago Record-Herald*, December 10, 1905; cited in Carol Ockman, "Dying Nightly: Sarah Bernhardt Plays the Orient," unpublished paper presented in *The Oriental Mirage: Orientalism in Context*, a symposium cosponsored by the Art Gallery of New South Wales, the Centre for Cross-Cultural Research, and the Australian National University, February 14, 1998, 7.

21. Alan Dale, "Sarah's Amazing Rejuvenation," July 16, 1904; cited in Glenn, *Female Spectacle*, 21.

22. Cited in Jane Abdy, "Sarah Bernhardt and Lalique: A Confusion of Evidence," *Apollo* 125, no. 303 (May 1987), 325.

23. Edward Burne-Jones to Graham Robertson; cited in Gold and Fizdale, *The Divine Sarah*, 239.

24. Luce Dalrue [Lucie Delarue-Mardrus], "Avant la première," *La fronde*, December 15, 1897; cited in Mary Louise Roberts, *Disruptive Acts: The New Woman in Fin-de-Siècle France* (Chicago: University of Chicago Press, 2002), 166–67.

25. Dame Ellen Terry, "The Story of My Life: The Glory of Sarah Bernhardt," *John O'London's Weekly*, January 14, 1928, 509.

26. George Jean Nathan, "The Divine Sarah and the Infernal Sally," *Smart Set* 33, no. 2 (February 1911), 157.

27. Ibid., 157–58.

28. Henry James, *The Tragic Muse*; cited in Glenn, *Female Spectacle*, 28–29.

29. *Professional Secrets: An Autobiography of Jean Cocteau, Drawn from His Lifetime Writings*, ed. Robert Phelps, trans. Richard Howard (New York: Farrar, Straus and Giroux, 1970), 35–36.

30. Cited in Roberts, *Disruptive Acts*, 203.

31. François Bournand and Raphaël Viau, *Les femmes d'Israël* (Paris: A. Pierret, 1898), 221; cited in Janis Bergman-Carton, "Negotiating the Categories: Sarah Bernhardt and the Possibilities of Jewishness," *Art Journal* 55, no. 2 (Summer 1996), 55.

32. Cited in Bergman-Carton, "Negotiating the Categories," 59; Glenn, *Female Spectacle*, 32.

33. Ernest Lys, "Sarah Bernhardt dans Jeanne d'Arc," *Gil Blas*, December 6, 1889; cited in Roberts, *Disruptive Acts*, 204.

34. Una Vincenzo, Lady Troubridge, "Hero-Worship" (unpublished essay); cited in Michael Baker, *Our Three Selves: The Life of Radclyffe Hall* (New York: William Morrow, 1985), 63. See also Martha Vicinus, "Turn-of-the-Century Male Impersonation: Rewriting the Roman Plot," in Andrew H. Miller and James Eli Adams, eds., *Sexualities in Victorian Britain* (Bloomington: Indiana University Press, 1996), 199.

35. Anatole Leroy-Beaulieu, *Israel among the Nations: A Study of the Jews and Antisemitism*, trans. Frances Hellman (New York: G. P. Putnam's Sons, 1895), 105; cited in Sander L. Gilman, "Salome, Syphilis, Sarah Bernhardt, and the Modern Jewess," in Linda Nochlin and Tamar Garb, eds., *The Jew in the Text: Modernity and the Construction of Identity* (London: Thames and Hudson, 1995), 111.

36. See Carol Ockman, "When Is a Jewish Star Just a Star? Interpreting Images of Sarah Bernhardt," in Nochlin and Garb, *The Jew in the Text*, 121–39.

37. Marie Colombier, *Les mémoires de Sarah Barnum* (Paris: Tous les libraires, 1883), 27, 57, 85, 142, 66; see Ockman, "When Is a Jewish Star Just a Star?" 127–28.

38. Obituary, *The Times* (London), March 28, 1923; cited in Pellegrini, *Performance Anxieties*, 41.

39. Daniel Lesueur, "Prêtresse de la beauté," *La fronde*, January 28, 1898; cited in Roberts, *Disruptive Acts*, 165.

40. Cited in Robert Horville, "The Stage Techniques of Sarah Bernhardt," in Eric Salmon, ed., *Bernhardt and the Theatre of Her Time* (Westport, Conn.: Greenwood, 1984), 51.

41. Cited in Gold and Fizdale, *The Divine Sarah*, 259.

42. *The Collected Letters of D. H. Lawrence*, ed. Harry T. Moore (New York: Viking, 1962), 17.

43. Cited in Carol Ockman, "Death and the Icon: Sarah Bernhardt's Nine Farewell Tours of America," in Christopher Balme, Robert Erenstein, and Cesare Molinari, eds., *European Theatre Iconography: Proceedings of the European Science Foundation Network* (Rome: Bulzoni, 2002), 21.

44. "Bernhardt's Banquet," *Puck*, October 27, 1880, 122; cited in Patricia Marks, *Sarah Bernhardt's First American Theatrical Tour, 1880–1881* (Jefferson, N.C.: McFarland, 2003), 31–32.

45. Henry Wadsworth Longfellow to G. W. Greene, April 3, 1881, *The Letters of Henry Wadsworth Longfellow, 1807–1882*, ed. Andrew Hilen (Cambridge, Mass.: Harvard University Press, 1966–72), vol. 4, 299; cited in Marks, *Sarah Bernhardt's First American Theatrical Tour, 1880–1881*, 69.

46. Jules Lemaître, "Madame Sarah Bernhardt," in *Literary Impressions*, trans. A. W. Evans (London: D. O'Connor, 1921; repr., Port Washington, N.Y.: Kennikat, 1971), 283–84.

47. Cited in Laurence Senelick, "Chekhov's Response to Bernhardt," in Salmon, *Bernhardt and the Theatre of Her Time*, 173.

48. Cited in Gail Marshall, *Actresses on the Victorian Stage: Feminine Performance and the Galatea Myth* (Cambridge: Cambridge University Press, 1998), 149.

49. Cited in Joanna Richardson, *Sarah Bernhardt and Her World* (New York: G. P. Putnam's Sons, 1977), 80.

50. Arsène Houssaye, *Les confessions: Souvenirs d'un demi-siècle, 1830–1880* (Paris: E. Dentu, 1885–91), vol. 4, 403; cited in Bradford, *Daughters of Eve*, 261.

51. Pierre Véron, "Monsieur Sarah Bernhardt," *Les coulisses artistiques* (Paris: E. Dentu, 1876), 131; cited in Roberts, *Disruptive Acts*, 173.

52. Cited in Gold and Fizdale, *The Divine Sarah*, 135–36.

53. Cited in Cornelia Otis Skinner, *Madame Sarah* (Boston: Houghton Mifflin, 1967), 98.

54. Cited ibid., 97.

55. Graham Robertson, "On the Death of Sarah Bernhardt, 1923," in *Letters from Graham Robertson*, ed. Kerrison Preston (London: H. Hamilton, 1953), 104.

Bernhardt in the New World

Epigraph: Sarah Bernhardt, *My Double Life: The Memoirs of Sarah Bernhardt*, trans. Victoria Tietze Larson (Albany: State University of New York Press, 1999), 251.

1. *Philadelphia Bulletin*, October 28 and 30, 1880; cited in Patricia Marks, *Sarah Bernhardt's First American Theatrical Tour, 1880–1881* (Jefferson, N.C.: McFarland, 2003), 24.

Bibliography

Printed Materials

Abdy, Jane. "Sarah Bernhardt and Lalique: A Confusion of Evidence." Apollo 117 (May 1987), 325–30.

———. Sarah Bernhardt, 1844–1923. London: Ferrers Art Gallery, 1973.

———. "Sarah Bernhardt's Role as a Sculptress." Christie's Review of the Year (1986).

Arwas, Victor, et al. Alphonse Mucha: The Spirit of Art Nouveau. Alexandria, Va.: Art Services International and Yale University Press, 1998.

Balk, Claudia. Theatergöttinen: Inszenierte Weiblichkeit—Clara Ziegler, Sarah Bernhardt, Eleonora Duse. Frankfurt: Stroemfeld/ Roter Stern, 1994.

Baring, Maurice. Sarah Bernhardt. New York: D. Appleton-Century, 1940.

Beerbohm, Max. Around Theatres. New York: Greenwood, 1930.

Bergman-Carton, Janis. "Negotiating the Categories: Sarah Bernhardt and the Possibilities of Jewishness." Art Journal 55, no. 2 (Summer 1996), 55–64.

Bernhardt, Lysiane. Sarah Bernhardt, My Grandmother. Trans. Vyvyan Holland. London: Hurst and Blackett, 1949.

Bernhardt, Sarah. L'art du théâtre. Monaco: Sauret, 1993.

———. The Art of the Theatre. Trans. H. J. Stenning. Freeport, N.Y.: Books for Libraries, 1969.

———. Dans les nuages: Impressions d'une chaise. Paris: G. Charpentier, 1878.

———. Ma double vie: Mémoires de Sarah Bernhardt. Ed. Claudine Hermann. Paris: Éditions des Femmes, 1980.

———. My Double Life: The Memoirs of Sarah Bernhardt. Trans. Victoria Tietze Larson. Albany: State University of New York Press, 1999.

Bernier, Georges. Sarah Bernhardt and Her Times. New York: Wildenstein, 1984.

Boyarin, Daniel, Daniel Itzkovitz, and Ann Pellegrini, eds. Queer Theory and the Jewish Question. New York: Columbia University Press, 2003.

Brandon, Ruth. *Being Divine: A Biography of Sarah Bernhardt.* London: Mandarin, 1992.

Brownstein, Rachel M. *Tragic Muse: Rachel of the Comédie Française.* New York: Alfred A. Knopf, 1993.

Brunhammer, Yvonne, ed. *René Lalique, bijoux, verre.* Paris: Musée des Arts Décoratifs/Réunion des Musées Nationaux, 1991.

Butler, Judith. "Performative Acts and Gender Constitution: An Essay in Phenomenology and Feminist Theory." *Theatre Journal* 40, no. 4 (December 1988), 519–31.

Castle, Terry. *The Apparitional Lesbian: Female Homosexuality and Modern Culture.* New York: Columbia University Press, 1993.

Chevalley, Sylvie. *Rachel.* Alençon: Calmann-Lévy, 1989.

Chevalley, Sylvie, Marie-Françoise Christout, Noëlle Guibert, et al., eds. *La Comédie-Française, 1680–1980.* Paris: Bibliothèque Nationale, 1980.

Cleto, Fabio, ed. *Camp: Queer Aesthetics and the Performing Subject, a Reader.* Ann Arbor: University of Michigan Press, 1999.

Cocteau, Jean. *Professional Secrets: An Autobiography of Jean Cocteau, Drawn from His Lifetime Writings.* Ed. Robert Phelps, trans. Richard Howard. New York: Farrar, Straus and Giroux, 1970.

Davis, Tracy C. *Actresses as Working Women: Their Social Identity in Victorian Culture.* New York: Routledge, 1991.

Diamond, Elin. *Performance and Cultural Politics.* New York: Routledge, 1996.

Dijkstra, Bram. *Idols of Perversity: Fantasies of Feminine Evil in Fin-de-Siècle Culture.* New York: Oxford University Press, 1986.

Dudden, Faye E. *Women in the American Theatre: Actresses and Audiences, 1790–1870.* New Haven and London: Yale University Press, 1994.

Dyer, Richard. *Heavenly Bodies: Film Stars and Society.* New York: St. Martin's, 1986.

Edmonds, Jill. "Prince Hamlet." In Vivien Gardner and Susan Rutherford, eds., *The New Woman and Her Sisters: Feminism and Theatre, 1850–1914.* Ann Arbor: University of Michigan Press, 1992.

Emboden, William A. *Sarah Bernhardt: Artist and Icon.* Irvine, Calif.: Severin Wunderman Museum, 1992.

Erdman, Harley. *Staging the Jew: The Performance of an American Ethnicity, 1860–1920.* New Brunswick, N.J.: Rutgers University Press, 1997.

Fraser, Corille. *Come to Dazzle: Sarah Bernhardt's Australian Tour.* Sydney: Currency, in association with the National Library of Australia, 1998.

Garb, Tamar. *Sisters of the Brush: Women's Artistic Culture in Late Nineteenth-Century Paris.* New Haven and London: Yale University Press, 1994.

Garber, Marjorie B. *Vested Interests: Cross-Dressing and Cultural Anxiety.* New York: Routledge, 1992.

Garelick, Rhonda K. *Rising Star: Dandyism, Gender, and Performance in the Fin de Siècle.* Princeton, N.J.: Princeton University Press, 1998.

Gever, Martha. *Entertaining Lesbians: Celebrity, Sexuality, and Self-Invention.* New York: Routledge, 2003.

Gilbert, Douglas. *American Vaudeville: Its Life and Times.* New York: Whittlesey House, 1940.

Gilman, Sander L. "Salome, Syphilis, Sarah Bernhardt, and the Modern Jewess." In Linda Nochlin and Tamar Garb, eds., *The Jew in the Text: Modernity and the Construction of Identity,* 97–120. New York: Thames and Hudson, 1995.

Glenn, Susan A. *Female Spectacle: The Theatrical Roots of Modern Feminism.* Cambridge, Mass.: Harvard University Press, 2000.

Gold, Arthur, and Robert Fizdale. *The Divine Sarah: A Life of Sarah Bernhardt.* New York: Alfred A. Knopf, 1991.

Greenhalgh, Paul, ed. *Art Nouveau: 1890–1914.* New York: Harry N. Abrams, 2000.

Guibert, Noëlle. *Chez Sarah Bernhardt dans les théâtres parisiens.* Arles: Lunes, 2002.

———, ed. *Portrait(s) de Sarah Bernhardt.* Paris: Bibliothèque Nationale de France, 2000.

Hahn, Reynaldo. *La grande Sarah: Souvenirs.* Paris: Hachette, 1930.

Hambourg, Maria Morris, Françoise Heilbrun, and Philippe Néagu. *Nadar.* New York: Metropolitan Museum of Art, 1995.

Hathorn, Ramon. *Our Lady of the Snows: Sarah Bernhardt in Canada.* New York: Peter Lang, 1996.

Huret, Jules. *Sarah Bernhardt.* Trans. G. A. Raper. London: Chapman and Hall, 1899.

Huyssen, Andreas. *After the Great Divide: Modernism, Mass Culture, Postmodernism.* London: Macmillan, 1988.

James, Henry. "The Comédie Française in London." In Allan Wade, ed., *The Scenic Art: Notes on Acting and the Drama, 1872–1901,* 128–29. New Brunswick, N.J.: Rutgers University Press, 1948.

Jenson, Robert. *Marketing Modernism in Fin-de-Siècle Europe.* Princeton, N.J.: Princeton University Press, 1994.

Joannis, Claudette. *Sarah Bernhardt: "Reine de l'attitude et princesse des gestes."* Paris: Payot, 2000.

Knepler, Henry. *The Gilded Stage: The Years of the Great International Actresses.* New York: William Morrow, 1968.

Lelieur, Anne-Claude, and Raymond Bachollet. Célébrités à l'affiche. Lausanne: Conti, 1989.

Lemaître, Jules. "Madame Sarah Bernhardt." In Lemaître, Literary Impressions, trans. A. W. Evans, 283–84. London: D. O'Connor, 1921; repr., Port Washington, N.Y.: Kennikat, 1971.

Mariani, Laura. Sarah Bernhardt, Colette e l'arte del travestimento. Bologna: Il Mulino, 1996.

Marks, Patricia. Sarah Bernhardt's First American Theatrical Tour, 1880–1881. Jefferson, N.C.: McFarland, 2003.

Marshall, Gail. Actresses on the Victorian Stage: Feminine Performance and the Galatea Myth. Cambridge: Cambridge University Press, 1998.

McCauley, Elizabeth Anne. Industrial Madness: Commercial Photography in Paris, 1848–1871. New Haven and London: Yale University Press, 1994.

McPherson, Heather. The Modern Portrait in Nineteenth-Century France. Cambridge: Cambridge University Press, 2001.

Menefee, David W. Sarah Bernhardt in the Theatre of Films and Sound Recordings. Jefferson, N.C.: McFarland, 2003.

Nectoux, Jean-Michel. Stars et monstres sacrés. Paris: Ministère de la Culture et de la Communication/Réunion des Musées Nationaux, 1986.

Ockman, Carol. "Sarah Bernhardt: Death and the Icon." In Christopher Balme, Robert Erenstein, and Cesare Molinari, eds., European Theatre Iconography: Proceedings of the European Science Foundation Network, 331–39. Rome: Bulzoni, 2002.

———. "When Is a Jewish Star Just a Star? Interpreting Images of Sarah Bernhardt." In Linda Nochlin and Tamar Garb, eds., The Jew in the Text: Modernity and the Construction of Identity, 121–39. New York: Thames and Hudson, 1995.

———. "Women, Icons and Power." In Aruna D'Souza, ed., Self and History: A Festschrift in Honor of Linda Nochlin, 103–15. New York: Thames and Hudson, 2001.

Parker, Andrew, and Eve Kosofsky Sedgwick, eds. Performativity and Performance. New York: Routledge, 1995.

Pellegrini, Ann. Performance Anxieties: Staging Psychoanalysis, Staging Race. New York: Routledge, 1997.

Pronier, Ernest. Une vie au théâtre. Geneva: Alexandre Jullien, n.d.

Rachel: Une vie pour le théâtre, 1821–1858. Paris: Musée d'Art et d'Histoire du Judaïsme, 2004.

Rennert, Jack, and Alain Weill. Alphonse Mucha: The Complete Posters and Panels. Boston: G. K. Hall, 1984.

Richardson, Joanna. Sarah Bernhardt and Her World. New York: G. P. Putnam's Sons, 1977.

Roberts, Mary Louise. Disruptive Acts: The New Woman in Fin-de-Siècle France. Chicago: University of Chicago Press, 2002.

Robertson, W. Graham. Life Was Worth Living. New York: Harper and Brothers, 1931.

Salmon, Eric, ed. Bernhardt and the Theatre of Her Time. Westport, Conn.: Greenwood, 1984.

Samuels, Charles, and Louise Samuels. Once upon a Stage: The Merry World of Vaudeville. New York: Dodd, Mead, 1974.

Saslow, James M. Pictures and Passions: A History of Homosexuality in the Visual Arts. New York: Viking, 1999.

Senelick, Laurence. The Changing Room: Sex, Drag and Theatre. London: Routledge, 2000.

Silverman, Debora L. Art Nouveau in Fin-de-Siècle France: Politics, Psychology, and Style. Berkeley: University of California Press, 1989.

Simon Bacchi, Catherine. Sarah Bernhardt: Mythe et réalité. Paris: SEDAG, 1984.

Skinner, Cornelia Otis. Madame Sarah. New York: Dell, 1966.

Solomon, Alisa. Re-dressing the Canon: Essays on Theatre and Gender. New York: Routledge, 1997.

Sontag, Susan. "Notes on Camp." In Sontag, Against Interpretation and Other Essays, 275–92. New York: Doubleday, 1966.

Steele, Valerie. Fashion and Eroticism: Ideals of Feminine Beauty from the Victorian Era to the Jazz Age. New York: Oxford University Press, 1985.

———. Paris Fashion: A Cultural History. New York: Oxford University Press, 1988.

Stokes, John. "Aspects of Bernhardt." Yearbook of English Studies 11 (1981), 143–60.

Stokes, John, Michael R. Booth, and Susan Bassnett. Bernhardt, Terry, Duse: The Actress in Her Time. Cambridge: Cambridge University Press, 1988.

Taranow, Gerda. The Bernhardt Hamlet: Culture and Context. Bern: Peter Lang, 1998.

———. Sarah Bernhardt: The Art within the Legend. Princeton, N.J.: Princeton University Press, 1972.

Verhagen, Marcus. "The Poster in Fin-de-Siècle Paris: That Mobile and Degenerate Art." In Leo Charney and Vanessa R. Schwartz, eds., Cinema and the Invention of Modern Life. Berkeley: University of California Press, 1995.

Verneuil, Louis. The Fabulous Life of Sarah Bernhardt. Trans. Ernest Boyd. New York: Harper and Brothers, 1942.

———. La vie merveilleuse de Sarah Bernhardt. Montreal: Éditions Variétés, 1942.

Vicinus, Martha. "The Adolescent Boy: Fin-de-Siècle Femme Fatale?" Journal of the History of Sexuality 5 (July 1994), 90–114.

———. "Turn-of-the-Century Male Impersonation: Rewriting the Roman Plot." In Andrew H. Miller and James Eli Adams, eds., *Sexualities in Victorian Britain*, 187–213. Bloomington: Indiana University Press, 1996.

Weisberg, Gabriel P., and Jane R. Becker, eds. *Overcoming All Obstacles: The Women of the Académie Julian*. New Brunswick, N.J.: Rutgers University Press, and New York: Dahesh Museum, 1999.

Williams, Rosalind. *Dream Worlds: Mass Consumption in Late Nineteenth-Century France*. Berkeley: University of California Press, 1982.

Woon, Basil (from material supplied by Madame Pierre Berton). *The Real Sarah Bernhardt, Whom Her Audiences Never Knew*. New York: Boni and Liveright, 1924.

Archival Collections

Bibliothèque-Musée de la Comédie-Française, Paris

Bibliothèque Nationale de France, Paris, Département des Arts du Spectacle, Département des Audiovisuels, Département des Estampes et de la Photographie, Département des Imprimés, Département des Manuscrits

Harry Ransom Humanities Research Center, The University of Texas at Austin

Harvard Theatre Collection, Cambridge, Massachusetts

Musée des Arts Décoratifs, Paris, Service de Documentation

Musée d'Orsay, Paris, Service de Documentation

Museum of the City of New York

The New York Public Library for the Performing Arts

Petit Palais, Musée des Beaux-Arts de la Ville de Paris, Service de Documentation

Contributors

Carol Ockman is Professor of Art History at Williams College. She is the author of *Ingres's Eroticized Bodies: Retracing the Serpentine Line* (1995) and of numerous essays on French art of the late eighteenth and nineteenth centuries, as well as contemporary art and culture. Her subjects include Sarah Bernhardt, the nude, portraiture, stereotypes, and Barbie. In addition to receiving the Fulbright-Hays Research Grant and the Samuel H. Kress Foundation Research Grant, she was awarded a Mary Ingraham Bunting Institute Fellowship in 1997–98. She received her Ph.D. from Yale University in 1982. Her next book is on the invention of the female nude in nineteenth-century France.

Kenneth E. Silver is Chairman of the Department of Fine Arts and Professor of Fine Arts at New York University and Contributing Editor to *Art in America*. He is the author of *Making Paradise: Art, Modernity and the Myth of the French Riviera* (2001). His other books include *Esprit de Corps: The First World War and the Art of the Parisian Avant-Garde* (1989), for which he won the Charles Rufus Morey Award from the College Art Association, and *David Hockney* (1994). He has co-organized two exhibitions for The Jewish Museum, *The Circle of Montparnasse* (1985) and *An Expressionist in Paris: The Paintings of Chaim Soutine* (1998), and has published numerous essays on French and twentieth-century art. He received his Ph.D. in 1981 from Yale University.

Janis Bergman-Carton, Associate Professor of Art History at Southern Methodist University, is the author of *The Woman of Ideas in French Art, 1830–1848* (1995) and numerous articles on nineteenth- and twentieth-century visual culture and contemporary Latin American art. She has received fellowships from the Woodrow Wilson, Samuel H. Kress, and J. Paul Getty Foundations and the Social Science Research Council of the American Council of Learned Societies. Her current book project is entitled *Art, Commerce, and Culture: La Revue Blanche and the French Fin-de-Siècle.*

Karen Levitov is Associate Curator at The Jewish Museum. She curated *My America: Art from The Jewish Museum Collection, 1900–1955* (2004) and *Contemporary Art/Recent Acquisitions* (2003) and co-curated *Voice, Image, Gesture: Selections from The Jewish Museum's Collection, 1945–2000* (2001). She was the museum's project director for the exhibitions *The City of K: Franz Kafka and Prague* (2003) and *New York: Capital of Photography* (2002). She holds an M.A. in Art History from the University of Wisconsin, Madison, and is a Ph.D. candidate at the State University of New York, Stony Brook.

Suzanne Schwarz Zuber is Curatorial Assistant at The Jewish Museum, where she worked on *Modigliani: Beyond the Myth* (2004). She assisted with the Neue Galerie New York's exhibition *New Worlds: German and Austrian Art, 1890–1940* (2002). At the Hirshhorn Museum and Sculpture Garden, Smithsonian Institution, she worked on exhibitions about William Kentridge (2001) and Ed Ruscha (2000). She received a B.A. in Art History from Hunter College, CUNY, in 2001, holds a degree in interior design from the Fashion Institute of Technology, and is completing her M.A. in Art History and Archaeology at New York University's Institute of Fine Arts.

Index

Illustration Credits

Boldface numerals refer to page numbers

Abbreviations

BNF	Bibliothèque Nationale de France, Paris
CF	© Collections de la Comédie-Française
HRC	Harry Ransom Humanities Research Center, The University of Texas at Austin
HTC	Harvard Theatre Collection, Houghton Library, Cambridge, Massachusetts
LSC	Laurence Senelick Collection of Theatrical Imagery, West Medford, Massachusetts, photo by Junius Beebe III © The Jewish Museum, New York
MCNY	Museum of the City of New York
MMA	The Metropolitan Museum of Art, New York
MNAF	© 2005 Mutuelle Nationale des Artistes, France, photo by Hervé Lamerre
MT	© Mucha Trust
NYPL	© 2003 The New York Public Library
PMVP	Photothèque des musées de la ville de Paris
PPI	Posters Please, Inc., New York
RMN	© Réunion des Musées Nationaux/Art Resource, New York
TJM	© The Jewish Museum, New York, photo by Richard Goodbody
VAM	V&A Images/Victoria and Albert Museum, London

Cover: BNF
Frontispiece: MT, courtesy of PPI
Back cover: TJM
Prologue: TJM

Introduction: **Frontispiece** BNF. **2** LSC. **3** MT, courtesy of PPI. **4** BNF. **5** Huntington Library, Art Collections, and Botanical Gardens, San Marino, California (left), CF/Patrick Lorette (right). **6–7** BNF. **9** PMVP. **10** BNF. **11** MNAF. **12** BNF. **13** From Claudia Balk, *Theatergöttinen: Inszenierte Weiblichkeit—Clara Ziegler, Sarah Bernhardt, Eleonora Duse* (Frankfurt: Stroemfeld/Roter Stern, 1994), p. 94 (left), VAM (top). **14** TJM. **15** © Sterling and Francine Clark Art Institute, Williamstown, Massachusetts. **16** From Arthur Gold and Robert Fizdale, *The Divine Sarah: A Life of Sarah Bernhardt* (New York: Alfred A. Knopf, 1991), fig. 26. **17** Collection of Mr. and Mrs. Jack Rennert, New York.

Entr'acte: Bernhardt Style: **18** PMVP, photo by Andreani. **19** Musée des Arts Décoratifs, Paris, photo by Laurent Sully Jaulmes (top), PMVP, photo by Ladet (bottom). **20** MNAF (top), BNF (bottom). **21** BNF.

Ockman Essay: **Frontispiece** *The Seven Year Itch* © 1955 Twentieth Century Fox. All rights reserved. TM 2005 Marilyn Monroe LLC by CMG Worldwide, Inc./www.MarilynMonroe.com. **25** MNAF. **26–28** BNF. **29** HRC (left), MCNY (top). **30** PMVP, photo by Pierrain. **31** BNF. **32** CF/Patrick Lorette. **33** HTC (left), from Gerda Taranow, *Sarah Bernhardt: The Art within the Legend* (Princeton, N.J.: Princeton University Press, 1972), pl. 3 m–o (right). **34–35** HTC. **36** PMVP, photo by Degraces (top), BNF (right). **37** BNF. **38** LSC (left), BNF (right). **39** PVMP, photo by Ladet. **40** HTC. **41** BNF. **42** HTC. **43** From Georges Bernier, *Sarah Bernhardt and Her Times* (New York: Wildenstein, 1984), p. 15. **44** HTC (left), Jane Voorhees Zimmerli Museum, Rutgers, The State University of New Jersey, New Brunswick, photo by Jack Abraham (right). **45** BNF. **46** © 2005 MMA. **47** BNF. **48** NYPL. **49–50** © 2004 Museum of Fine Arts, Boston. **51–52** BNF. **53** RMN, photo by H. Lewandowski. **55** HTC. **56** BNF. **57** MT, courtesy of PPI. **58** BNF. **59** HTC. **60** MT, courtesy of PPI. **61** MT. **62–63** MT, courtesy of PPI. **64** BNF. **65** MCNY. **66** HTC. **67** HTC (left), BNF (top). **69** BNF. **70–71** MCNY. **72** Courtesy of the Academy of Motion Picture Arts and Sciences. **73** Photofest.

Silver Essay: **Frontispiece** BNF. **76** HTC. **77** BNF. **78** TJM. **79** From Christian Genty, *Histoire du Théâtre national de l'Odéon: Journal de bord, 1782–1982* (Paris : Fischbacher, 1981). **80** HTC. **81** MNAF. **82** LSC. **84** From Noëlle Guibert, ed., *Portrait(s) de Sarah Bernhardt* (Paris: Bibliothèque Nationale de France, 2000), p. 198. **85** BNF. **87** NYPL. **89–90** BNF. **92** Bibliothèque Forney, Ville de Paris. **93** MCNY. **95** MT. **96** BNF.

Bergman-Carton Essay: **Frontispiece** Collection of Robert A. Zehil, Monte Carlo. **100** CF (top), MNAF (right). **102** MT, courtesy of PPI. **103** Musée de la Publicité, Paris. **104** VAM. **106–7** BNF. **108** HTC. **109** From Georges Bernier,

Sarah Bernhardt and Her Times (New York: Wildenstein, 1984), p. 136. **110** BNF. **111** © Centre des Monuments Nationaux, Paris. **112** TJM. **113** TJM (top), Collection of Robert A. Zehil, Monte Carlo (bottom). **114** MMA. **115** TJM. **116** HTC. **117** © 2005 MMA. **119** MNAF. **122** LSC.

Levitov Essay: **Frontispiece** RMN, photo by R. G. Ojeda. **126** PMVP, photo by Degraces. **127** PMVP, photo by Ladet. **128** © 2005 MMA. **130** HTC. **131** Posters Please, Inc., New York. **132** BNF. **133** From Arthur Gold and Robert Fizdale, *The Divine Sarah: A Life of Sarah Bernhardt* (New York: Alfred A. Knopf, 1991), fig. 46. **135** NYPL. **136** BNF. **138–39** BNF. **141** PMVP, photo by Pierrain. **142** RMN, photo by Jean Schormans.

Entr'acte: Bernhardt and Advertising: **144** LSC. **145** BNF. **146** BNF (left), HTC (right). **147** LSC (top), HTC (bottom).

Bernhardt in the New World: **Frontispiece** MT, courtesy of PPI. **150** NYPL (top right), HTC (bottom right and left). **151** HTC. **152–53** Library of Congress, Prints and Photographs Division, Washington, D.C. **154** MCNY. **155** HTC. **156** HRC (top), BNF (bottom). **157** Library of Congress, Prints and Photographs Division, Washington, D.C. (top), The Shubert Archive, New York (bottom). **158** PMVP, photo by Degraces (top), BNF (bottom). **159** MCNY. **160** HTC (left), MCNY (right). **161** BNF. **162** MCNY (top), CF/Patrick Lorette (bottom). **163–65** HTC.

Chronology: **Frontispiece** HTC. **169** HTC (left), BNF (bottom). **171** BNF. **172** HTC. **173** VAM. **174** BNF (top), The Armand Hammer Collection, Gift of the Armand Hammer Foundation, Hammer Museum, Los Angeles, photo by Robert Wedemeyer (bottom). BNF (bottom). **175** HTC (left), PMVP, photo by Pierrain (right). **177** HTC. **178** BNF. **179** Cinémathèque Française, Bois d'Arcy, France.